Lothario's Corpse

TRANSITS:
LITERATURE, THOUGHT & CULTURE, 1650–1850

Series Editors
Kathryn Parker, University of Wisconsin–La Crosse
Miriam Wallace, New College of Florida

Transits is a series of scholarly monographs and edited volumes publishing beautiful and surprising work. Without ideological bias, the series seeks transformative readings of the literary, artistic, cultural, and historical interconnections between Britain, Europe, the Far East, Oceania, and the Americas between the years 1650 and 1850, and as their implications extend down to the present time. In addition to literature, art, and history, such "global" perspectives might entail considerations of time, space, nature, economics, politics, environment, gender, sex, race, bodies, and material culture, and might necessitate the development of new modes of critical imagination. At the same time, the series welcomes considerations of the local and the national, for original new work on particular writers and readers in particular places in time continues to be foundational to the discipline.

Recent titles in the *Transits* series:

Lothario's Corpse: Libertine Drama and the Long-Running Restoration, 1700–1832
Daniel Gustafson

Romantic Automata: Exhibitions, Figures, Organisms
Michael Demson and Christopher R. Clason, eds.

Beside the Bard: Scottish Lowland Poetry in the Age of Burns
George S. Christian

The Novel Stage: Narrative Form from the Restoration to Jane Austen
Marcie Frank

The Imprisoned Traveler: Joseph Forsyth and Napoleon's Italy
Keith Crook

Fire on the Water: Sailors, Slaves, and Insurrection in Early American Literature, 1789–1886
Lenora Warren

Community and Solitude: New Essays on Johnson's Circle
Anthony W. Lee, ed.

The Global Wordsworth: Romanticism Out of Place
Katherine Bergren

For a full list of *Transits* titles visit www.bucknelluniversitypress.org.

Lothario's Corpse

LIBERTINE DRAMA AND THE LONG-RUNNING RESTORATION, 1700–1832

DANIEL GUSTAFSON

Bucknell UNIVERSITY | UNIVERSITY PRESS
LEWISBURG, PENNSYLVANIA

Library of Congress Cataloging-in-Publication Data

Names: Gustafson, Daniel, author.
Title: Lothario's corpse : libertine drama and the long-running Restoration, 1700–1832 / Daniel Gustafson.
Description: Lewisburg, Pennsylvania : Bucknell University Press, [2020] | Series: Transits : literature, thought & culture, 1650–1850 | Includes bibliographical references and index.
Identifiers: LCCN 2019036604 | ISBN 9781684482122 (hardback) | ISBN 9781684482115 (paperback) | ISBN 9781684482139 (epub) | ISBN 9781684482146 (mobi) | ISBN 9781684482153 (pdf)
Subjects: LCSH: Libertines in literature. | Libertinism in literature. | English drama—18th century—History and criticism. | English drama—19th century—History and criticism. | Theater and society—Great Britain—History—18th century. | Theater and society—Great Britain—History—19th century.
Classification: LCC PR708.L52 G87 2020 | DDC 822/.509—dc23
LC record available at https://lccn.loc.gov/2019036604

A British Cataloging-in-Publication record for this book is available from the British Library.

∞ The paper used in this publication meets the requirements of the American National Standard for Information Sciences—Permanence of Paper for Printed Library Materials, ANSI Z39.48-1992.

www.bucknelluniversitypress.org

Distributed worldwide by Rutgers University Press

Manufactured in the United States of America

For Serena

CONTENTS

Lothario's Corpse

INTRODUCTION

The Long-Running Restoration

PREFACE

Between 1826 and 1827, *The New Monthly Magazine* published a semiregular column dedicated to a dialogue between two friends regarding politics, the beau monde, and theater in London. In the July 1827 issue, their conversation turned to recollections of Robert Coates, an amateur actor notorious for his outlandish death scenes of Shakespeare's Romeo and Nicholas Rowe's Lothario, the seductive libertine villain of *The Fair Penitent* (1703). As Lothario, Coates's atrocious acting turned the play's tragedy to farce, much to the glee of audiences:

> [Coates] kept the house in a right joyous humour, until the climax of all mirth was attained by the dying scene of "the gallant and the gay [Lothario]"; but who shall describe the prolonged agonies of the dark seducer! his platted hair escaping from the comb that held it, and the dark crineous cordage that flapped upon his shoulders in the convulsions of his dying moments, and the cries of the people for medical aid to accomplish his eternal exit. Then, when in his last throes, his bonnet fell, it was miraculous to see the defunct arise, and after he had spread a nice handkerchief on the stage, and there deposited his head-dress, free from impurity, philosophically resume his dead condition; but it was not yet over, for the exigent audience, not content "that when the man was dead, why there an end," insisted on a repetition of the awful scene, which the highly flattered corpse executed three several times to the gratification of the cruel and torment-loving assembly.[1]

Coates played his un-self-consciously campy Lothario at London's Haymarket Theatre a number of times between 1811 and 1814, almost always with the effect of being "entreated to die twice, or if he pleased, a dozen times."[2]

Coates's performance is one of sustained "corpsing." Traditionally, corpsing occurs when an actor accidentally shatters the illusion of the theatrical fiction through effectively "killing" the character she or he represents and thus ending the show. Coates's corpsing is somewhat unique. First, the mimetic illusion of

Lothario is upset from the start; the "cruel and torment-loving" audience is not there to enjoy the effects of the fourth wall (a concept still in its embryonic stages in the early nineteenth century) but to enjoy Coates as Coates, an actor in the throes of self-deluded, spectacular failure. His corpsing does not bring the show to a close, but constitutes the show itself. Second, the character that is corpsed at the culmination of this anecdote is, mimetically, a dead body. The theatrical illusion is broken in that Lothario is shown to be Coates, but also in that Lothario's corpse reanimates only to die and return repeatedly to life: a feedback loop of reenactments that precludes the temporal linearity and finality built into such moments of death in scripted drama.

As the theatrical fiction promptly ends but is just as promptly reset, what returns to life in these encores is Lothario (however ridiculously represented in the eyes of Regency audiences), a character whose death bears a particular importance in the theater history of the long eighteenth century in Britain. Familiar today as a name synonymous with a seducer, Lothario first emerged at the end of the Restoration and—as I will argue at greater length in chapter 1—embodied the sexual and sociopolitical excesses for which that period's dramatic corpus, its libertine court, and its absolutist Stuart kings, Charles II and James II, were remembered. For the Whig playwright Rowe, whose political leanings corresponded to the values of the 1688 revolution that ousted the Catholic Stuarts and their culture from the national stage, the death of the suave but dangerously self-willed Lothario symbolizes an overcoming of this turbulent past. Its enactment in the theater, increasingly a site imagined for its capacity to regulate the public, bears a disciplinary force on the social body of the audience who are asked to see, in Lothario's death, his attractions as at once self-destructive and characteristic of a licentious Restoration past that is firmly over.[3] In revivals such as Coates's, however, where the "defunct" libertine "arise[s]" again and again, death is not an end and one's "eternal exit" is qualified by one's encore. The play's regulatory effect is thus suitably upended: hardly disciplined in any sense, the audience desires Coates/Lothario to live again, his unruliness never to be quite over. Neither fully alive nor fully dead in this moment of corpsing, the libertine exists in a liminal state of constant returns.

I begin with this anecdote of Lothario's corpse (dead but subject to reanimating encores) because it is emblematic of this book's argument about Restoration libertine drama's place in British cultural history between 1700 and 1832, the desire it fosters in subjects of this long eighteenth century, and the relation such desire bears to ideas of governance in the period. To remain with Lothario as our example for the moment, pronouncements of his cultural demise resound in litany across the period's thinking about its theater history. Samuel Johnson offers a telling example in his biographical life of Rowe, where he reads Lothario as the predecessor of the rapist Lovelace in Samuel Richardson's masterwork of libertine death, *Clarissa* (1747–1748). Noting the similarities between Lovelace and Lothario (both seductive, amoral, aristocratic rakes who meet their ends in a duel), Johnson contends nonetheless that Richardson "has excelled his original in the moral effect of the fiction. Lothario, with gaiety which cannot be hated, and bravery which cannot be despised, retains too much of the spectator's kindness. It was in the power of Richardson alone to teach us at once esteem and detestation, to make virtuous resentment overpower all the benevolence which wit, and elegance, and courage, naturally excite; and to lose at last the hero in the villain."[4] Johnson's distinguishing of Lovelace from Lothario implicitly separates page from stage, attributing the power to inculcate true moral virtue in readers to print and the power to muddy it to embodied performance. Why Lovelace succeeds at producing "virtuous resentment" and Lothario fails has entirely to do with the latter libertine's theatrically live presence exceeding the moral design of Rowe's script. It is the physically present spectator's "kindness," and not that of the reader restrained to the mimetic register, that Johnson emphasizes as being engendered by Lothario's charismatic purchase on the features of the Restoration stage rake hero: "bravery," "gaiety," "wit," and "elegance." *Clarissa*'s recasting of the rake's life and death causes Lothario's reign to be over "at last."

At the same time, this passage registers an anxiety that the spectator's appreciative regard for the features of the Restoration stage libertine lingers in the present, stymieing the finality of this figure's demonization. Johnson's remarks reiterate a now familiar way of understanding the cultural chronology of the eighteenth century: the displacement of the theater by the novel (with its ties to bourgeois notions of virtue and social regulation) as the dominant cultural institution of the period. The decline in popularity of the Restoration rake and the culture of Restoration drama has been a part of that story. It is thus easy to take Johnson at his word that *Clarissa* succeeds in presiding over the Restoration rake's cultural demise and to give little thought to the spectator's "kindness" other than as a target for the social and moral work of the bourgeois novel. But the passage nonetheless emphasizes the persistent attraction of the Restoration libertine stage, especially for eighteenth-century subjects produced under new regimes of governance. This book is about that attraction.

Lothario's Corpse contends that, both metaphorically and literally, moments of corpsing involving Restoration libertine drama occur throughout the eighteenth and early nineteenth centuries in ways that challenge an axiomatic understanding of this drama's post-1700 history. Traditional theater history claims that the plays of such major Restoration dramatists as George Etherege, William Wycherley, and Aphra Behn disappeared from Britain's repertory stages in the eighteenth century, the anticivil ethos of their rakish heroes inimical to the values of Whig liberalism: bourgeois moderation, sociability, and constitutional rule of law. In contrast, in this book's focus on a wider spectrum of performances, it argues for the Restoration stage rake's unruly persistence in eighteenth-century culture, revealing the continued circulation of the Stuarts' theatrical legacy and thus recasting the cultural history of the era. It unearths the performance history of Restoration libertine drama in the century following its supposed demise, attending particularly to how its characters and scenarios occupied the cultural imaginary in ways that contributed to a series of extended debates over political liberty, theatrical culture, and modern institutions of social discipline.

Restoration drama describes the plays produced in England between the restoration of the monarchy in 1660 and, typically, one of two debatable end dates: the 1688 revolution that ousted James II from the throne or the year 1700, which saw the death of John Dryden and the debut of William Congreve's final comedy, *The Way of the World.* Though libertine plays form only one subsection of Restoration drama's corpus, libertine attitudes and activities were widely portrayed and debated in the theater. From the anti-Puritan comedies of the 1660s, Dryden's *Marriage A-la-Mode* (1671), and the "libertine offensive" of the late 1670s (which included William Wycherley's *The Country Wife* [1675], George Etherege's *The Man of Mode* [1676], and Aphra Behn's *The Rover* [1677]) to the political plays of the 1680s (Edward Ravenscroft's *The London Cuckolds* [1681] and Thomas Otway's tragedies) and Whiggish critiques of Stuart culture (Thomas Shadwell's *The Libertine* [1675] and the work of Congreve and John Vanbrugh), libertine representations often served as a barometer for the period's shifting social and political currents.[5] In general, as B. A. Kachur argues, Restoration libertinism involved "a revolt against society's customs, conventions and institutions in favour of a more naturalistic state which allowed an individual free and uncensored expression of desires and drives."[6] Often expressed in the hedonistic behaviors such as drinking, gambling, violence, and sexual adventuring embraced by the "court wits" associated with the licentious reign of Charles II (Lord Rochester, the Duke of Buckingham, and Etherege, among others), libertinism purported to query the governing norms of society. This is reflected in the drama, often in the presence of a libertine hero possessed of a lawless yet seductive wit and charisma whose intellectual cynicism, cultural elitism, and self-licensed will defies the strictures of patrilinear marriage, bourgeois morality, and even monarchical authority itself. At the same time that the rake asserts his liberty in recognizing no authority beyond the desires of the self, his rule-breaking and refusal to accept communal bonds display an aristocratic privilege often figured in terms of the absolutist sovereignty associated with the Stuart kings and their court. "Mine is a life monarchs might envy," boasts the eponymous hero of *The Libertine*.[7] The problematic co-implication of the discourse of personal liberty and sovereign absolutism is, in fact, at the heart of much of what Restoration libertine drama explores.

The gradual disappearance of Restoration libertine drama from the national repertory over the course of the long eighteenth century has been attributed in part to broad sociopolitical and epistemological changes surrounding the post-1688 eclipse of Stuart sovereignty. Since at least the nineteenth-century writings of Thomas Babington Macaulay, Whig history has coupled an image of a licentious Restoration theatrical culture with the arbitrary rule of its monarchs, claiming both to have been expelled in the 1688 revolution that supposedly replaced the political and cultural avatars of Stuart absolutism with the liberal values of limited consensual government, toleration, and a respect for the rights and liberties of the freeborn subject. Revisionist historians have long challenged this narrative of Whig history. But they continue to uphold a chronological divide between the Stuart absolutist past and the rise of hegemonic liberalism after 1688, documenting new facets of sociopolitical organization at odds with the monarchy that dominated Restoration culture. Readings of changes in theatrical culture tend to embed themselves in such histories, considering the Restoration stage and its avatars of Stuart sovereignty and libertinism irrelevant to eighteenth-century modernity.

This book does not contest the revisionist narrative of hegemonic liberalism's emergence in the eighteenth century but rather suggests that its dispersal of Stuart absolutism produces outcomes we have yet to explore, particularly a persistent fantasy of and fascination with the autonomy of sovereign rule embedded within a discourse of personal liberty and political rights. This fantasy is embodied in the continued popularity of the Restoration stage rake over the course of the eighteenth century. Rather than read him as a monologic emblem of tyranny and antisocial extravagance distinct from the values of liberal subjectivity, I uncover the ways in which the Restoration stage rake served as a model that was attractive to eighteenth-century writers and performers otherwise repelled by his affiliations with the Stuart political past. The rake persists for a culturally and politically diverse host of writers and performers—from Whig theater critics and radicals such as John Dennis and John Wilkes to Tory nostalgics such as James Boswell—who recycle and adapt diverse scenarios from Restoration libertine drama throughout the long eighteenth century: from the rake's lawless exploits of aristocratic license and antisocial wit, to his displays of republican antimonarchism and philosophical skepticism, to his downright revolutionary anticapitalist radicalism. These writers and performers repurposed the behaviors of the Restoration rake as a means of exploring, on the one hand, the powers of the freeborn British subject and, on the other, the affordances and limits of liberal institutions. The rake's popularity across the eighteenth century, I argue, was driven by the way his assertions of personal sovereignty appealed to a desire to enact, test, and contest the postrevolutionary claim of the liberty of the subject and the power of liberal Enlightenment institutions to govern that subject. Yet, as the rake's sovereign autonomy resonated with the liberal subjectivity that supplanted it, it never lost its association with the Stuart absolutist past; instead it became a means of exploring the tension, rather than the linear transition, between absolute sovereignty in rule and absolute sovereignty over the self. The rake was not simply celebrated or demonized, but became a powerful generator of cultural argument: he was a critical force who opened up a set of debates about the relation of the liberty-loving British subject to key forms of liberal power (including bourgeois rule of law, the commercial public sphere, and the institution of the stage itself) and—in a manner that anticipates the disturbingly persistent desire for the absolutist strongman in twenty-first-century democratic communities—about the allure of lawless sovereign power in the liberal imagination.

Thus, *Lothario's Corpse* reveals how the Restoration's theatrical legacy served as a cultural idiom in debates concerning the very nature of British liberty, governance, and the sovereign subject in the century following the end of Stuart rule. It concurs with recent scholarship in viewing the Restoration not just as the early part of the "long" eighteenth century but as actually "long" in its own right, but it further suggests that the Restoration is also "long-running"; its constantly revived and revised performances are at the heart of what makes post-1688 Britain modern.[8] In the rest of this introduction, I analyze the dominance—from the eighteenth century until now—of the narrative that dictates Stuart sovereign absolutism and libertine drama to be "over" in post-Restoration Britain. In turn, I suggest how performance theory may help us to question the validity of this view and thus rethink the contours of theatrical and political culture of the period between 1700 and 1832. Seeing theater history and the history of political subjectivity in this way means seeing Restoration drama as "long-running": not over but ongoing, subject—like Lothario's corpse—to unexpected revivals.

A BRIEF HISTORY OF GETTING OVER RESTORATION DRAMA

To describe Restoration libertine drama as "long-running" may seem counterintuitive given the lengthy history of pronouncements and enactments of its demise. According to one standard narrative of British theater history, the story of Restoration drama between, roughly, 1700 and 1832 unfolds as a kind of vanishing act, its relevance defined in negative terms of its defamation in the cultural imaginary and its disappearance from the national repertory. Charles Lamb testified to this memorably in his elegiac essay "On the Artificial Comedy of the Last Century" (1822): "The artificial Comedy, or Comedy of Manners, is quite extinct on our stage. Congreve and Farquhar show their heads once in seven years only, to be exploded and put down instantly. The times cannot bear them."[9] Lamb may be channeling Georges Cuvier here, but he is also certainly conjuring Samuel Johnson, who defines "extinct" in his dictionary as "at a stop; without progressive succession."[10] Restoration drama, like the Stuart dynasty that produced it, is subject to a succession crisis—not only at the culminating moment in which Lamb's essay appeared but also gradually as the long eighteenth century progresses.

Methodologically, modern theater studies tends to corroborate Lamb's personal experience of loss as quantifiable fact, ensuring that the disappearance of Restoration libertine drama from the stage remains a primary feature of its reception history.[11] The empirical decline of the plays' popularity has been accounted for in ways that indicate just how much older twentieth-century criticism remains in Lamb's genealogical ambit. For Lamb, the "stage libertine playing his loose pranks" in an imaginative "fairy-land" has been supplanted by "the exclusive and all devouring drama of common life; where the moral point is every thing; where, instead of the fictitious half-believed personages of the stage (the phantoms of old comedy) we recognize ourselves."[12] Restoration drama abdicates under the invasion of middle-class morality and identities into theater. Putting aside Lamb's Romantic correlation of the plays with fantasy, he describes a regime change that reenacts a pattern of Stuart history still accepted in today's scholarship: the displacement of a licentious aristocratic court and stage by the staunchly moral, bourgeois-leaning culture of the Williamites and Hanoverians.[13] As Richard Bevis writes, echoing Lamb, "the demise or radical alteration" of Restoration drama "was the inevitable result of the infiltration of the theater by the bourgeoisie. . . . As the social class of the audiences became more heterogeneous and workaday, spectators were less interested in seeing titled rakes and idle toasts onstage: they wanted to see themselves."[14] Other theater historians are less sanguine about the clear-cut lines of audiences' class constitution, but they nonetheless concur that new dramatic output after 1688 began increasingly to reflect middle-class tastes in a way that precipitated the obsolescence of earlier Restoration modes.[15]

More recently, the work of Lisa Freeman, Daniel O'Quinn, and others has initiated a welcome renaissance in Georgian theater studies, at once revising the positivist methods of earlier scholarship and complicating the story of a straightforward bourgeois-moral ascendancy at the turn of the century.[16] But it has also produced the unintended consequence of further entrenching the idea that

Restoration libertine drama bears decreasing weight within the post-1700 theatrical world. As Freeman puts it:

> The periods and the concerns of the drama in each period [Restoration and Georgian] are quite distinct. In the most general sense, Restoration drama, influenced by the discursive necessities of a new monarchist imperative, concerns itself with the reconstitution of both political legitimacy and the authority of language. Eighteenth-century drama, on the other hand, turns in the wake of the political settlements of 1688 and the financial revolution of the 1690s to considerations of the new social, economic, and political relations among and between the different classes and of the impact of consumer culture and commercial interests on social, moral, and literary values.[17]

Such studies as Freeman's are savvy in their challenge to the Whiggish narrative of liberalization that once motivated historical thought on the transition from monarchist to bourgeois interests. Their revisionism stops short, however, in their continued impulse to map a linear development of theater history against changing contexts, one that puts Restoration libertine drama outside the chronological pale of eighteenth-century modernity.

Freeman's dissociation of the Stuart past from new Georgian dramatic interests, with the issue of sovereignty as its crux, accords broadly with trends in eighteenth-century scholarship beyond the confines of theater studies. The diminishing of sovereign absolutism in the wake of post-1688 liberal shifts has been a fundamental feature of British literary and historical master narratives shaping the period.[18] Michael McKeon's account of the "devolution of absolutism" gestures in this direction; he describes the period as host to "a progressive detachment of the normatively absolute from its presumed locale in royal absolutism and its experimental relocation in 'the people,' the family, women, the individual, personal identity, and the absolute subject," in which "the indefinite transferability of royal absolutism fed the notion that even, perhaps only, the individual was endowed with an absolute authority."[19] This new absolute subject is a type of Lockean individual who values self-ownership and self-determination but whose purchase on these qualities does not interfere with the liberties of fellow subjects authorized by sociopolitical formations such as civil society, a rational public sphere, and representative contractual government. Along with a privileging of the authority of the subject, scholars likewise posit a rise in the eighteenth century of new structures of liberal "governmentality" in which diffuse, consensual, and extrajuridical technologies of power—such as commercial culture, domesticity, fashion, and the arts and sciences—competed with the declining forces of absolutism.[20] With the inception of such liberal subjectivities and structures, the monarchical sovereignty that was perceived to hold sway under the later Stuarts undergoes dispersal and depersonalization in an expanding body politic.

Libertines—particularly those associated with the Stuarts—are generally thought to fare poorly in this cultural and political landscape. As Erin Mackie suggests, the rake is an avatar of Stuart rule and defined by a commitment to "the exercise of personal will self-licensed as absolute authority."[21] The rake engages in a theatrics of arbitrary power in his social relations that is at once reminiscent of the experiments in personal rule by Charles II and James II and contradictory to the postrevolutionary values that supplanted them: king-in-parliament government and the protection of the liberties and property of the English subject. As Michael Neill and Warren Chernaik have argued, even when mouthing the "rhetoric of liberty," the rake is "an instinctive 'tyrant' whose insurrection against the civil order of society aims at the usurpation of absolute authority"; his political ideology is one of hypocritical paradox as he "justif[ies] oppression in the name of freedom, liberating the will to possess and destroy."[22] The political settlement established in 1688 and reasserted with the Hanoverian succession in 1714 opposed the return of Stuart absolutism and signaled the demise of the rake's political relevance.

Thus, many scholars have found William Hogarth's visual satire *A Rake's Progress* (1735) to be a useful analogue for thinking about the historical trajectory of this character. Dethroned from the heights of popularity on the 1670s stage, the rake undergoes a "decline into insignificance," as Elaine McGirr puts it, as the long eighteenth century progresses from the Restoration of the monarchy to the political reforms of the 1830s.[23] One of the most popular cultural narratives of the Restoration rake, in fact, centered on the possibility of his reform, and best-selling works from Gilbert Burnet's documentation of Lord Rochester's deathbed repentance (1680) to Samuel Richardson's *Clarissa* ensured that reform was equated with death. McGirr's claim that *Clarissa*'s ideological purpose lay in its exorcism of Stuart autocratic and aesthetic excesses—"Lovelace must die"—is widely applicable to many authors who took up the subject of the Restoration rake.[24] Eighteenth-century drama—at least the comic varieties—tended to kill its libertines less often, but it proved no less adept at eradicating their ethos. Reform-minded fashionable plays such as Colley Cibber's *Love's Last Shift* (1696), Richard Steele's *The Conscious Lovers* (1722), and Edward Moore's *The Foundling* (1748) enacted a metaphorical death of the Restoration rake by ideologically consolidating his outmodedness, forcing such characters to get with the times, to conform to new models of social and sexual behavior, or to become obsolete.

While the idioms and interests of Georgian theater are undeniably distinct from those of theater under the Stuarts, it is my contention that Restoration drama is never so definitively left behind. The scholarship just outlined witnesses Restoration libertine drama's obsolescence in the statistical dearth of revivals and in the succession of new genres with new cultural imperatives on the national stages. Its focus remains on the text, the play, and the conditions of production, all read against a sociocultural backdrop shifting ever away from the Stuart past. Interrogating these methods, I suggest, is necessary in order to realize the long-running nature of the Restoration. What does it mean to say—as scholars have done, tacitly or explicitly, with their pervasive focus on linear change, ends, and disappearance—that Restoration drama is "over" after the watershed dates of 1688, 1700, or 1714? How instead might we see how it acts as a residual force—in Raymond Williams's specific sense of the term—within eighteenth- and early nineteenth-century culture?[25] To pursue these questions demands that we shift our attention from the sites of evidence of theater history to those of performance history.

PERFORMANCE, HISTORY, AND RESTORATION DRAMA

For the purposes of this book, two crucial aspects of performance history to note are its desire to explore the bridge between the aesthetic and the everyday (how actions, behaviors, and gestures migrate from the realm of drama or the stage and are appropriated and reenacted within broader arenas of culture) and its suspicion of claims of the past's irrecoverability. As a discipline drawn to questions of temporality, performance history has evolved in the recent turn in performance studies that queries a pervasive late twentieth-century notion of performance as that which disappears as soon as it is produced. In describing the temporal relations embedded in reenacted events and behaviors, performance historians do not dispute performance-as-disappearing-act as much as they rethink disappearance as a precursor to or opportunity for inevitable reappearance rather than as a vector of absolute loss.[26] Along such lines, in her work on American historical reenactment, Rebecca Schneider reads "overness" as an ideological disposition (not a temporal fact) that obscures the way historical time remains open-ended and alterable: "Being 'over' is one of the ways a secular, linear, or progress-oriented Enlightenment model of time disciplines our orientation to events that appear to precede the present. And yet . . . it is the very pastness of the past that is never complete, never completely finished, but incomplete: cast into the future as a matter for ritual negotiation and as yet undecided interpretive acts of *reworking*. In this way, events are given to be past, or to become past, by virtue of both their ongoingness and their partialness, their incompleteness in the present."[27] In other words, historical time might be said to spill over rather than ever truly to be over. That we do not readily recognize this is due to an Enlightenment-inherited historical consciousness that favors linearity and an "experience of acceleration," in Reinhart Koselleck's words, "by means of which one's own time is distinguished from the preceding time."[28]

Schneider rereads performance's theoretical association with recurrence—from Richard Schechner's "twice-behaved behavior" to Marvin Carlson's "ghosting"—as a way of bringing the past's "ongoingness" into view and upsetting the disciplinary mechanism of "overness."[29] The habituation to Enlightenment linearity frames the "now" as normative and inevitable, characterizing any alternatives as behind the times and foreclosing the "what if" that inheres in an understanding of the past as not discrete, as not containable as reified object in the archive, but rather as open for interpretive "reworking" in the present. But acts of recurrence, Schneider claims, can "contest tightly stitched Enlightenment claims to the forward-driven linearity of temporality, the continuity of time, and challenge, as well, an attitude toward death as necessarily irrecoverable loss."[30]

Schneider's suspicion of "overness," however, itself relies on linearity. For her, the Enlightenment serves as a temporal straw man, a straightforward past moment when "modern Western conventions of linear temporality" got initially "stitched," only now in the twenty-first century to be followed by scholars' embrace of queer historiographies. On the one hand, her notion of the Enlightenment's imposition on the present speaks to Joseph Roach's idea of the "deep" eighteenth century as a past that "isn't over yet."[31] On the other hand, she ignores how the Enlightenment past may be a time not just of linear stitching but of unstitching as well. As a period in the political history of Enlightenment, the Restoration particularly reveals this. To take just one example, accompanying Charles II's ascension to the throne was the 1660 Act of Oblivion, a mandate to the nation to forget the violent events of the civil wars and Interregnum. In its plea for erasure, Oblivion presumed that a disruptive past could be forgotten so as to secure the fiction of monarchical succession; it implicitly claimed that history could be put back in order—an order defined by the current political state of things—by declaring this past to be so over as to never have existed. But as historians of the period have documented, contemporaries were fond of remarking on the religious and constitutional crises between 1660 and 1688 as a kind of twice-behaved behavior, an acknowledgment of the past's refusal to stay put.[32] Later Stuart playwrights actively participated in this, staging second Restorations nightly in their thematic (*The Comical Revenge*, *The Conquest of Granada*), allegorical (*Albion and Albanius*), and occasionally unabashedly historical (*The Rump*, *The Roundheads*) productions. Jonathan Scott claims the Restoration to be "a prisoner of memory," its political conflicts a traumatic working through of the unresolved issues of the national psyche.[33] But we might also think of such interpretations and performances as "reworkings": attempts to redo, alter, or complete what was perceived as an ongoing past, as Schneider says of American Civil War reenactors, the way it "should have been."[34] Oblivion's attempt at getting "over" the nation's troubled past by leaving it behind was accompanied by, and perhaps even conjured up, its insistent returns.

The history of Restoration libertine drama between 1700 and 1832 that I examine is similarly one of entangled "overness," recurrence, and reworking in performative moments that extend beyond that drama's revival on the national stage. Performance history may of course refer to the chronicling and culturally materialist analysis of staged productions over time of a given play. But, as a discipline, it also involves unpacking what Michel de Certeau calls "the practices of everyday life": the ways in which routine activities, gestures, behaviors, or bodily enactments are enmeshed in a field of social and cultural production.[35] My analysis lingers not on the organically whole text or play, but on the smaller performative elements essential to and repeated throughout the corpus of Stuart libertine drama—the repertoires of behavior associated with the figure of the rake—and on the ways in which these elements circulated in the post-Restoration British cultural imaginary: in literature (dramatic and otherwise), in cultural and political debate, and in the everyday performances of bodies.

The primary means by which Restoration drama remains "incomplete" in the eighteenth-century present, these performative elements surface throughout this book in three forms: the figure of the rake, the poses associated with him, and the habitual scenarios in which he engages. The figure is, in one sense, the most straightforward keyword here, referring to the characters that populate a literary or dramatic text. Etymologically indebted not only to shapes and patterns, but also to persons of distinction, in another sense, a figure suggests a character that has become so iconic as to bear metonymically an archetypal signification. Lothario—the seducer—remains a familiar case in point, but in the eighteenth century other figures also emerged. Charles Lamb's essay "Modern Gallantry" (1822), for example, satirically labels lower-class individuals practiced in the ways of upper-class "refinement" as "Dorimants in humbler life," suggesting the extent to which the libertine hero of Etherege's *The Man of Mode* (the focus of chapter 2) remained a part of cultural memory well after the last known revival of the play in 1766.[36] As they enter the cultural lexicon as idiomatic expression, unmoored in various ways from the texts that originally produced them, figures reveal the literary past as subject to revival and revision in everyday patterns of (linguistic) behavior.

Though poses are attached to the figures who strike them, they are a much more deliberate type of performance that even further troubles the supposed "overness" of the past. The linguistic origins of "pose" are loaded with referents to theatricality and time (evolved from the Latin verbs *pausare* and *ponere*, "to pause" and "to show off," respectively), and a pose is a consciously aesthetic staging of one's bodily situation in a manner that is, as Schneider theorizes it, "reenactive": there is "a citational quality to posing due to the fact that a pose is arrested, even momentarily, in what is otherwise experienced as a flow in time."[37] Interrupting the flow of linear time, the pose also undoes it, if only for a moment; in its physical stillness, it reveals the temporal still-ness of the past, its penchant for persisting or being still here in the present. Whether a pose is struck to adopt its referent as part of the poser's identity or to distance oneself, aesthetically and temporally, from the referent, it is a behavior that gestures to the "ongoingness" of the past. If the eighteenth century is increasingly bereft of Restoration revivals in terms of plays fully produced on the repertory stages, it is replete with literary-theatrical characters (as we will see with Rowe's Lothario and John Gay's Macheath in chapters 1 and 2) and real historical persons (as we will see with John Wilkes and James Boswell in chapter 3) striking poses indebted to and invested in the behaviors, figures, and concerns of Stuart libertine drama.

Finally, on a broader scale than figures and poses, there are scenarios. I borrow the term from Diana Taylor's study of performance and cultural memory, *The Archive and the Repertoire* (2003). For Taylor, scenarios describe stageable "meaning-making paradigms that structure social environments, behaviors, and potential outcomes"; performative by nature, they encompass largely formulaic plot structures, situations, settings, and gestures that—recognizable within a culture's heritage at a given historical moment—organize and interpret social conflict and the production or suppression of certain values and perspectives.[38] Bordering on the archetypal, scenarios derive their "explanatory and affective power" from their transferability through time. Their "portable framework bears the weight of accumulative repeats. The scenario makes visible, yet again, what is already there: the ghosts, the images, the stereotypes."[39] Taylor's rendering of the scenario as revelatory of an undead past haunting the present thus accords with Schneider's understanding of time that evades the strictly linear—the past (even if imaginary) here structures the present as the scenario serves as a conduit through which cultural knowledge and traditions recur and are transmitted through time. But this concept of the scenario also gestures to Schneider's idea of the nonlinearity of embodied performance as affording an alternative view to what is ordinarily visible in the now. If scenarios "predispose certain outcomes" in their predictable repeatability,

Taylor argues, ultimately their embodiedness "allow[s] for reversal, parody, and change": they "are passed on and remain remarkably coherent paradigms of seemingly unchanging attitudes and values. Yet, they adapt constantly to reigning conditions."[40] Open to live participation as narrative is not, scenarios are not only energized with the possibility of changing the script (as we saw earlier with Coates's moment of corpsing), but also suggestive of just how incomplete and ongoing the past is, as its very repetition is what makes it susceptible to change.

I linger on these theories of performance because they mark the possibility of bodily enactment as a site in which the past may be preserved in the present rather than lost to time's progress. Exploring Restoration drama through these performative sites of evidence (figures, poses, scenarios) reveals how its vanishing from the stage and its demonization in a canonical reception history coincide with important instances of its reappearance. Recognizing its reappearances allows us, on the one hand, to expand the purview of theater history itself beyond the play and the playhouse and, on the other, to widen our vision of how drama exists not just as an aesthetic form or institution of mass entertainment for the eighteenth century but as a foundational means of structuring the period's conflicts.

Specifically, the argument of this book turns on how the performance history of the Restoration stage rake features fundamentally in eighteenth-century contests over the powers and contours of the postrevolutionary liberal subject. If traditional theatrical or political histories of the period suggest how power "shift[s] away from the will of the sovereign to the desire of the subject," then the long-running nature of Restoration libertine drama that I uncover asks us to modify this formulation.[41] The texts and performances that I examine indicate, rather, that in the eighteenth century the desire of the subject is often a desire for the will of the sovereign. The personal sovereignty that the Stuart rake flaunts and that his drama explores retains an appeal to eighteenth-century subjects as a performative means of negotiating the promises and problems of individual liberty and governance embedded in the succession of liberal ideals. Charting a performance history of Restoration libertine drama, then, offers a new angle on the way we understand the eighteenth century's place in a history of liberal modernity: as much an era that engenders absolutist sovereignty's reappearances as one responsible for its disappearance.

SOVEREIGN DESIRE IN THE LONG-RUNNING RESTORATION

The eighteenth-century subject's desire for the sovereign—mediated through the figure of the Stuart rake—is exemplified in the following short and selective history of theater reviews of John Vanbrugh's libertine play *The Provoked Wife* (1697). *The Provoked Wife*'s fortunes at the midcentury were mixed. On the one hand, even after being shorn of its more incendiary religious and risqué passages by Vanbrugh and later revisers, the play prompted moral backlash. *The London Magazine*, in 1771, summed up half a century's worth of censure in its indictment of the play's "indecency" and queried its resistance to the cultural death experienced by other Restoration rake drama, asking, "what can have so long preserved that most impeachable of compositions, The Provoked Wife, from a disagreeable oblivion?" The play's antihero, the drunken would-be rake Sir John Brute, was singled out as particularly offensive: "[He] is so great a brute, that we do not feel a ray of compassion for him."[42] On the other hand, onstage representations kept *The Provoked Wife* alive in the acting repertory. Sir John was, ironically, a perennially popular role of David Garrick, the actor-manager most responsible for purging the London theaters of Restoration libertine plays; reviews of his interpretation of the character ranged much more positively. Though condemning "the Looseness of [Vanbrugh's] Principles" overall, *The London Chronicle* admired Garrick's jovial Sir John: "How full of frolic Festivity is he in the Tavern scene, when free from Women, and elevated by Wine and my Lord Rake! Even Temperance and Sobriety wish to be of the Party, and to enjoy the Knight's Company."[43] Recognition of the carnivalesque allure with which Garrick endowed the role—capable of tempting even the personification of moral values themselves—was echoed in another *London Chronicle* review: "[Garrick's Sir John] is the greatest favourite in the play; such a joyous agreeable wicked dog, that we never think we can have enough of his company; and when he drinks confusion to all order, there is scarce a man in the house, I believe, who is not for that moment a reprobate in his heart."[44]

Such anecdotes vex the Restoration rake's standard role in eighteenth-century political thought when we consider the scene to which the audiences are reacting. In this "tavern scene," Sir John and his companions toast "Confusion to all order," and Sir John drunkenly justifies indulgence in his libertine desires with antithetical assertions of sovereign absolutism and subjects' rights: "I am within a hair's breadth as absolute by my privileges as the King of France is by his prerogative. . . . Liberty and property and old England, huzza!"[45] In one sense, the reception of this scene accords with Erin Mackie's theorization of the rake's status within a pantheon of eighteenth-century literary characters who, while anachronistic in their sociopolitical values, persist appealingly in the cultural consciousness for their charismatic masculine outlawry. For Mackie, "rakish criminality is linked through nostalgic compensation to aristocratic ideals of peerless privilege and through competition to emerging ideals of the polite gentleman"; at the same time, the character's lasting prestige stems from this very "maintenance of forms of absolutism discredited in both the political and social realms."[46] Her reading relies on the formulations of Michael McKeon and Catherine Gallagher, in which, in devolved form, the sovereign "becomes a figure for the self-enclosed, autonomous nature of any person" at the vanishing point of absolute rule itself as a center of authority and knowledge.[47] The audiences' reaction to Garrick's Sir John in this particular scene suggests that the appeal of the criminal rake coincides with the "discredited" desire to imagine the self's powers as sovereign: autonomous and outside the bounds of law and social reciprocity.

Yet I question whether Sir John—and the Restoration stage rake in general—operates strictly as a figure of anachronism. For Mackie, the rake remains distinct from the liberal subject in that subject's ultimate disavowal of the sovereign self's place in modernity; the rake's prestige thus resides in his fundamentally romanticized status and is produced through gestures of nostalgia that indicate a sense of the past as never recurring.[48] These anecdotes suggest, however, the power of libertine performances to stymie distinctions of past and present, absolutist ruler and liberal subject. The key phrase in *The London Chronicle* reviews is "for that moment"; it signals the power of Garrick's enactment to pause the flow of time, to create momentarily a space in which the temporal and ideological differences between a "reprobate" Restoration rake and a moral midcentury playgoer could be collapsed. The true "confusion to all order" of the scene—and that which audiences arguably find so tantalizing in Garrick's rendition—resides in Sir John's elision of the 1688 Whiggish value for the subject's "liberty and property" with the "prerogative" of an absolutist monarch. In Sir John's performance, the liberal ideals of "liberty and property" do not supplant absolutism in the standard chronology of English political history but rather conjure absolutist behavior, in the model of the rake invested with sovereign powers, as the means of their enactment. This scene of rakish provocation indicates that the desire to imagine one's rights in terms of absolutist sovereign prerogative is not just a confusion of Sir John's, but potentially a fantasy of the modern eighteenth-century subject as well.

This book aims to show that the draw of sovereign will embodied in the Restoration rake (rather than being exhibited in the performances of the anachronistic or nostalgic Tory-Jacobite or those of the romanticized or demonized outlaw) is manifested in those of the entirely modern figure that I call the postrevolutionary subject: those Whiggish or Hanoverian individuals who support the values of the 1688 revolution (liberty of the subject, property, representative government) as bulwarks against Stuart absolutism and its imagined returns. This paradoxical affinity may be explained when we recall that, within the vast corpus of Restoration drama, the libertine's associations extend beyond (if never fully escaping) sexual violence, class privilege, and royal tyranny.[49] Sir John's insistence on personal autonomy, for instance, was a feature of many seventeenth-century radical republicans and Whig revolutionaries whose antiabsolutist political convictions became the inheritance of the eighteenth-century liberal. The republican Algernon Sidney's declaration that "every Man is a King" belongs as much to the Restoration stage rake as it does to the radical or the self-owning postrevolutionary subject, a congruence revelatory of absolutist sovereignty's potential to haunt its liberal descendants.[50]

Thus, one major strand of my argument is that the eighteenth-century appeal of Restoration libertine drama evolves from its leading figures' claim to a discourse of personal liberty that the postrevolutionary subject borrows and repurposes. A model for the sovereign subject endowed with the right to self-rule, the rake harbors a repertoire of behaviors useful in challenging not only absolutism but the forms of liberal governmentality that operated in the wake of Stuart sovereignty's decline and that were perceived by some writers and performers as detrimental to the 1688 promise of the liberty of the subject. The figures, poses, and scenarios affiliated with the libertine energies of Restoration theater—from the rake's attacks on bourgeois-Puritan culture, civility, and monarchy to his purchase on fashion, wit, and taste—offer a set of oppositional tactics to the discourses and sites that joined with juridical forces in regulating the eighteenth-century subject: bourgeois-capitalist hegemony, sociability, civil society and the rational public sphere, reformist morality. The rake's rebellion against norms and conventions may be ironic and never full-fledged, given that his self-interested manipulation of such norms and conventions is what accords him the privilege of transgression in the first place. But his provocations, I suggest, are redirected to the purpose of querying the modes and institutions of an eighteenth-century liberal modernity under which the postrevolutionary subject subsists and is conditioned. Restoration libertine drama offers a repository of figures, poses, and scenarios that individuals mobilized, at least purportedly, in the name of the British subject's right to freedom under these new contexts of governance.[51]

Yet if postrevolutionary subjectivity borrows from the dramatic libertine's repertoire in this way, then it also remains haunted (as we can see with Sir John) by the rake's absolutism and its damaging effect on the body politic. The Restoration rake's poses and scenarios are thus simultaneously mobilized to expose the liberal subject as the vehicle by which sovereign violence haunts the eighteenth-century present. Such potential is harbored in another of the Restoration rake's familiar attributes: his suspicion of the very discourse of autonomy that he voices. As Michael Neill notes, libertine plays were part of a literary culture of "skeptical deflation"—encompassing everything from the mock-heroic to Rochester's antimonarchism and self-directed ironies—that routinely derided Restoration society's claims to the superiority of the human individual and its institutions.[52] In puncturing pretensions to sovereign self-will, the plays gesture toward the crux of the political act of the 1660 Restoration itself, in which the Stuart monarchy returns but only as demystified copy of its earlier naturalized, authentic power, its reappearance conjuring a parodic response to the desire to put sovereign order back in place. This double bind of sovereign desire and its accompanying deflation forms the heart of the long-running Restoration as materialized in the performances of the postrevolutionary subject.

The long-running nature of Restoration drama, then, is revealed in how the poses and scenarios of its sovereign libertine figures—unmoored from but never transcending their original contexts in the plays—are adopted and adapted by eighteenth-century writers and performers as they interrogate the post-1688 discourse of British liberty, new forms of liberal governmentality, and new subject positions to which these forms give rise. Seeing the continued draw of this theatrical legacy, moreover, makes visible the varied ways in which the emergent forces of hegemonic liberalism revive rather than dispel sovereign desire in the period. My contention here builds on the thought of contemporary political theorists, since Michel Foucault, invested in locating the underpinnings of liberal modernity in the persistence of sovereign violence. For eighteenth-century studies in particular, Foucault's work has been crucial in advancing claims that the Enlightenment advent of liberalism is inseparable from the emergence of extrajuridical technologies of power that began to supplant the institutions of a centralized sovereign state in determining discourses of truth and knowledge and processes of subjectivation. But at the same time, Foucault acknowledges that the specter of sovereignty is never fully exorcised; its recurrence and intensification in the twentieth and twenty-first centuries, in fact, have become a preoccupation of political theorists ever since.[53] Only very recently have eighteenth-century scholars begun to assess this lingering in the Enlightenment, analyzing how sovereignty's questions of legitimacy and violence are enmeshed in burgeoning liberal discourse, in colonial production, and in literary and aesthetic forms.[54]

To such explorations of sovereignty's endurance as a form of power or rule, my account of Restoration libertine drama adds the idea that sovereignty (particularly in the form of Stuart absolutism) persists in the eighteenth century as a style of performance. Imagining the authority of the self in the mode of privileged sovereign autonomy is, as Judith Butler intimates, a desire spurred by modern shifts in the conceptualization of power: "The difficulty of describing power as a sovereign formation [in modernity] in no way precludes fantasizing or figuring power in precisely that way; to the contrary, the historical loss of the sovereign organization of power appears to occasion the fantasy of its return."[55] Despite liberal governmentality's displacement of sovereignty in the seventeenth and eighteenth centuries, Western epistemology, Foucault likewise claims, continues to refuse "to cut off the King's head."[56] Even after the forceful end of monarchical absolutism emblematized in the beheading of Charles I or Louis XVI, sovereignty "continued to exist as . . . an ideology of right."[57] Indeed, Foucault explains how the desire for sovereignty is an essential feature of an individual faced with the operations of governmentality: "When we want to make some objection against disciplines and all the knowledge-effects and power-effects that are bound up with them, what do we do in concrete terms? What do we do in real life? . . . We obviously invoke right, the famous old formal, bourgeois right. And it is in reality the right of sovereignty."[58] For Foucault and Butler, the fantasy of sovereignty is resurrected in the modern subject's performance of the very rights and liberties that, historically, contested the absolutism of the Stuarts. The way that the Enlightenment subject's desire for a purchase on postrevolutionary freedom coincides with and produces a fantasy of sovereign will is made palpable in the figure of the Restoration stage rake, a fact that explains his hold on the British cultural imaginary deep into the nineteenth century.

Ultimately, then, what the circulation of Restoration theatrical figures, poses, and scenarios in the long eighteenth century reveals is the extent to which absolutist sovereignty and burgeoning liberal culture are co-implicated in a genealogy of liberty. The Restoration rake's lingering appeal to Whiggish liberal individuals looking to enact the ideals of postrevolutionary liberty, I argue, productively muddies the ideological and chronological distinctions between absolutist and liberal forms of subjectivity that so often structure our view of the period. In unearthing the inheritances of the Stuart sovereign past in the contours of eighteenth-century liberal subjects and institutions, this book's performance history speaks to an ongoing scholarly analysis of how the Enlightenment production of an ideal of liberty is predicated on facets that such an ideal would deny: privilege, exclusion, authoritarianism, and the general delimitation of full political or human subjectivity. Moreover, this history offers an eighteenth-century perspective on one of the more disturbing problems of sovereignty in twenty-first-century liberal society: the persistent appeal of the authoritarian strongman among subjects of supposedly liberal democracies looking to safeguard their rights and freedoms. The history of long-running Restoration drama that I propose in this book—housed equally in theatrical and social performances, the literary imagination, and political discourses—suggests not that the killing off or reform of the Stuart libertine did not happen, but rather that such cultural events bear outcomes other than disappearance, demonization, and nostalgia. Restoration libertine drama's very "overness" after 1700 is in fact what sets the stage for its encore. This encore is what *Lothario's Corpse* explores.

A TABLE OF CONTENTS

Lothario's Corpse diverges from prior studies of Restoration drama largely concerned with traditional literary analysis and the historicizing of individual plays. What readers of the ensuing chapters should not expect is a systematic catalog of all Restoration productions on the post-1700 British stage. Staged revivals of select plays by Behn, Wycherley, Congreve, and Vanbrugh have been documented and analyzed in works of more traditional theater history, and factual information on them resides as well in the pages of *The London Stage*.[59] The "revivals" that constitute my examples, alternately, operate outside the theater space as well as within it. While some chapters attend in part to revived Stuart-era productions on the repertory stages, my unit of analysis is primarily not the play or the text but the figure of the rake and the scenarios and repertoires of behavior associated with him in the corpus of Restoration drama. Nor do I attend in great detail to close readings of the Restoration plays from which these characters and behaviors derive. My interest lies instead with the drama's eighteenth-century reception history: the readings and misreadings, surrogations and substitute genealogies that are built around its cultural memories and reinterpretations in post-Restoration Britain.

I take seriously Robert Hume's argument that canonical libertine plays (primarily the sex comedy of Etherege, Wycherley, Congreve, and Behn) are hardly representative of the diverse range of drama produced between the 1660s and 1690s.[60] Nonetheless, it is such plays and their connection to the politics of the Stuart monarchy and court that resurface in the cultural memories that structure the debates about liberty that I analyze. Even within the narrow scope of this type of drama, however, I do not pretend to comprehensiveness. This book does not proceed in play-by-play fashion through the libertine canon, exploring each one's afterlife. Each chapter focuses on a distinct moment in cultural history wherein the Restoration stage and its rakes are declared dead and, reading an assemblage of texts, figures, and performances within these moments, underscores how the drama's disappearance at once evokes its revival. Sporadic, uneven, and contingent on the availability of the right conditions and actors—much like the operations of the eighteenth-century repertory stages themselves—these revivals demonstrate one way of seeing the Restoration's history as long-running.

Chapter 1 explores how the eighteenth-century appeal of the Restoration stage rake emerges at the precise moment of the post-1688 moral-bourgeois revolution that supposedly precipitates his demise. The 1690s and early 1700s were home to a backlash against Stuart political and cultural excess for which Restoration comedy (with its cynical satire, aristocratic elitism, and sexual licentiousness) served as a convenient index. An expansive look at writing for and about the theater in this period, however, suggests that the Restoration rake's socially and economically extravagant behaviors (cit-cuckolding, antibourgeois wastefulness, self-inflating wit) were also widely co-opted to expose the rule of law and moral order as an obfuscation of a capitalist rule of property that delimited the postrevolutionary promise of liberty. The text and performance history of Rowe's *The Fair Penitent* are important here for their reflection of, and critical take on, the rake's revived attraction as anticapitalist radical. A fantasy of killing off the charismatic but absolutist Stuart avatar, Lothario's death is nonetheless matched in the play by the appeal of his assertions of self-sovereignty against exclusionary bourgeois rule, especially for characters such as the heroine Calista, who embraces a Whig ideology of personal liberty. Rowe's tragedy thus revolves around the susceptibility of postrevolutionary values to absolutism's seductiveness. At the same time, as the moments of unruly "corpsing" that haunt the play's stage history coincide with disruptions of the bourgeois regulation of the body public, *The Fair Penitent* reveals the extent of Restoration comedy's power to subvert structures of moral and capitalist governance.

Chapter 2 describes the resilience of George Etherege's play *The Man of Mode* (1676) and its libertine hero, Dorimant, in the era of Whig cultural and political ascendancy following the 1714 Hanoverian succession. Attacked on moral and aesthetic grounds by Richard Steele in the popular *Tatler* and *Spectator* papers (1709–1711, 1711–1712), Etherege's play is usually thought to have been successfully banished from the stage, the result of growing eighteenth-century taste for sentimental comedy and a hallmark of the supposed decline in popularity of Restoration libertine drama. *The Man of Mode* surprisingly remains in the repertory under Steele's tenure as manager of Drury Lane theater, however, its persistence a sign of the gap between the liberty-loving English subject and burgeoning sites of cultural governance, particularly the commercial theaters and the polite bourgeois public sphere. Beginning with John Dennis's dispute with Steele over the merits of Dorimant, I analyze a set of texts—from the works of Steele, Dennis, and Daniel Defoe to a series of contemporary newspapers and periodicals—that show how Etherege's rake's anticivility is remodeled as a mode of resistance to the perceived commercialization of national taste by Whiggish cultural authorities. The end of the chapter turns to a reading of John Gay's *The Beggar's Opera* (1728) and its immediate reception, arguing that the furor that this play and its libertine-highwayman protagonist Macheath caused must be understood in context of the earlier debate over Dorimant and the cultural policing of taste.

The third chapter explores the reenactment of the behaviors of the Restoration stage rake as a widespread response to the corruption of liberty and resurgence of Stuart-era absolutism imaginatively harbored in both the Jacobite uprising of 1745 and George III's "personal rule" in the 1760s. Distinct from earlier decades when Restoration libertine drama still experienced sporadic theatrical revivals, the midcentury marks a time when all but the most anesthetized representations of the Stuart rake had vanished from the boards. Yet the draw of the sovereign rake lingers—embodied specifically in characters descended from him, such as Vanbrugh's Sir John Brute, Gay's Macheath, and Rowe's Lothario—paradoxically in the performances of subjects who challenge the period's figures of arbitrary rule with a radical ideology of the rule of the people. I juxtapose readings of David Garrick's anti-Jacobite theatrical performances, the sociopolitical provocations of Wilkite radicals and their opponents, and the journalistic self-fashioning of James Boswell to show how the rake's republican antimonarchism, behaviors of carnivalesque misrule, and rhetoric of liberty are appropriated to resist cultural figurations of authoritarianism on a number of registers while at the same time uncovering how the liberal values of popular sovereignty are predicated on the popularity of the prerogatives of the sovereign individual.

In the final chapter I turn to Restoration drama's role in the rise of modern liberalism, specifically in the discourse of theatrical reform and in a series of historical comedies (set in the Restoration and featuring cameos by Charles II and his leading court rakes Lord Rochester and the Duke of Buckingham) of the era between Waterloo and the 1832 Reform Bill. Against foundational statements of theater history such as Charles Lamb's regarding the vanishing of Restoration comedy during this era, the Restoration rake was actually everywhere on the stage, the dialectical problem he posed between the poles of liberty and tyranny absolutely essential to the liberal agenda of theatrical rights. The later Romantic era was marked by pervasive calls for the reform of the corrupt politics of the ruling elite. London's national theatrical culture had been tied to the throne ever since the Restoration—its companies effectively acting as "His Majesty's Servants"—and it became subject to similar calls for restructuring by liberal playwrights desiring the freedom to ply their trade outside the bounds of state control. I begin by reading the performances and speeches of chief reformers such as William Hazlitt, Douglas Jerrold, and Edward Bulwer Lytton, contending that their case for theatrical rights hung on a carefully constructed historical narrative about the long-running Restoration, the upshot of which was that the theater was the place in modern liberal Britain where the corrupt Stuarts could be said still to reign. Such propaganda was both purveyed and contested on the stage in a set of historical comedies involving scenarios of reformation of Charles II and his courtiers, some of which used the figure of the tyrannical rake openly to forward liberal reform's agenda, while some others, from a more radical vantage, used this figure to critique burgeoning liberal ideology itself as a reanimation of Stuart absolutist sovereignty. Looking at plays by Jerrold, John Howard Payne, and particularly William Thomas Moncrieff's *Rochester* (1818), I argue that this corpus at once frustrates the standard account of Restoration drama's disappearance from the theaters and complicates the chronological distinction between absolutist and liberal forms of rule.

1

CORPSING LOTHARIO

THE EPILOGUE TO NICHOLAS ROWE'S TRAGEDY *Jane Shore* (1714) marks a significant moment in the succession between Stuart and postrevolutionary theatrical culture. Spoken by Anne Oldfield, who played the titular Jane, an adulteress, the epilogue playfully apologizes to the audience's "modest matrons" and "virtuous wives" for its heroine's sin—"cuckold-making"—but pleads for a compassionate handling due to her distinction from women of a bolder sort:

> This matter here was proved against poor Jane:
> She never once denied it, but in short,
> Whimpered, and cried, "Sweet sir, I'm sorry for't."
> 'Twas well she met a kind, good-natured soul;
> We are not all so easy to control.
> I fancy one might find in this good town
> Some would ha' told the gentleman his own;
> Have answered smart, "To what do you pretend,
> Blockhead! As if I mustn't see a friend!
> Tell me of hackney-coaches, jaunts to th' City,
> Where I should buy my china—Faith, I'll fit ye!"
> Our wife was of a milder, meeker spirit:
> You! Lords and masters! was not that some merit?[1]

Rowe preserves Jane's essential docility and goodness, despite her sexual transgression, by opposing her to a wife who rebels against her husband's domestic and commercial domination and who more than a little resembles the women of William Wycherley's Restoration sex comedy *The Country Wife* (1675). The wife's implication that she will take sexual revenge on her husband for dictating where she shops refers to a particularly high watermark of Restoration theatrical bawdiness, *The Country Wife*'s "china scene," wherein china serves as a pervasive euphemism in an audacious act of cuckoldry between the libertine hero, Horner, and Lady Fidget. As the scene was notorious in its own right, and made more so by Wycherley's sardonic self-reference to it as the epitome of everything wrong with the Restoration stage in *The Plain Dealer* (1676), Rowe could rely on the allusion as convenient shorthand not only for a kind of sexual aggressiveness that his Jane rejects but for the corruptions of sex, satire, and aristocratic license in Britain's Restoration theatrical past.[2]

The allusion to *The Country Wife* is followed by Oldfield calling for the displacement on stage of Wycherley's libertine style by Rowe's preferred idiom, sentiment:

> If the reforming stage should fall to shaming
> Ill-nature, pride, hypocrisy, and gaming,
> The poets frequently might move compassion,
> And with she-tragedies o'errun the nation.
> Then judge the fair offender, with good nature;
> And let your fellow-feeling curb your satire.[3]

Tongue-in-cheek as the image of a nation "o'errun" with "she-tragedies" may be, the epilogue describes a familiar story of post-Restoration theatrical succession: "fellow-feeling" supplanting "satire," sentimental drama supplanting cynical Stuart sex comedy. That Rowe's contemporaries understood this to be the effect of his dramatic work more largely is suggested in a memorial tribute by Charles Beckingham that celebrates Rowe's 1703 tragedy *The Fair Penitent*. First depicting Rowe as a poet dedicated to "the Publick Good"—"To Virtue steddy, to thy Country true, / We read the Poet, and the Patriot too"—Beckingham goes on to describe his patriotism to reside in his putting an end to the stage libertine's reign:

> The Libertine in Love exults a-while
> On violated Charms, and ravish'd spoil;
> But soon his Triumphs find a timely Date;
> The Villain's Crimes receive the Villain's fate.[4]

Beckingham's textual gloss on these lines indicates that the "Libertine" in question is *The Fair Penitent*'s villain, Lothario, whose "fate," after seducing the protagonist, Calista, and cuckolding her husband, is to end the play as a corpse. The poem confirms Rowe's loyalty to the post-Stuart state in the playwright's putting a "timely Date" to an avatar of Stuart theatrical culture, criminalizing and punishing Lothario for the kind of behaviors that drew audiences to the likes of Wycherley's rakish heroes only a few decades earlier.

Both the epilogue to *Jane Shore* and Beckingham's panegyric equate Rowe with the "reforming stage," a reading borne out in modern scholarship of eighteenth-century theater. His plays are the final nail in the coffin of the cit-cuckolding dramas of the 1670s and 1680s (which turned on scenarios of class conflict in which aristocratic rakes seduced the wives of middling-class citizens, or "cits"), illustrative of a more widespread cultural succession in the early 1700s that elevates a bourgeois, moral, and sentimental aesthetic over one of the aristocratic and the heroic and the sex comedies with which it is ideologically paired. As with Beckingham's association between patriotism and the Stuart libertine's "timely Date," such narratives of progressive cultural change bear a politics. As they refute any serious future for the theatrical forms of Restoration libertine comedy, they hew closely to sociopolitical readings of the period instituting either a liberal or a bourgeois-capitalist hegemony, a distinct shift away from Stuart absolutism and the aristocratic ethos of Restoration court society. Revisionists have questioned the older assumptions of Whig and Marxist historians regarding the political transformations established in the wake of the 1688 revolution, William III's accession to the throne, and the dwindling of the Stuart dynasty into Jacobitism. A comparable revisionism, however, has yet to be fully extended to this period in British theater history, insofar as the "timely Date" on the postrevolutionary stage of the Restoration comic rake—and the figure's fate as index for linear ideological change—is a story that has gone largely unchallenged.

In this chapter, I take a wide look at the Stuart libertine in writing for and about the stage in the late 1690s and early 1700s, arguing that the performances of Restoration comedy retained a persistent appeal that resides, paradoxically, in the draw of the aristocratic sovereign self-license of the very cit-cuckolding comic heroes that Rowe and his contemporaries found distasteful. The declarations of the "overness" of Restoration libertine comedy promulgated widely under Williamite culture are neither so simple nor so final but mask a conflicted afterlife in which Restoration libertine comedy is uneasily harnessed in challenge to new forces of moral-bourgeois governance. This theatrical lineage, I argue, possessed radical potential as its charismatic anticapitalist rakes, and their battle with bourgeois cits, were lifted from its plays' immediate contexts and repurposed anew by a host of writers as part of an assessment of the inclusivity of the rights of liberty, property, and rule of law under the Williamite succession. In tracing this appeal of the rake, my goal is to bring into view how the very terms and texts of this cultural succession that demonize and dismiss the Restoration theatrical libertine simultaneously conjure this figure's revival.

To argue this, I turn first to the reactions in Williamite culture of the late 1690s to the troubled ideological alliance of the aristocratic rake and political radicalism that marked much of Stuart comedy. For a host of writers on the cultural politics of the stage—from Jeremy Collier and Richard Blackmore to John Vanbrugh and Tom Brown—rehearsing the staple battle of "wit versus cit" embedded in much Restoration comedy became a means either to uphold the moral middle-class values of the Williamite succession or to cast them as a dangerous appendage of the exclusions of bourgeois-capitalist rule. In the last sections of the chapter, I return to Rowe's *The Fair Penitent*, reading both its text and its performance history in the eighteenth century for the way it comments on the supposed radical appeal of the aristocratic stage rake. Lothario is the central figure here; one of the century's most famous theatrical corpses and one that refused to stay dead, both metaphorically and literally, he is indicative of the problem of definitively asserting the "overness" of the Stuart theatrical past. Part of a moment of theatrical and political reform in the late 1690s and early 1700s, I argue, the performances of the aristocratic rake revived in figures such as Lothario disrupt linear succession, revealing, in a larger theoretical sense, some of the implications behind thinking of historical progress in terms of theatrical revival.

BOURGEOIS-CAPITALIST SUCCESS(ION) AND ITS DISCONTENTS

Beckingham's assessment of the politics behind Rowe's giving a "timely Date" to stage libertines such as Lothario is best understood in the context of the entwined moral and political backlash against Stuart culture that peaked in the 1690s and early 1700s. Commenting on the political and economic advantages of the marriage at the center of *The Fair Penitent*, Altamont, the cuckolded husband and Lothario's political and sexual rival, celebrates them as instituting "a better order of succeeding days" for himself and his family.[5] By 1703, when Lothario and Altamont first hit the London stage, from a Whig perspective, historical events seemed to have ushered in "a better order of succeeding days" for the nation. In ousting James II, the 1688 revolution was perceived as a victory of Whig political philosophy, the defeat of Stuart absolutism by the values of contractual government, constitutional law, limited monarchy, and subjects' rights. The 1701 Act of Settlement further secured the English throne for the Protestant Hanoverian line, allowing, for a time, fears of a renewed succession crisis to be quieted, if not truly quelled.[6] These political changes were reinforced by widespread calls for social reform that, as Brett Wilson puts it, were "frequently and self-consciously conceived as a reaction against the cultural excesses of the Stuart dynasty."[7] The libertinism of the Restoration court had been provoking moral outrage since 1660; but various campaigns for the reform of English morals and manners intensified noticeably after 1688. William III's state policies encouraged the suppression of national vice, often represented as inherited from the corrupt courts of Charles II and James II, as a prop to the new king's tenuous political legitimacy, while Reformation societies, backed by influential clergymen such as Gilbert Burnet and Edward Stillingfleet, lobbied for laws against public misbehavior. As a number of scholars have documented, the Stuarts were increasingly demonized under William's "godly revolution" as the epitome of social indecency and sexual tyranny, made to oppose the virtues of marital fidelity, piety, and toleration that Williamite culture claimed as its own.[8]

Such attempts to put the Stuarts outside the pale of politics and to effect a concomitant moral-cultural revolution were mirrored in the push for theatrical reform. Theater historians have distinguished the 1690s and early 1700s as host to a number of aesthetic reactions, especially in comedy, unfriendly to the Stuart era: from the popularity of reformed-rake plots such as Colley Cibber's *Love's Last Shift* (1696) or renderings of the rake's power as fraudulent such as Mary Pix's *The Beau Defeated* (1700) to the socializing of the rake's energies, in the works of William Congreve and Susanna Centlivre, within a new order of Whig civil society.[9] Accompanying these aesthetic changes was a flood of reformist rhetoric in print. As an institution particularly beholden to Charles II, the London stage was frequently charged with propagating libertine practices left over from the Stuarts in a way that was damaging to the health of state and nation. One of the Reformation societies' recurring demands was "that the public Play-Houses may be suppressed" for their tendency to produce a populace "indefatigable in raking out of . . . our modern Plays, all Expressions that may seem to favour . . . Licentiousness."[10] The anxiety that rakish theatrical representation led to a public permeated with libertine activity was seconded by writers such as Daniel Defoe, Richard Blackmore, Jeremy Collier, and George Ridpath whose antitheatrical writings targeted specific "Bawdy Play[s]" of Stuart dramatists and their Williamite inheritors.[11]

Politically, the motivating principles behind such calls for theatrical reform were disparate. As Lisa Freeman has shown, while the puritanical Ridpath and the high Anglican nonjuring Collier could concur in their condemnation of the stage, the former did so because of a perceived alliance of libertine theater with the "Lascivious and Arbitrary Humours" of the tyrannical Stuarts, while the latter saw in the stage rake a breakdown of traditional social order that was mirrored in William's de facto government, a reveling in the "Arbitrary Pleasure" of the absolute subject that could lead to the Hobbesian nightmare of social anarchy.[12] Nonetheless, what theatrical reformers of all stripes seemed to share was a feeling that Restoration comedy's threat lay in its relation to misrule, its power to evoke the fraught kinship between the rake and political subversion. Collier's *Short View of the Immorality and Profaneness of the English Stage* (1698), for example, accuses playwrights of both fostering the "Success . . . in Debauchery" familiar to Restoration rake comedy and desiring "to revive the old Project of Levelling," thus describing the effect of William's succession as a return of civil war radicalism in the guise of libertine lawlessness.[13] Alternately, for Blackmore—a middling-class physician whose poetic panegyrics to William earned him a knighthood and a professional appointment in the royal household—comedy carried the menace of Jacobitism. Targeting the libertinism of "modern comedies" specifically in the preface to *Prince Arthur* (1695), Blackmore argues that "our Poets seem engag'd in a general Confederacy to ruin the End of their own Art, to expose Religion and Virtue, and bring Vice and Corruption of Manners into Esteem and Reputation. The Poets that write for the Stage (at least a great part of 'em) seem deeply concern'd in this Conspiracy."[14] Such passages mark libertine drama as a conspiratorial threat to the existing state (imagined conversely as virtuous, chaste, and therefore legitimate), an ideological vehicle for the staging of Jacobite radicalism in a decade witness to a number of plots to forcibly remove William from the throne. Despite the conflicting opinions over what constituted the legitimate political order, Stuart libertine comedy came to serve as a broad index for all that needed banishing from it.

Postrevolutionary culture, however, did not just seek to distance itself from Restoration comedy; it remained drawn to this dramatic heritage, using its scenarios and libertine performances in ways that complicate the narrative of a chronologically straightforward cultural succession away from the Stuart past. If twentieth-century revisionist historians have specifically singled out the political and religious facets of 1690s Williamite rule in their reconsideration of 1688 as the hallmark moment of liberal Whig history (with its traditional emphasis on the shifting axes of class power, religious toleration, the rise of progressive democratic institutions), they have yet conceded 1688 to have ushered in something of a bourgeois revolution. As Steve Pincus claims, 1688 inaugurated "a bourgeois revolution in a cultural and political sense," giving new importance to a bureaucratic program of economic imperialism and to the middle-class values of exchange, commercialization of culture, and moral propriety.[15] More broadly, 1688 stands as one of the seventeenth- and eighteenth-century revolutionary moments described by Michael Hardt and Antonio Negri as foundational for the modern "republic of property," a pervasive political organization wherein "the establishment of the constitutional order and the rule of law served to defend and legitimate private property."[16] For Hardt and Negri, the period's bourgeois revolutions institute a rule of property masquerading as a rule of law, concealing the operation of biopolitical capitalism's disenfranchisement of the commons under the republican discourse of popular rights. Under such circumstances, the Stuart libertine's comic subversions—specifically as figured in opposition to puritanical and bourgeois-capitalist rule—might be imagined to serve those individuals either excluded from the new centers of socioeconomic power or otherwise critical of the effects of Williamite cultural reform.

Laura Brown has suggested as much, arguing that the Restoration stage rake harbors a set of "ideological material[s]" aligned with revolutionary identities that would have repelled most mainstream Williamite Whigs. Drawing a series of parallels between the Stuart libertine's performances and those of seventeenth-century radical sects such as the Ranters and the True Levellers (a shared opposition to the sanctity of marriage, Protestant social and sexual mores, the middle classes, and social hierarchy), Brown reminds us that the rake is poised "for a radical assessment not only of the bourgeois, moderate Presbyterians, but also of the monarchy and the aristocracy itself, especially in their accommodation to capitalist society. The libertine advocacy of freedom, with its deliberate subversion of social order and hierarchy, constitutes an implicitly radical attack upon the status quo, launched from an ideological vantage point outside an increasingly capitalist society."[17] Such a directed assault is essential in the Restoration libertine's Stuart lineage. From midcentury cavalier poetry to the Tory cit-cuckolding comedies of the Exclusion Crisis, the royalist preoccupation with gentlemanly ease, wit, and free sexuality served at once as an ideological foil to and competitive engagement with the powers of Whig puritanism and capitalism that had proved more than capable of upsetting the aristocratic and monarchic foundations of the Stuart state. As Anita Pacheco describes it, the comically rendered sexual and social affront of upper-class Tories against citizen Whigs that was a staple of the royalist imaginary "enacts the inherent superiority and right to power of the Stuart dynasty and its ruling elite."[18]

If the radical potential of the rake's performances (notably in cit-cuckolding) remained just that—potential, never intended to upset the socioeconomic hierarchy on which the rake's power depended—it was nonetheless capable of being manipulated by other subjects within the purview of the burgeoning Whig republic of property. The repertoire of the 1670s and 1680s stage libertine was, in fact, mined extensively during the Williamite period for its radical possibilities. In part, this explains the seemingly paradoxical attraction of Whig playwrights to the traditions of early Restoration rake drama evident in the "minor resurgence of sex comedy" in the later 1690s, comprising the works of William Congreve, John Vanbrugh, Thomas Southerne, Thomas D'Urfey, and Catharine Trotter.[19] For Congreve, respectively in *Love for Love* (1695) and *The Way of the World* (1700), the courtship plots of Valentine and Angelica and Mirabell and Millamant rehearse the revolution settlement in their emphasis on how the Lockean values of sociable exchange, trust, and contractualism may prevail in structuring the social order over against the outmoded performances of Stuart absolutist will and libertine self-aggrandizing. At the same time, as Richard Braverman has argued, Congreve endows heroes such as Mirabell with the linguistic wit and sexual magnetism of the comic Stuart rake, adopting yet also adapting such traits for the service of revolution principles.[20]

Vanbrugh's and Trotter's use of rake drama proved more subversive; their assumption of the Restoration's scenarios of comic seduction in *The Relapse* (1696), *The Provoked Wife* (1697), and *Love at a Loss* (1700) signals an unnerving skepticism toward the Williamite axis of moral reform, bourgeois property, and Whig politics. "Virtue," claims Constant, the married Lady Brute's would-be seducer in *The Provoked Wife*, "consists in goodness, honour, gratitude, sincerity and pity, and not in peevish, snarling, strait-laced chastity."[21] Both an able critique of the Williamite symbol of marital fidelity and a rhetorical ploy to get Lady Brute into bed, Constant's remark reveals how the rake's sexual libertarianism, however specious, might retain attraction as a radical alternative to the politics of confining morality. Vanbrugh underscores bourgeois virtue's insidiousness in Sir John Brute's trust that his wife's virtue will only serve to make her more securely his sole property. *Love at a Loss*, alternately, concludes in the reluctant marriage of the rakish Beaumine to Lesbia (whom he had previously seduced), which is brought about not through a mutual agreement forged in ritual courtship or the reform of the libertine but, in a parody of representative parliamentary government, "by vote" of the other characters, which infringes on the individual wills of the couple.[22] Rather than these comedies resolving their courtship entanglements in stable marriage, they employ the adulterous energies and libertine cynicism familiar from earlier Restoration drama to undercut the patriarchalist tenet of reformist culture that a virtuous civil society may be forged out of the powers of contract, consent, and liberal representative government. While the plays are equally skeptical of their philandering leading men, they nonetheless use their rakes' provocations to probe and ultimately unmask the republic of property that subtends the ideological building blocks of Williamite cultural and political reform.

For non-dramatic authors as well, taking a radical stance against the new cultural constitution under Williamite reform was the aim behind reviving the legacy of Restoration libertine comedy. At the turn of the century, the concept of wit—the Stuart rake's traditional stock in trade—became the center of a major literary controversy that consciously reenacted an important primal scene of Restoration comedy itself: the confrontation of the rake with the emergent forces of bourgeois capitalism. In part a rebuttal to the ridicule the author had received from

John Dryden, John Dennis, and Samuel Garth for his pretensions to epic verse in *Prince Arthur*, Blackmore's *Satyr against Wit* (1699) was the cause of this poetic war. The *Satyr* operates in the same discursive vein that we have seen in Blackmore's earlier reformist writings, aligning tropes that Whig writers would label as "Stuart" or "Jacobite"—licentiousness, arbitrary government, rebellion—against the Williamite privileging of virtue, regulation, and law. Taking ad hominem aim at his critics, playwrights such as Congreve, Vanbrugh, and Wycherley and a host of others affiliated with Will's coffeehouse, a center of wit culture in the 1690s, Blackmore attacked wit as the cultural analogue to a morally bankrupt, frivolous, and subversive polity that would betray the revolution settlement:

> Wit does of Virtue sure Destruction make;
> Who can produce a Wit and not a Rake?
> Wise Magistrates leud Wit do therefore hate,
> The Bane of Virtue's Treason to the State.
> . . . .
> What well-form'd Government or State can last,
> When Wit has laid the Peoples Virtue wast?[23]

In rejoinder, the patrons of Will's, led by Tom Brown, shot back with the mock *Commendatory Verses, on the Author of the Two Arthurs, and the Satyr against Wit* (1700), which in turn provoked a number of defenses of Blackmore, such as the *Discommendatory Verses, on Those which are truly Commendatory, on the Author of the Two Arthurs, and the Satyr against Wit* (1700) and *An Epistle to Sr. Richard Blackmore* (1700), as well as some bemusedly neutral commentary on the escalating quarrel, notably Defoe's *The Pacificator* (1700) and Abel Boyer's *Letters of Wit, Politicks and Morality* (1701).[24]

More than Blackmore's transparently pro-Williamite propagandizing, what is interesting, for our purposes, about his *Satyr* is the way the wits' reaction to it played out in terms of the class conflicts of Restoration comedy. Ostensibly about Blackmore's poetic merit, the controversy, as Abigail Williams has described it, was rooted in a sociopolitical struggle for cultural supremacy, enacted as a contest between a moralistic, unrefined middle class and a set of glib but stylishly aristocratic gentlemen.[25] The wits caricatured Blackmore as "the Cheapside Knight" and "the City Bard," mobilizing in the *Commendatory Verses* an arsenal of anti-Whig satirical tropes (unsociability, hypocrisy, puritan enthusiasm, pedantry, commercialism) to imply that his associations with London's unfashionable middle-class citizenry made him a poor poet and an unqualified cultural arbiter.[26] Fashioned as a stereotypical "cit," he is also subject to jokes about "cuckoldom," a nod to the traditions of earlier Restoration comedy in which, as we saw earlier, sociopolitical conflict is enacted in terms of masculine potency.[27]

Less remarked on has been the way the wits not only lampooned Blackmore as a version of the stage cit but also themselves adopted the self-stylizations of the Restoration stage rake in opposition to him. In place of the cit's stolid focus on "Business," the wits, boasted Tom Brown, pursued a "gay *Carousing Trade*" of convivial leisure, theatergoing, drinking, women, and satire.[28] Brown's preface to the *Commendatory Verses*, written from the ironic perspective of a London tradesman, identifies the wits as "those flashy Fellows, your *Covent-Garden* Poets . . . good for nothing, but to run into our Debts, lye with our Wives, and break unmannerly Jests upon us as Citizens."[29] The poems in the ensuing volume follow through on this representation, incorporating classist ribaldry and extolling the "manly Pleasures" of a blithely genteel lifestyle.[30] Whether or not the wits actually engaged in such acts (Brown did), they cultivated an affiliation with the performances of cit-cuckolding, gentlemanly ease, and economic extravagance that were fixtures of the Restoration comic rake as a means of asserting their social superiority.[31] These behaviors are, moreover, consciously linked by contemporaries to the heyday of the Restoration stage through their venue of choice. Will's coffeehouse was a site haunted by Stuart libertine history, as it had been frequented "by the first-rate Wits that flourish'd in King *Charles* II's Reign, such as the late Earl of *Rochester*, . . . Sir *George Etherege*, Mr. *Dryden*, Mr. *Wycherly*, and some few others."[32]

We should be hesitant to read the wits' response to the *Satyr* strictly along party political lines, however. While their satiric thrust seems anti-Whig, its function may be better read as a tactical resistance to Blackmore's marriage of cultural succession with the republic of property.[33] Denying the denigrating connotations associated with the term, the *Satyr* reinvents the "cit" role, exalting "Discreet and Grave" individuals who were "for Business born" as protectors of "the Glory of *Britannia's* Isle." The bourgeois class values of industry, exchange, and moderation are here aligned with England's imperial prestige and opposed to "useless, . . . sauntering empty Wit."[34] To remedy wit's wastefulness, Blackmore calls to "erect a Bank for Wit" and imagines the consequences that such a scheme would produce. The bank would be regulated by a group of reformist ministers who would "exert [their] Soveraign Power" to ensure that "false Wit" would "lose its currency" by taking it in to be melted down, recoined, and circulated back into the market for the benefit of the nation's cultural economy. Whig and Tory poets alike—Congreve, Vanbrugh, Southerne, Wycherley, and Dryden are listed—will fare poorly under these economic regulations if at all aligned with the libertine productions that

Blackmore was out to eradicate, their "false Species" of wit producing fewer returns in marketable sterling silver. In addition, the *Satyr* gives gleeful permission for these new economic regulators to "chastise the Poets who our Laws invade," contriving punitive measures such as branding as fit punishment for the libertine writers who will become too poor to survive under these conditions and thus turn to larceny, fraud, and treason.[35] Blackmore's bank thus relies for its governing power on capitalist strategies that underwrite how the state functions to include or exclude subjects from its realm, ensuring that poetic liberty and even poetic survival in the commonwealth of the muses are determined by a metric of financial and moral value set by a reformist ministry.

It is this redefinition of the promise of law and liberty along capitalist and violently disciplinary lines that provokes the wits' recourse to the Stuart libertine pose. If in Restoration comedy, as Laura Brown and others have shown, the rake's radicalism must ultimately be repudiated as self-destructive (the libertine is as much served by the sociopolitical status quo as he is repulsed by it), this is not necessarily the case with the wits, for whom the appeal of the rake's repertoire of behaviors lies in its ability to contest the republic of property attached to reformist culture. The *Satyr* recognizes their radical potential, their ideological resemblance to revolutionary groups such as the True Levellers or the Ranters, in its indictment of the wits as a mob who have "broke [the Muses'] Inclosures."[36] Alluding to the very contemporary issue of enclosure—the state-sanctioned expropriation and privatization of previously communally open lands—Blackmore renders the poetic realm as legally held private property and the wits as a collective of lawless commoners who, displaced from it, are bent on pulling down its borders. The authors of the *Commendatory Verses*, while not inviting such comparisons to the masses, nonetheless stress that such radical disruption of enclosure is precisely the point. Countering Blackmore's insistence on property, his pervasive imagery of economic structures and strictures, wit, they contend, must be "unconfin'd as Air," an image that accords with their pose as carefree breakers of social and economic bounds.[37] In their self-fashioning, the wits access an idea of absolute liberty in a prelapsarian state of nature, borrowed from a tradition of cavalier poetry that later Stuart libertinism uses to justify its more raucous assault on capitalist logic. Though the Restoration rake's repertoire is courtly rather than common, it nevertheless grants the wits a language of radical challenge to the perceived capitalist perversions of the Williamite moral revolution. As much as the wits' response to Blackmore enacts a class struggle for cultural supremacy, then, it wrests the discourse of the post-revolutionary liberty of the subject away from its union with an ideology of enclosure by conjoining it with the performances of aristocratic rakish license that were resistant to emergent capitalist biopolitical regimes.

Rehearsing the battle of "wit versus cit," a staple of the very Restoration comedies that had initially sparked theatrical reform, the controversy surrounding the *Satyr* reveals that this dramatic repository could be turned toward oppositionist ends. Reform culture's emphatic demonization of Restoration comedy obscures how elements of that comic legacy simultaneously retained its appeal, especially in their ability to unleash the radicalism latent in the rake's purchase on freedom and resistance. Of course, the wits, as with the Stuart rakes they emulate, do not go as far as Gerrard Winstanley in their attack on the republic of property. Their fantasy of gentlemanly autonomy relies implicitly on the capitalist structures against which they explicitly protest. Many of the wits, however, were not of genteel background, and very few of them were aligned with the Stuart cause. This suggests a more widespread draw of the fantasy of aristocratic will housed in the Restoration comic rake's heritage, its appeal as a model of behavior capable of launching a cultural critique even for those writers not affiliated with its class roots or politics. What such ghosting of the Restoration rake offers, I suggest, is a mode of performing and redefining postrevolutionary liberty that can vex, however incompletely, the biopolitical basis of the Williamite cultural succession and that belies that succession's success in demolishing the appeal of the Stuarts' dramatic past.

Looking back on the wit controversy in the 1701 preface to *The Christian Hero*, Richard Steele—who contributed to the *Commendatory Verses* himself—effectively summarizes the paradox of Restoration comedy's attractive persistence. Positing that "the World is divided between two sorts of People, the Men of Wit and the Men of Business," Steele claims that the former have achieved an "almost irresistible Dominion" over "the Government of Mankind" by a charisma reminiscent of the Stuarts:

> While the Man of Wit speaks, he bestows upon his Hearers, by an apt Representation of his Thoughts, all the Happiness and Pleasure of being such as he is, and quickens our heavier Life into Joys we should never of ourselves have tasted, so that we are for our own sakes his Slaves and Followers: But indeed they generally use this charming Force with the utmost Tyranny, and as 'tis too much in their Power, misplace our Love, our Hatred, our Desires and Aversions, on improper Objects; so that . . . they have stamp'd a Kind of praise and Gallantrey on some vices and half persuaded us that a Whore may be still a Beauty, and an Adulterer no Villain. . . . In Imitation of those we have mentioned, there daily arise so many Pretenders to do Mischief, that what seem'd at first but a Conspiracy, is now a General Insurrection against Virtue.[38]

Steele would seem to channel Rochester here: "Men of wit are dangerous tools, / And ever fatal to admiring fools."[39] Marshaling a series of Jacobite allusions—

"Pretenders," "Conspiracy," "Insurrection"—he compares the wit's "charming Force" to the dangers of Stuart "Tyranny" and usurpation, but also aligns it with what Joseph Roach has called "it": an uncanny stylistic allure, manifested here in an ability to make willing "Slaves" of the public, to reinstitute licentious arbitrary rule—supposedly expelled in the wake of William's godly revolution—not in the realm of high politics but in that of cultural taste.[40] A charismatic tyrant, the man of wit restores the mesmerizingly lawless behavior of the Stuart rake, his reign producing something like the world of Restoration comedy in which the transgressors, not the regulators, of sexual or social values retain supremacy. On the one hand, Steele recognizes the lure of this pose to lie in its purchase on liberty; we admire the man of wit "for our own sakes," desiring to imitate his sovereign power to render his world as he pleases. Yet, on the other hand, this imagined freedom of the absolute subject is what subjugates us. If, in terms of the narrative offered by traditional Whig history, the Williamite succession tames Stuart personal rule in favor of the liberty of the subject, Steele registers the worry that it is tragically in the subject's very desire for liberty—manifested in a self-consuming attraction to the social power of the Restoration rake—that such progress away from the dangers of Stuart sovereignty may be troubled.

Such anxiety that Stuart absolutism and the Restoration rake who so often serves as its analogue lie at the heart of postrevolutionary culture is an obsession of *The Fair Penitent* as well. In what follows, I turn to a reading of Rowe's play and its libertine villain, Lothario, with these contexts of Restoration comedy's role in debates about theater, cultural change, and competing versions of Whig liberty in mind. Like Steele, Rowe was marginally affiliated with the wits at Will's coffeehouse, and his presentation of Lothario recalls *The Christian Hero*'s skepticism of the wit's self-destructive appeal.[41] Rowe's play, however, is hardly a straightforward defense of the Williamite moral revolution against the licentious and outmoded form of Restoration comedy; rather, it implicates post-1688 culture itself for reanimating the allure of the comic Restoration rake and thus dangerously collapsing the distinction between Stuart past and Williamite present that Whig history would draw. In the fate of its villain, *The Fair Penitent* does not so much dismiss the appeal of the Stuart rake's radical potential as uncover the impossibility of such an effect, revealing it to be a tragic consequence of the period's cultural succession.

LOTHARIO'S CORPSE AND THE RADICAL COMMONS

The Fair Penitent is a tragedy about succession and the libertine performances that threaten to alter it. "A melancholy tale of private woes," as Rowe's prologue proclaims, the play details domestic strife in the household of the Genoese nobleman Sciolto and his daughter, Calista, the eponymous heroine (5). Eager for a male heir, Sciolto has married Calista against her will to a young political ally, the good-natured but insipid Altamont; unbeknownst to her family, however, Calista has been seduced and abandoned by Lothario, an aristocratic rake and enemy to Altamont's house for whom she harbors a lingering attraction. Amid Lothario's attempts to use the fact of their affair as vengeance against Altamont and Calista's protests of the tyrannical treatment she has suffered at the hands of the play's men, her secret is exposed. Altamont kills Lothario in a duel, which leads ultimately to a factional uprising in Genoa and Calista's suicide. Sciolto dies as well, bequeathing his estate to a grieving Altamont, his sister Lavinia, and her husband Horatio. Patrilinear succession proceeds, but it is not without its sacrifices.

This simple plot proved enduring. By midcentury, *The Fair Penitent* was one of the period's most frequently revived tragedies, in large part due to its appeal as an acting vehicle for London's theatrical celebrities.[42] For some recent scholars, its popularity is explained in its essentially private and domestic displays of emotion and female sexuality and the ways in which such spectacles were co-opted for an emergent bourgeois ideology. For others, the tragedy bears thematically or even directly on the political issues of sovereignty and succession that obsessed the later Stuart era.[43] Implicitly or explicitly, for many of these readings *The Fair Penitent*'s representation of how domestic, familial, and sexual politics may regulate individual behavior registers a broader epistemic shift from coercive juridical rule to forms of governmentality that construct and control subjects' bodies. Calista is often the crux on which such readings turn. Throughout, she deplores her objectified status in a power play between men: "How hard is the condition of our sex, / Through ev'ry state of life the slaves of man!" (34). Calista's lament drives much of the tragedy's emotional power while also being ripe for politicization. Her sexual and vocal deviation from autocratic rule evokes an older Whiggish discourse of resistance, rights, and consent, but at the same time her assertions of autonomy alienate her from a new Whiggish regime whose consolidation of political power depends on the affective bonds of civil society and the patriarchal policing of gendered behavior.[44]

Though Lothario is recognized for contributing to *The Fair Penitent*'s success—and for achieving a cultural longevity of his own—he has received far less attention than Calista, even from critics who have set their sights on the she-tragedy's men. In part, such relative neglect results from the conventionality that was to make his name synonymous with seducer. Lothario is often considered a fairly straightforward example of the Restoration stage rake—slightly belated perhaps, but typical, and thus not requiring much explanation.[45] His behaviors and rhetoric establish him within this dramatic heritage: he exhibits a self-willed desire "to break through law, and spurn at sacred order" (28); he abandons Calista after sleeping with her; he roundly rejects "the marriage chain" (14). To justify his absolutist approach to social life, Lothario mouths a Rochesterian philosophy of the reasonableness of unrestrained desire, proclaiming the irresistibility of man's natural impulses in language familiar from Restoration libertine culture.[46] To Calista's accusation that he would have her "live / A slave to base desires and brutal pleasure, / To be a wretched wanton for thy leisure," he responds cavalierly, "The driving storm of passion will have way, / And I must yield before it" (49).

Unlike so many of the villainous libertine tyrants who served as emblems of Stuart excess in the period's tragedy, however, Lothario retains much of the Restoration comic rake.[47] If the play's other men tend to be modest, sententious, and pathos ridden, Lothario is recognized as "haughty, gallant, [and] gay" (62). He exudes the wit, potency, and allure often found in his comic predecessors and associated with what Richard Braverman has termed "the Stuart élan," the "charismatic vitality associated with the [restored Stuart] court," a performative erotics of power that may be construed as a prop for either legitimate or coercive rule.[48] Lothario engages in "gayer thoughts" and "let[s] laughter loose" (30). He flaunts his witty prowess in verbal bantering with Horatio and Calista's maid, and his speeches to Calista herself abound with a language of seductive potency and recall the comic rake's privileging of present indulgence over forward-looking industry.[49] "To a long oblivion give thy cares," he encourages her, "And let us melt the present hour in bliss" (47). Indeed, Lothario would seem to join Shadwell's Don John in his assertion, "My business is my pleasure."[50]

As with the comic Restoration rake, such recourse to present pleasure is better read not as an opposition to business but as a blind to the business of sociopolitical conflict. While not puritans and cits in the traditional sense, Rowe's male protagonists inherit something of these characters in their moral and economic interests and in their desire to forge Altamont's "better order of succeeding days" beyond the pale of a corrupt court. Lothario's seductive potency and his preemptive cuckolding of Altamont threaten to alter this new order. Behind his expressions of sensual abandon lies a contest for the power and social legitimacy perceived to come with succession to Sciolto's estate and a desire for "vengeance" against the men who have barred him from it, "the dull, doting husband" Altamont and the morally stringent Horatio (28).

Lothario is so often overlooked, then, I would argue, because he is so familiar to us: an archetypal libertine character of Stuart cavalier descent. But at this date in theater history, when rake tyrants hardly ever carried the charm of the 1670s comic libertine, Rowe's call back to this heritage in his villain demands further interrogation. One possible way of reading here is to understand the play as a targeted reversal of the politics of earlier Restoration cuckolding comedies, a forging of what we might call a cit-cuckolding tragedy. Brett Wilson has suggested as much; riffing on Braverman's coinage, he proposes—in a way reminiscent of Beckingham's assertion of the rake's "timely Date" and the ousting of libertine excess by social bonds à la the epilogue to *Jane Shore*—that the play's "defeat of Lothario obliterates 'Stuart élan' from Rowe's stage, displacing it with Whiggish sympathy."[51] I would suggest, alternately, that while Rowe's political intent may be such as Wilson describes, the play also functions to question the finality of such obliteration. If, in Lothario's corpse, *The Fair Penitent* banishes the comic rake under the cultural succession of new Whiggish interests, it also registers an anxiety over the possibility of a long-running Restoration, the failure of that succession embodied in his continued appeal in Whig culture. The play makes tragic the consequences of the Williamite cultural succession, particularly the way sovereign desire lingers as a self-consuming avenue of radical resistance to the republic of property that mars the extension of liberty to the nation.

That *The Fair Penitent* was peculiarly subject to the ghosts of Restoration rake comedy was remarked on by Rowe's critics. One of the most immediate reactions to the play in print was an anonymous satirical prologue that, à la Steele's indictment of the effects of wit, accused Rowe of misdirecting the nation's admiration onto licentious characters. The prologue levels a specific complaint against Altamont, the "Hero cuckold" who has been inappropriately raised to tragic heights:

> Confederate Cuckolds then come Clap this Play!
> Our lucky Bard to You devotes this Day.
> No *Doodle*, *Dashwood*, *Wiseacre* is here,
> Or any of the puny Race, that us'd t'appear;
> The Cuckold now assumes a haughtier Air.[52]

With this comparison of Altamont, the play's "dull, doting husband," to the three cit dupes of Edward Ravenscroft's *The London Cuckolds* (1681), *The Fair Penitent* is made to feature in and ultimately to exceed a genealogy of Stuart comedy. The author of the prologue recognizes in Rowe's work—albeit disapprovingly—what Laura Rosenthal has shrewdly shown to be an effect of Restoration sex comedies: the elevation of the cuckold to the status of guardian of social hierarchy, his ability to shrug off the libertine's sexual usurpation representative of the nation's need to ritualistically forget the specter of rebellion that the rake embodies.[53] If, in Restoration comedy proper, this elevation remains somewhat implicit, Rowe makes it as overt as the prologue's author suggests, heroizing his cuckold in his affiliation with marriage, family, and private property, new forces of governmentality that were increasingly responsible for regulating the nation. Read in this fashion, *The Fair Penitent* might be considered not as a reaction against rake comedy but as the genre's logical apotheosis.

Regarding its rake, *The Fair Penitent* similarly pushes to the limits Restoration comedy's usual tactics for allaying his radical challenge. Lothario's libertine acts are not ultimately self-consuming of his own power, as are those of Wycherley's Horner, nor is he resocialized through an impending marriage to an equivalently witty female lead, as are George Etherege's Dorimant and Aphra Behn's Willmore. He is instead blatantly killed off in a contest of arms that leaves the cuckolded Altamont momentarily victorious. Lothario's death at Altamont's hands in the fourth act is followed quickly by his rearrival on the scene as a corpse. The stage directions that open the fifth act explicitly call for the return of "Lothario's body on a bier" along with a disheveled and mourning Calista, who promptly soliloquizes over her lover's now-faded élan:

> But here's a sight is terrible indeed:
> Is this that haughty, gallant, gay Lothario,
> That dear perfidious—Ah!—how pale he looks!
> How grim with clotted blood, and those dead eyes! (61–62)

A symbolic stage prop, Lothario's corpse serves as exemplum of the Restoration comic rake's fate in postrevolutionary culture: the libertine who in the past embodied aristocratic charm, power, and pleasure has become immobilized and almost unrecognizable in the present. Dead and isolated with only the suicidal Calista at his side—in what is perhaps a grim parody of the marriages that usually end Restoration comedies—Lothario represents Rowe's rejection of the rake under the new conditions of social compact embodied by the play's other men.

That these scenes of the rake's demise were the symbolic heart of the play's ideological design for Rowe's contemporaries is suggested in how often they appeared in frontispiece illustration. Beginning with the 1714 reprint of *The Fair Penitent* and extending into early nineteenth-century editions of Rowe's works, Calista's fifth-act mourning over Lothario's corpse was the standard image that readers would have encountered upon opening the play text. It was seconded only by illustrations of Lothario's dead body immediately following the duel with Altamont.[54] Such salient visual reminders would seem to be at odds with Lothario's fate, textually, at the end of the script. Rowe keeps his corpse onstage for the entirety of the fifth act, but after Calista's set-piece mourning speech, it is never mentioned in the dialogue or stage directions again. In reading the play, in other words, it is easy to forget that Lothario's corpse is still there, its initial symbolic significance gradually overshadowed by the rest of the characters acting out the tragic denouement. The contrast between the corpse's visual presence in illustration and its disappearance from textual denotation is suggestive of Rosenthal's reading of the free play of memory and forgetting in Restoration comedy's treatment of the libertine. Lothario's corpse—as it appears in these various ways in print—serves as a reminder of the national need to forget the rake, to consign his insurgent energies to a distanced past. In killing off its libertine—rather than socializing him as in older Restoration comedy or resignifying his powers for a Whiggish regime as in *The Way of the World*—*The Fair Penitent* literalizes this ideological effect, asking audiences to imagine the Stuart rake as dead and gone.

As equally important, however, as the ideological play of the absence and presence of Lothario's corpse is the fatal attraction that Calista continues to bear toward it. In the concluding act, Calista is in the charnel house to mourn Lothario, and she does so in terms that recall in equal parts her disgust and her admiration for his libertine pose, his vulnerability in death and his vitality in life: he is "perfidious" yet "dear," "pale" with "dead eyes" yet still evocative of once being "haughty, gallant, [and] gay."[55] Her unwillingness to let go of her past with Lothario is, moreover, contrasted to the logic of succession that drives Sciolto, Altamont, and Horatio. Calista quite literally refuses to succeed to the new man whom her father has chosen for her, disclosing to Lothario during their final exchange, "hadst thou been true . . . Nor Altamont but thou hadst been my lord" (49). If Rowe's intent is to dismiss the Stuart élan in the rake's death, to ask us to forget the Stuart cultural past, then this point has been effectually lost on his heroine, who, for all her scorn at his libertine infidelities, remains drawn to him.

Wherein, though, does Calista's persistent attraction to Lothario lie? Beyond their sexual attraction forming the basis for its domestic tragedy, *The Fair Penitent* draws the pair together, I suggest, in such a way as to explore the politics of their shared affinity for the possibilities of liberty and autonomy harbored in the libertine's sovereign pose. The specific terms of Calista's remembrance over the corpse—"haughty, gallant, gay"—indicate that part of the allure, for her, lies in this very cavalier aristocratic posturing that, as we saw earlier, was also the means by which the wits of the *Commendatory Verses* responded to Williamite moral reform. Rowe's play constructs Lothario as a representation of the concurrent attraction and menace of wit culture and its revival of a set of comic Restoration performances that toe a line between liberty and absolute authority.

This is best exemplified in Lothario's altercation with Horatio, a scene resonant of the cultural struggles between wit and reform in the years leading up to the play's production. Encountering Lothario on the verges of Sciolto's garden in act 2, Horatio confronts him with an indictment of his libertine lifestyle that could have come straight out of anti-wit discourse. Just as Blackmore renders wit as frivolous, vain, and ultimately unlawful, Horatio accuses Lothario of being "unworthy of a man" in his disrespect for "law" and "sacred order," chastising him as member of a "skipping, dancing, worthless tribe" of upper-class rakes who, "too lavish," have been "bred at home in idleness and riot" and who talk only of superficial and low subjects: "of your dress, / of dice, of whores, of horses, and yourselves" (28–30). Compounding anticivil "riot" with self-centric "idleness" and pleasure, Horatio's charges not only index contemporary attacks on wit culture but also recall John Milton's depiction of the newly restored Stuart courtiers in *Paradise Lost* (1667): "Sons of Belial" who are "flown with insolence and wine" and who "riot" in "Court and Palaces" and "in luxurious Cities."[56] Lothario plays the part quite willingly. The scene opens with a parallel to book 4 of *Paradise Lost*, specifically the conflict between the angel Gabriel and Satan. Like Milton's angelic guardian of Eden, Horatio warns Lothario that Sciolto's garden is a "forbidden place" and that he must "expect a punishment" if found there again; Lothario, in his turn, repeats Satan's contemptuous address to Gabriel—"Know ye not mee?"—upon first seeing Horatio:[57]

> Ha! Dost thou know me, that I am Lothario?
> As great a name as this proud city boasts of. (27, 30)

The scene then executes a seamless transition from Lothario as haughty warrior-aristocrat to Lothario as Stuart comic wit. He mocks Horatio's moral-reformist language and his "solemn order" to avoid Sciolto's residence with taunts about "cuckold[s]" and the promise to "indulge our gayer thoughts, and let laughter loose, / And use [Horatio's] sacred friendship [to Altamont] for our mirth" (30).

Rendering in serious terms the comic battle of wit versus cit here, the same scene also underscores how the wit's libertine pose may manifest itself in a politically dangerous perversion of the Whiggish idea of liberty. When, amid the rising verbal conflict, Horatio indicts Lothario for being inappropriately "pleasant," Lothario cuts him off and wittily appropriates the allusion to "pleasure" to make a claim about the revolutionary grounds of his libertine will:

> By the joys
> Which yet my soul has uncontrolled pursued,
> I would not turn aside from my least pleasure,
> Though all thy force were armed to bar my way,
> But like the birds, great Nature's happy commoners

> That haunt in woods, in meads, and flow'ry gardens,
> Rifle the sweets and taste the choicest fruits
> Yet scorn to ask the lordly owner's leave. (30)

Specifically, Lothario's bird simile might remind us of Willmore's comic defense of his sexual profligacy to Angellica Bianca in *The Rover*: "I must, like cheerful birds, sing in all groves, / And perch on every bough."[58] More generally, it recalls the Restoration aristocratic rake's rhetorical privileging of the liberties of "great Nature" over social bounds. The familiar libertine recourse to nature, however, is delivered in Lothario's speech in starkly political terms reminiscent of the questions of capitalism that shaped the wits' reaction to Blackmore's proposals for cultural reform. As one of the "happy commoners," Lothario imagines the pursuit of his libertine will as an act of radical politics, a revolutionary wresting of the communal rights to the land from the private enclosure of "the lordly owner." It is a vision, moreover, that accords with the policies of radical leveling of older seventeenth-century revolutionary sects and that were often attributed, in 1690s ideological warfare, to the more extremist versions of Whig republicanism. In the state of nature that Lothario professes, it is not the centralized Stuart monarchy that is the target of radical activity, but capitalism's republic of property, embodied in moral and social enclosers like Horatio. *The Fair Penitent* reveals part of Lothario's élan to be his ability to spin the Restoration rake's performance of absolute will as the desirable culmination of the Whig doctrine of the liberty of the subject.

Ultimately, Rowe expects his readers to see Lothario's wit in the way that Steele might: its charismatic powers of representation make us "misplace our Love, our Hatred, our Desires and Aversions, on improper Objects." Lothario's self-fashioning as a heroic advocate of the liberty of the commons is undercut by the way his insistence on his own "uncontrolled" pursuit of sexual pleasure turns a pastoral vision of the state of nature to a Hobbesian one in which individuals have a "Right to every thing; even to one anothers body."[59] In Lothario's purposeful confusions, *The Fair Penitent* shows an effect of libertine wit to be the collapse of the liberty of the subject into licentious absolutism of the self-willed individual. Moreover, as scholars have noted of the Restoration rake's assertions of personal and political liberty more generally, Lothario's desire to break "lordly" socioeconomic bounds is self-consuming in that it betrays the only real power base—his class privilege—from which the libertine can launch his subversive performances. Furthering the Miltonic parallel that structures this scene, Rowe portrays Lothario in terms of Gabriel's epithet for Satan: a "sly hypocrite, who now wouldst seem / Patron of liberty."[60] Lothario's Satanism extends beyond his role as Calista's tempter in a retelling of the biblical fall narrative and encompasses his stance as a corrupter of liberty.[61]

Through Lothario's defense of a kind of Whiggish freedom, *The Fair Penitent* poses an ideological kinship between the wit/rake and the extremist republican radical in their mutual commitment to—as one 1690s pamphleteer put it—"lawless liberty."[62] With the Whigs' transition from the opposition party under Charles II and James II to the court party under William, many Whigs of the 1690s and early 1700s began to detach themselves from the antimonarchist revolutionary attitudes that had been a staple of their heritage. In turn—and especially in the context of the financial crises and standing army debates that rocked England in the wake of the 1697 peace of Ryswick—other Whigs who were more critical of William's sovereignty formed a tenuous rhetorical alliance with Tory and Jacobite "country" interests, reviving the revolutionary principles of resistance and freedom from domination but also inadvertently encouraging associations with civil war–era zealotry and a breakdown of social order often attached to the specter of republicanism.[63] By 1703, the resurgence of Whig radicalism that had marked the late 1690s was itself called into question, as the new war with France and Anne's ascension to the throne somewhat allayed fears of an over-mighty executive at home. As John Dennis declared in his prologue to Charles Gildon's *The Patriot* (1703)—an adaptation of Nathaniel Lee's republican-leaning *Lucius Junius Brutus* (1680)—for a playwright to espouse revolutionary "Anti-Regal Principles" in the modern era "would be now unjust."[64] These were sentiments to which Rowe could ascribe; J. Douglas Canfield notes that in the first decade of the eighteenth century, Rowe's allegiances underwent a marked shift from "country" to "court."[65] *The Fair Penitent* similarly seems to dismiss older strands of Whig revolutionary ideology in having them voiced by an insidious yet charismatic figure of the self-centric absolutist rake marked by the stamp of leveling so often used by moderate Williamite Whigs to derogate unpopular strands of resistance theory and popular sovereignty. The play's attribution of such ideas to the wit Lothario serves as an indictment of the recent trend in English cultural history of flirting with the revival of the Restoration comic rake as an avatar through which to take a radical stance against the republic of property and moral reform at the heart of Williamite cultural politics.

The misguided appeal of a radical assertion of the liberty of the subject that *The Fair Penitent* registers in contemporary English culture is embodied in Calista. Her fatal attraction is not to the rake's sexual charms, but to his revolutionary ones. This is evinced in the discursive similarities that she shares with Lothario; particularly in the opening of act 3, Calista repeatedly protests her treatment by the play's men in the Whiggish terms of autonomy and resistance.[66] Confronted first in this scene by Sciolto's accusation that her "sullen" behavior toward Altamont makes her "wayward" and "perverse," Calista asks:

> Has not your daughter giv'n herself to Altamont,
> Yielded the native freedom of her will
> To an imperious husband's lordly rule,
> To gratify a father's stern command? (33)

Juxtaposed with Lothario's speech to Horatio at the end of act 2, Calista's argument here relies similarly on the polemic of natural liberty, emphasizing an inherent conflict between "the native freedom of her will" and the "lordly rule" of husbands and fathers. In the soliloquy that follows, her complaint mounts to an assault on the republic of property and the institution of marriage as the bedrock of an arbitrary patriarchy's subjugation of a disenfranchised commons of women:

> How hard is the condition of our sex!
> Through ev'ry state of life the slaves of man.
> In all the dear delightful days of youth
> A rigid father dictates to our wills
> And deals out pleasure with a scanty hand.
> To his, the tyrant husband's reign succeeds:
> Proud with opinion of superior reason,
> He holds domestic bus'ness and devotion
> All we are capable to know, and shuts us,
> Like cloistered idiots, from the world's acquaintance
> And all the joys of freedom. Wherefore are we
> Born with high souls but to assert ourselves,
> Shake off this vile obedience they exact,
> And claim an equal empire o'er the world? (34)

Calista voices some of the standard tenets of Whig resistance theory in her representation of the rule of "rigid father" and "tyrant husband." As the "slaves of man," women are dispossessed by an arbitrary government of their "wills" and "pleasure," their rights to self-ownership, consent, and autonomy. Subjected in this way, for Calista, women are not only the property of men but also disenfranchised of their own common-law rights to self-possession. The image of the tyrants' "scanty hand[s]" discloses an economic angle to Calista's speech: male tyranny is caught up with and determined by the unequally gendered distribution of private property within the patriarchal household.

In the emphasis of Calista's revolutionary Whig language on the play of property and freedom, enclosure and openness, it recycles much of what Lothario voices in his own act of subversion of Horatio's similarly "stern command" against encroaching on Sciolto's territory. With the comparison of women to "cloistered idiots," Calista suggests the exclusion of her sex from the enclosed rights to "freedom" supposedly housed in the political settlements meant to curtail tyranny. Her resistance to "lordly rule" relies on a claim of "equal empire o'er the world," an image of shared, common rights to a natural landscape that mirrors Lothario's own protest against Horatio's imperious "lordly owner." In a later argument with Horatio, Calista again rehearses these ideas of slavery and freedom through the trope of dispossession from the land, likening herself to a "poor captive in a foreign realm" who longs for "the dear native land" that she could once call her own (35). For Calista, as for earlier seventeenth-century radicals, enclosure and exclusion are the dominant tropes for how social rules foster a tyrannical polity in which the people have no representative status.

In the end, like Lothario, Calista too seeks to be "free from the marriage chain," another image by which she condemns the way social institutions perpetuate a tyrannical regime of enclosure and slavery (40). *The Fair Penitent*, in fact, goes to great length to emphasize the way its heroine and villain draw similarly on radical idioms that endorse freedom of the individual will, popular rights, and resistance. This parallel makes Calista's recourse to such radical language suspect in its proximity to the Stuart libertine's self-centric perversions of liberty. Modern readers might recognize a fundamental ideological distinction between Calista's liberal proto-feminism and Lothario's licentiousness, but it is important to note that Rowe's protagonists consistently do not. For Horatio especially, Calista's radicalism makes her akin to Lothario in his self-willed pursuit of pleasure: Horatio can see her only as a "fatally fair" female libertine, "false [and] luxurious in [her] appetites," enamored of a "variety" of lovers, and constantly "contriving riot and loose scapes of love" (18, 20). Attracted to the revolutionary language in which Lothario casts his specious call to resistance, Calista is subject to the same trajectory as her lover, her defense of revolutionary liberty collapsing into a bid for riotous self-license in the eyes of the other characters. Her pleas for subjects' rights and the commons are, moreover, shot through with aristocratic overtones that betray her association of freedom with popular and equitably gendered sovereignty. Upon Horatio accusing her directly of loose sexual behavior, her rebuttal echoes Lothario's warrior-aristocrat posturing:

> Dishonor blast thee, base, unmannered slave,
> That dar'st forget my birth and sex. (38)

The stress she lays on her "birth" and her "high soul" suggests an aristocratic privilege attached to her desire for individual autonomy. In these moments, Calista's rhetoric approaches that of Artemisia in Rowe's *The Ambitious Step-mother* (1700), who at one point in the play levels a feminist-sounding critique aligned more clearly with lawless self-license:

> Could Fate e'er mean
> Me, for a Wife, a Slave to *Tiribasus*!
> To such a Thing as he! a Wretch! a Husband!
> Therefore in just Assertion of my self,
> I shook him off, and past those narrow limits,
> Which Laws contrive in vain for Souls born great.[67]

Calista's attempt at autonomy and "equal empire" threatens similarly to devolve into a solipsistic performance of the lawless pose of the absolutist subject. *The Fair Penitent* thus operates as part of the hegemonic reforms of establishment Whig culture, aligning radical and Stuart libertine values as twinned versions of "lawless liberty."

Calista's story, I suggest, is the story of postrevolutionary culture's resignification of the Restoration comic rake's performances, their persistent appeal under new Williamite conditions of moral and sociopolitical governance. Just as Steele describes a nation led astray by a false promise of liberty in wit culture's genealogical connection to Stuart comedy, so too is Calista seduced by the attractions of a Stuart libertine wit that prove self-destructive. What Lothario offers Calista is the temptation of a revolutionary brand of liberty that bears within it a serpent's sting of Stuart arbitrary rule. In the end, *The Fair Penitent* articulates the corrupting potential of the rake's glamorous display of a supposedly radical egalitarianism and reveals how possible it is for the Whiggish performances of the rights-bearing subject to reanimate Stuart absolutism in the realm of social relations; the play does not so much destroy the Stuart rake's élan as reveal how that élan survives in contemporary culture in an alluring yet tragic form of the self-consuming liberty of the subject. An analogue to the nation's continued infatuation with the Restoration libertine, Calista's fatal attraction to Lothario is the tragedy of radical Whig principles in post-1688 circumstances: the tragedy of how an older political discourse of autonomy and resistance, intended to protect the commons from tyrannical encroachments, results in the lawlessness of the absolutist subject. *The Fair Penitent* extends tragic sympathy to Calista—and to the historical Whig principles to which she adheres—but ultimately, through the association of those principles with libertine sovereign desire, it also suggests the necessity of abandoning them in favor of rule of law embodied in social contract, sentiment, and moral reform.

If, however, *The Fair Penitent* marks Lothario and Calista as archaisms of a tumultuous seventeenth-century past that Whig modernity would banish, it also registers the anxiety that their sovereign desire is generated by the very terms of the Williamite cultural and political succession, particularly as those terms rely fundamentally on the concept of property. As we have seen, Lothario's and Calista's rhetoric of resistance relies on images of private ownership and enclosure of the commons, and, indeed, these are the operating metaphors that the play associates with Sciolto's domestic rule. At the start, for example, the social contract that binds together Sciolto's extended family is physically represented in a series of embraces that he offers Altamont and Horatio and suggests how their polity is based on sociability, a value that, by the early eighteenth century, was beginning to inform modern Whig cultural politics.[68] At the same time, the text emphasizes the possessive nature of such affective gestures as Sciolto glories in making Altamont "mine," telling him further:

> I set thee down and sealed thee for my own;
> Thou art my son, ev'n near me as Calista.
> Horatio and Lavinia too are mine. (10)

The passage justifies Sciolto's sovereignty as contractual and sociable but conjoins it with the language of personal ownership over other people, providing a more benevolent mirror image of the republic of property that Calista laments. Moreover, the backdrop for Sciolto's embraces further emphasizes the enclosure at the base of his politics: his garden estate, walled off from an "ungrateful Genoa" (8). Natural and harmonious, the garden represents not only the Edenic remove that Lothario's Satanism will infiltrate, but also a site of private property and law as it is significantly withdrawn from public disorderliness. The setting thus serves as a spatialization both of the property relations that undergird the play's Whig ideology and of the temporal break across the 1688 succession, with the garden's naturalized enclosure representing the present's orderliness in contrast to a courtly and competitive factionalism that is distinctly reminiscent of a Williamite view of the Restoration past.

The exclusionary nature at the heart of Whig ideology thus imagined is ultimately what drives Lothario's particular response. Confiding to Rossano—his only ally, to whom he has no motive to be specious—Lothario admits early on, "I liked [Calista], and would have married her, / But that it pleased her father to refuse me, / To make this honorable fool her husband" (12). The denial of his marriage suit amounts to being cut out of the garden, the play's site of law and property, and it precipitates his decision not just to seduce Calista but, as he later boasts to

Horatio, to make the knowledge of the act "as public / As is the noonday sun, air, earth, or water / Or any common benefit of nature" (28). Lothario's vengeance is a means to expose Sciolto's naturalized enclosure to a real state of nature and upset his privilege, to make his familial property "common" rather than privately owned. Playing opposite Lothario's performance of the Restoration aristocratic libertine, then, Rowe's other men appear as symbolic cits, not simply because of their role in the cuckolding plot but because of how their revolutionary ideology is made to depend on capitalist bourgeois values.

Lothario's defense of the commons as a space of egalitarian natural liberty is certainly specious (he is as obsessed by ownership as Sciolto is), but the ideological material latent within it is capable of being put to more genuinely radical ends; this is evinced in Calista's resistance to the Whig liberalism of Sciolto's polity. If Lothario is excluded outside the propertied enclosure of marriage and the contractual family, Calista is excluded from full liberty of the subject from within these very institutions designed to secure it. She views the marriage contract as a sovereign "force" that

> May bind two bodies in one wretched chain;
> But minds will still look back to their own choice.
> So the poor captive in a foreign realm
> Stands on the shore, and sends his wishes back
> To the dear native land from whence he came. (35)

Like Lothario, Calista counters images of natural freedom (open shores and native lands) and choice to a motif of marriage as binding enclosure, unmasking the impasse at the heart of Williamite political symbolism: if the contractual family represents the elevation of rule of law and the liberty of the subject against the licentious absolutism of the Stuarts, it is also an instrument of the biopolitical fashioning of social life, especially for the Whigs, who, as Rachel Weil argues, saw it as site for regulating "property, population growth and economic productivity."[69] Sciolto's prioritization of the contractual family unit over individual desire—he threatens to "cast [Calista] off as one whose impious hands / Had rent asunder nature's nearest ties" (34)—is not just evidence of his "Roman strictness," his adherence to a stoic honor culture, but more importantly an example of the way marriage and contract are captured within the republic of property (53). What Calista's body can produce biologically and socially in forging bonds between the play's propertied men is more essential than her own place in the commons. The play reveals that her attraction to Lothario's libertine rhetoric is conditioned by how the property-centric nature of Whig ideology delimits the possibility of freedom.

As *The Fair Penitent* uncovers the capitalist base of Williamite political values and their cultural symbols—contract and rule of law, marriage and sociable exchange—it gestures to how the antibourgeois behaviors of the Restoration stage rake may find new purchase after 1688. The Whig liberalism of Sciolto's contractual family establishes an anti-Stuart polity, but its enclosing and exclusionary nature generates a response in the form of libertine aristocratic self-fashioning as a vehicle for accessing the liberty denied under capitalist sovereignty. While the play does not amount to a straightforward critique, on Rowe's part, of this facet of the new Whig establishment, it nonetheless offers a glimpse of how the Restoration stage rake's anticapitalist behaviors may be resignified (spuriously for Lothario, genuinely for Calista) not as a rearguard aristocratic defense against a turning tide of bourgeois modernity but as radical resistance to the republic of property. Lothario and Calista fail as true representatives of the commons, their adoption of the Restoration libertine's pose ultimately devolving into a self-consuming form of Hobbesian absolutism and thus reinscribing a regime of property in the self-possessed aristocratic body. But what the rake's theatrical heritage offers, nonetheless, is the charismatic fantasy of the possibility of resistance to the republic of property's inflections of law and liberty, opening up a space of desire that can contest the supposed end of Restoration libertine comedy's cultural pertinence.

The ultimate tragedy of *The Fair Penitent* is how postrevolutionary Whig culture, in attempting to banish the Stuart political and theatrical past, actually sets the stage for its return. As the liberalizing values that sustain the 1688 settlement and its subsequent Williamite cultural reforms are entangled with a republic of property that encloses law and liberty with capitalist privilege, they call forth the lawless, anticapitalist, cit-cuckolding Restoration libertine as a newly attractive model for enacting the subject's release from such inegalitarian constraints. If for Tom Brown and the wits this could be celebrated as a comic re-righting of the state of nature, for Rowe it produces only tragedy, as Stuart absolutism is paradoxically revived as an unintended effect of the Williamite cultural revolution.

Read in the contexts of 1690s theatrical and cultural reform, then, *The Fair Penitent* is less about the obliteration of the Stuart élan than it is about the anxiety that such obliteration will never be finalized. While Rowe's polemical intent may indeed be to firmly establish his villain's attractive Stuart cavalier credentials only to later emphasize his death as symbolic of their outmodedness, the text itself offers an alternate story. It attempts not only to delegitimize an older brand of republican politics and its alignment with the "lawless liberty" of Stuart and radical culture but also to comment on the persistence of the Restoration aristocratic rake, particularly the way in which his challenge to the rule of law is resignified as a challenge to the rule of property. This issue of the Restoration rake's banishment echoes finally in Lothario's dying speech to Altamont:

> My fierce ambitious soul
> Declining droops, and all her fires grow pale,
> Yet let not this advantage swell thy pride:
> I conquered in my turn, in love I triumphed.
> Those joys are lodged beyond the reach of fate;
> That sweet revenge comes smiling to my thoughts,
> Adorns my fall, and cheers my heart in dying. (50)

Even in dying, Lothario does not lose the enduring charisma of the Restoration comic rake. Sounding just as "haughty, gallant, [and] gay" as ever, his deathbed taunt posits the impossibility of Altamont's "better order of succeeding days": it is a promise of the future's inability to adequately forget the rake's radical challenge. As the very moment of Lothario's death becomes a moment of the rake's lingering hold on the future, *The Fair Penitent* registers not the end of Restoration libertine drama but its long-running nature.

CORPSING LOTHARIO IN PERFORMANCE

If, as text, *The Fair Penitent* frets over the Restoration rake's threat to cultural succession, then as performance, the play itself bears the potential to bring that threat to life. Summarizing a long legacy of thought in performance studies on the entwined issues of embodiment and signification, Elizabeth Dillon contends that "the signifying economy of the theatre operates in two registers: one that is *ontic* (thingly, material, resolutely present) and one that is *mimetic* (referential, immaterial, gesturing toward a scene located elsewhere)." For Dillon, the value of this dual perspective lies in recognizing how the ontic, material conditions of performance "can begin to unwind mimesis" and "offer a challenge to the very script that is being performed."[70] In a way distinct from the immaterial signifiers of print, the world of things on the stage offers a chance to reframe or fracture the mimetic fabric out of which ideologies are fashioned and subjects governed. In this final section, I turn to a seminal moment in *The Fair Penitent*'s eighteenth-century performance history (its debut) in which such ontic aspects of the theater, particularly the effect and affect of Lothario's body onstage, confound the hegemonic drive of Rowe's script, collapsing the linear distance between Stuart past and postrevolutionary present and evoking the long-running Restoration. While Rowe's text may try to put Lothario's disruptive energies to rest by killing him off, its performance history reveals his corpse's occasionally quite literal refusal to stay dead.

As part of the script, the substitution of the corpse for the once radically autonomous libertine accords with the regulatory objective that, as I noted earlier, scholars have read in the text's treatment of social and gendered norms. Lothario's bodily fate is tied up with the play's mobilization of its sociopolitical agenda. Emblematic of the disciplining that the Stuart rake faces under the new standards of civility and masculinity, the spectacle of Lothario's corpse in the fourth and fifth acts is indicative of the eighteenth-century theater's ability to compete with the sovereign powers of church and state as a site of governmentality, that is, a site effective in noncoercively regulating the body public.[71] Indeed, much as the annual revival of Rowe's *Tamerlane* (1701) on November 5 served as a ritual celebration of the nation's deliverance from Stuart and French tyranny in the 1688 revolution, *The Fair Penitent*'s perennial popularity in the acting repertory may speak to the esteem audiences had for its political message, thus supporting the traditional reading of it as marking a shift in theater history away from Restoration culture.[72]

But elements of *The Fair Penitent*'s stage history suggest that, with regard to its potential for governing subjects, its success was double-edged at best. Elizabeth Dillon, Kathleen Wilson, and Susan Cannon Harris, for instance, have variously traced how, outside of the London metropole, individual performances of the play could become as much occasions for contesting British imperialism as they were hegemonic operatives of it.[73] The mimetic stakes of Rowe's drama of cultural succession were challenged at home too, the possibilities embedded within its staging a latent threat to its social utility in governing the body public. *The Fair Penitent*'s script contains the prospect of its own theatrical undoing in the ontic status of Lothario's corpse as a prop in the fifth act. "Invisible on the page except as textual signifiers," Andrew Sofer reminds us, "props seduce our attention in the playhouse."[74] When confronted with the printed text, readers may very well forget Lothario's presence in the final act; but in live performance, the longer Lothario's body lingers onstage, the more it may distract audiences from the scene's moral and sociopolitical aims. Despite Sciolto's dying injunction to the remaining members of the cast to forget Lothario's and Calista's transgressions in looking away from their dead bodies—"O, turn thee from the fatal object" (69)—the lingering presence of the corpse retains an ontic potential that may exceed the play text's pretensions to its banishment.

According to popular theatrical lore, such a potential was actualized in the 1703 premiere of *The Fair Penitent* at Lincoln's Inn Fields when Lothario's corpse—personated by a live actor—got up and walked off in the middle of the fifth act. The anecdote is originally retailed by William Rufus Chetwood, longtime prompter at Drury Lane, in his *General History of the Stage* (1749) and is worth quoting at length:

> I shall mention, as my last Note, an Accident that fell out at this Play, the first Season it was perform'd, in the Year 1699 which I gather'd from that Stage Chronicle, Mr. *John Bowman*.
>
> *Lothario*, after he is kill'd by *Altamont* in the 4th Act, lies dead by Proxy in the 5th, raised on a Bier covered with Black by the *Property-man*, and the Face whitened by the Barber, the Coat and Perriwig generally filled by one of the Dressers. Most of the capital Actors in the establish'd Theatres have generally a Dresser to themselves, tho' they are paid by the Manager, to be ready, on all Occasions, for Stage-guards, Attendance, &c.
>
> Mr. *Powell* played *Lothario*, and one *Warren*, his Dresser claimed a Right of lying for his Master, and performing the dead Part of *Lothario*, which he proposed to act to the best Advantage; tho' *Powell* was ignorant of the Matter. The Fifth Act began, and went on, as usual, with Applause; but, about the Middle of the distressful Scene, *Powell* called aloud for his Man *Warren*, who so loudly replied, from the Bier on the Stage, *Here, Sir! Powell* (who, as I said before, was ignorant of the Part his Man was doing) repeated, without Loss of Time, *Come here this Moment, you Son of a Whore! or I'll break all the Bones in your Skin*. *Warren* knew his hasty Temper; therefore, without any Reply, jump'd off, with all his Sables about him, which, unfortunately, were tied fast to the Handles of the Bier, and dragg'd after him. But this was not all; the Laugh and Roar began in the Audience, till it frighten'd poor *Warren* so much, that, with the Bier at his Tail, he threw down *Calista* (Mrs. *Barry*), and overwhelm'd her with the Table, Lamp, Book, Bones, together with all the Lumber of the Charnel-house. He tugg'd, till he broke off his Trammels, and made his Escape; and the Play, at once, ended with immoderate Fits of Laughter: Even the grave Mr. *Betterton*
>
> *Smil'd in the Tumult, and enjoy'd the Storm*.
>
> But he would not let the *Fair Penitent* be play'd any more that Season, till poor *Warren*'s Misconduct was something forgot.[75]

The accuracy of Chetwood's account is difficult to verify—his dating wrongly places *The Fair Penitent*'s debut in the seventeenth century, and it remains the only confirmation of such a spectacular mishap. Nonetheless, the anecdote has since been codified in a number of stage histories, and it provides an amusing and feasible explanation as to why this otherwise very popular play went unperformed for twelve years after an initial one-night run.[76] It puts the blame for the play's disappearance from the repertory on a moment of corpsing—thespian slang for onstage bloopers that inadvertently turn tragedy into farce. As a verb and as a theatrical event, to "corpse" means for an actor, by accidentally breaking the fourth wall in some way, to "kill" the character he or she represents in the mimetic world of the play. It is, as Nicholas Ridout argues, an event almost always connected with laughter, with death, and "with the irruption of the real and the suspension of proper order."[77] Chetwood's account presents a unique example of this phenomenon, however, in that what is "corpsed" is a corpse itself; the failure of the play's mimetic fabric produces a moment of death that is simultaneously a moment of return to life.

Such failures are best conceived not as blunders to be regretted but, as a number of recent scholars of performance have argued, as constitutive of the theatrical medium itself, its error-prone and risky liveness a source of its very identity and power. Indebted, in part, to a post-positivist understanding of failure to achieve sovereign plenitude as fundamental to the processes of representation and the production of subjectivity, many theorists of failure describe their subject as subversive. As with parody, theatrical failure's power lies in its capacity to expose as constructed conceptions of "the real," "the natural," or "the correct" and to undermine the ideologies that turn on them.[78] As much as theater may serve to hegemonically disseminate a particular social, cultural, or political order, in its ever-looming potential for mimetic breakdown, it may also generate unexpected alternatives to that order. As such "failures" move unpredictably off script, they call the rightness of "success" to account. Sara Jane Bailes puts it nicely: theatrical "failure *produces*, and does so in a roguish manner."[79]

What is produced, roguishly, in Lothario's corpsing is an undoing of the success of historical succession. The ontic failure to finalize the rake's demise both lays bare the postrevolutionary Whiggish declaration of the eclipse of Stuart culture as ideological, not factual, and, for a moment, enacts an alternative possibility of history's outcome: the return of Restoration libertine drama and its latent radicalism. This effect appears first in Chetwood's description of the scene between George Powell and his manservant, which is suffused with something uncannily Rochesterian. Though Powell was known best for his portrayals of ranting tragedy villains, he had played his share of Restoration rakes—Don John in *The Libertine* (1675), Willmore in *The Rover*, Ramble in *The London Cuckolds*, and Jupiter in *Amphitryon* (1690)—some of whom, like Shadwell's and Behn's, were known to be modeled after Lord Rochester.[80] Such roles bled into his personal life, which Colley Cibber, John Vanbrugh, and others recalled for its "licentious Courses"—a history of brawling, inebriety, hauteur, and idleness.[81] Chetwood's anecdote vividly describes a particular instance of this in how Powell speaks to Warren; the cursing and the threat of violence that mark Powell's "hasty Temper" in their exchange evoke Rochester's habit of cursing out his servants, a trait that Shadwell immortalized in the brutal language of Don John and that Rochester himself self-ironically endowed in the libertine speakers of his poetry.[82] In this moment of corpsing, the (mimetic) death of the Stuart rake is comically upstaged by that figure's (ontic) revival in the form of Powell restoring his behavior, a real-life Restoration drama emerging to reverse the script's attempt to banish its characters and legacy.

The collapse of mimetic and ontic registers in Warren's accident not only shatters the theatrical illusion but also speaks to how the material conditions of the stage can expose that illusion as an agent of governmentality. The ontic subject who emerges from the mimetic corpse is, in social terms, one whose will is displaced from his self. Warren, unlike the self-possessed sovereign libertine (or what remains of him) that he plays, is literally not his own man but a servant, property of another's will. In one sense, we might read this collapse of Lothario into Warren as fortuitously in line with the Whiggish impetus of the play, as an exposing and containing of the Stuart libertine's dangerously autonomous energies in the ontic suggestion that all such characters of sovereign pretensions are, deep down, servants to some higher power. But in another sense, the details of Warren's corpsing offer a more sweeping reveal of the political conditions of the stage itself as disciplinary mechanism. Corpsing, Ridout speculates, "occurs on occasions where the self is operating with particular self-consciousness as the agent of a discourse of discipline or control" and in which that discourse comes undone: "What we experience as affect in these moments of undoing is an apprehension of our own position in relation to the economic and political conditions of our theatregoing."[83] For Ridout, theater is a medium that covers up the labor of its aesthetic and, in its inevitable failures, reveals that cover-up, unearthing the sociopolitical relations that motivate it. Warren's transformation from aristocrat to servant highlights theater as not merely an aesthetic activity, but also a space of social regulation. It does so by reminding us that Powell too—underneath the veneer of the mimetic self-possessed aristocrats whom he personates—is also ultimately a servant, a laborer in the service of Her Majesty Queen Anne's household, responsible for the regulating of the body public through the discipline of bodies on and around the stage. As Warren's corpsing uncovers a long line of laborers undergirding the play's mimetic fiction, it makes explicit the drama's role as laborer for a political order in its attempts to render Lothario dead.

As this moment of corpsing disrupts this labor, it in turn hinders the ideological success of the specific political order that, as we have seen, Rowe's text instantiates. Chetwood's anecdote details the breakdown of discipline as an effect of the corpse's comic rebellion. The rebellion is made possible, first, by Warren's liminal status between properly human and properly prop, between ontic acting agent and mimetic inanimate object. The anecdote lingers on this confusion in the way it depicts his relation to other stage props. Literally "tied fast to the Handles of the Bier," a position that causes his body to merge with the table, lamp, book, and bones in the general disarray, Warren becomes just one prop among the many that set the tone for Calista's mourning scene. His personhood similarly merges with descriptions of Lothario's clothes, signs of the character's aristocratic status. Chetwood's phrasing, in fact, prioritizes the clothes—the "Coat and Perriwig" are "filled" with the passive body of the dresser. Filler rather than animating force, his person emphasizes the emptiness of the Stuart aristocratic rake: all style and no substance. Suggestive of the cultural and political obliteration of the rake, as scripted, these props contribute to the play's governmental drive to regulate the social body. Warren-as-prop works equally to this end, but his concurrent ontic status shows him in service to a different master altogether, the Rochesterian rake in the figure of the offstage Powell. His literal upheaval of the stage amounts to a revolt (albeit unconscious) against the governmentality of the stage via the revival of a live Restoration libertine scenario, the very cultural artifact against which the play militates. The anecdote dramatizes a conflict between postrevolutionary theatrical culture and Stuart theatrical culture, with the latter clearly stealing the show.

In the audience's response to this onstage disorderliness, the standard wisdom of eighteenth-century theater history is reversed. Restoration comedy—with its self-licensed and antisocial rake heroes—still manages to hold mass appeal, insofar as it is restored in the exchange between Powell and his servant. An effect of Lothario's corpsing, the play's discourse of fifth-act tragic morality that would discipline viewers to a moral-bourgeois regime of sexual and social moderation is literally dissolved in "Fits of Laughter" so "immoderate" that not only does the present performance end, but Betterton bans it from production in the immediate future. In this return of Restoration comedy in the form of Lothario's corpsing, the ordering of the body public comes apart; the failure of *The Fair Penitent*'s performance to go as scripted results not in a willful forgetting of the Stuart rake, but in a need for the very play that would dismiss him and the sociopolitical regime that he symbolizes to be "something forgot."

Finally, however, what the anecdote suggests is not simply the continuing appeal of Restoration comic libertine behavior, but the actualization of the communal power of his latent radicalism. As the disorderliness onstage infects the behavior of the audience, it transforms them from an assemblage of individual subjects formed by the regulatory powers of affective spectacle into an unruly collective—not necessarily the unthinking rabble that eighteenth-century authors loved to deride, but a version of what Elizabeth Dillon calls a "performative commons" that can represent themselves in material challenge to the disciplinary pitch of the script.[84] Restoration comedy and its radical challenge to postrevolutionary order haunt the theatrical space of Chetwood's anecdote and show up that order as only one possible way of conceiving a representative public. Though Lothario and Calista mouth the language of the commons against the enclosing moral-bourgeois order on display in Sciolto and Altamont's hoped-for succession, they fail, in the play, as true representatives of the commons, their desire for liberal autonomy dissolving into sovereign absolutism. But in the failure of Warren and Powell as Lothario to fulfill the rake's scripted destiny, the possibility of the commons is produced, if only for a moment, in the audience whose "Laugh and Roar" signal resistance to the ideological regime that the text would forward and that the corpsing lays bare. Reneged time and again in the texts of Restoration comic drama—and even more so in Rowe's apotheosis of this genre—the promise of the rake's radicalism to subvert governance in the name of the people manifests itself in this moment of spectacular failure.

When *The Fair Penitent* is considered in relation to its performance history, I would argue, it never kills off the Restoration rake at all. Instead, it offers a glimpse of the long-running Restoration that showcases the lingering appeal of the aristocratic rake and contests the dominance of the Whig-bourgeois cultural succession in the early 1700s. The failure of Lothario's corpse to perform the governance function accorded to it in the script opens up a space where the Restoration libertine stage thrives again. The productivity of the script's particular ontic failures resides in the Stuart élan not being banished, in the Whiggish succession not being completely successful, and in the utility of aristocratic Stuart theatrical culture for popular resistance to the new regimes of order—particularly instantiated in the republic of property—that such a succession would institute.

2
DEBATING DORIMANT

IN THE YEARS SURROUNDING the Hanoverian succession of 1714, Richard Steele and John Dennis published a series of critical exchanges about George Etherege's libertine comedy *The Man of Mode; or, Sir Fopling Flutter* (1676). The two writers had much in common; both were playwrights, literary critics, Whig partisans, and loyal supporters of the recent political settlement that debarred the exiled Stuarts from the British throne. Yet their views on Etherege's masterpiece and its libertine hero, Dorimant, could not have differed more widely. Steele, in *The Spectator* no. 65, criticizes Dorimant for failing to uphold the decorum of "a fine Gentleman" and concludes that "this whole celebrated Piece is a perfect Contradiction to good Manners, good Sense, and common Honesty."[1] Years later, Dennis defends Dorimant's gentility, arguing that the play admirably "answer[s] the two Ends of Comedy, Pleasure and Instruction."[2] Theater history largely acknowledges Steele to have "won" the debate. The blockbuster success of his new model of exemplary and sentimental comedy, *The Conscious Lovers* (1722), marks a transition to eighteenth-century modernity in which the satiric and aristocratically rakish modes of the Restoration stage are rejected in favor of sociable and increasingly bourgeois ones. The "rake's progress" on the early eighteenth-century stage is one of declining cultural relevance, and such developments in theatrical culture are understood by current scholars as helping to articulate and solidify the ideological values of the post-1688 Whig regime.[3]

While *The Man of Mode* tends to factor into eighteenth-century theater history primarily for the way it disappears from the acting repertory, its libertine hero, Dorimant, like Lothario, might be best characterized by his insinuating reappearance in the British cultural imaginary. Dorimant's very name, as Horace Walpole and Charles Lamb attest, became synonymous with the very idea of gentility as the century progressed.[4] In this chapter, I want to assess the broader literary and political contexts of Steele and Dennis's debate over the fate of Etherege's play, particularly as the modernization of theatrical culture coincides with a simultaneous modernization in the political history of subjectivity during the transitional period between Stuart and Hanoverian rule. Robert D. Hume has questioned the teleological narrative in which the later Stuart libertine dramas by Etherege, Wycherley, Dryden, and Behn are replaced by sentimental or bourgeois comedy in the 1710s. Such accounts, Hume argues, do not consider that the London stages at the time functioned as repertory theaters; nor do they effectively "reckon with the old plays that dominated the repertory at all times."[5] Hume's observation implicitly suggests that new modes of drama such as *The Conscious Lovers* are not the only aesthetic artifacts that might condition or reflect concurrent modernizations in political ideology. What, then, does it mean—for literary history and the history of subjectivity—that such older models of Restoration drama linger in revival?

In turning to the writings of Steele and Dennis and their effect on a decade of theater criticism and dramatic work to follow, including John Gay's *The Beggar's Opera* (1728), I argue that the contest over the repertory of the early eighteenth-century commercial theaters—and specifically over the "rake's progress" within that repertory—is an arena in which the relation between older models of political subjectivity tied to Stuart absolutism and burgeoning models of liberal subjectivity may be defined and negotiated by the new arbiters of Whig culture. Attending to the revival of the Stuart libertine in such contests, we can see that the period's concerns lie not so much with moral or aesthetic reforms, but with the question of how cultural authorities can uphold the ideals of self-possession and English liberty while simultaneously requiring the self's submission within proper social and political bounds.

For my purposes, the word "repertoire" not only describes the day-to-day functioning of the London stages but also signals the theoretical concept—recently put into dialogue with the "archive" by Diana Taylor—of an embodied system of knowledge that may be transmitted and modified as cultures negotiate their sense of identity through time. Repertoires contain sets of past practices, performances, and behaviors that may be "restored" in the present, both repeated and revised.[6] In eighteenth-century studies, Joseph Roach and Thomas King have revealed how style, gestures, and other embodied acts exist as resignifications of a repertoire in the process of "ongoing negotiation and revision of accumulated meanings through their restoring and recoding of behavior in the progression of everyday performance."[7] The repertory of London's commercial theaters may itself be imagined thus as not only a repository of plays but a locus in which political and social behaviors are restored, revived, and negotiated on a daily basis. In what follows, I turn to the debates over the persistence of Etherege's rake in the theatrical repertory—from Dennis and Steele to the pages of a host of newsprint theatrical criticism to *The Conscious Lovers* and *The Beggar's Opera*—in order to suggest not only how the Stuart rake's ideology of personal rule imaginatively persists after 1688 but also how it forms a model of behavior for the very liberal subjectivity that alleges to supplant it. In Dorimant's revival in the era surrounding the Hanoverian succession, the performances of personal sovereignty associated with him are co-opted to help the autonomous liberal subject navigate new structures of governmentality attached to sociable civil society and commercialized cultural taste. Instead of relying, as Erin Mackie does, on the glamour of criminality to explain the rake's continued draw after 1688, I suggest that the character's performance of personal sovereignty proves contentious and occasionally appealing to the very arbiters of a new Whiggish culture of sociability.[8] The rake does not always stand in strict competition with the sociable gentleman as a nostalgically distanced figure, as Mackie would have it; rather, the sociable gentleman actually restores some of the rake's behavior—particularly his autonomy—in the formulation of his own role as a self-possessing English subject. Such restored behavior is revealed both in the debates over the direction of the theatrical repertory in the early eighteenth century and in the performances of the Whig cultural arbiters themselves.

DEBATING DORIMANT I: STEELE

When it comes to the Restoration rake's place in a living theatrical tradition in the early eighteenth century, we think of him as more dead than alive, killed off by attacks on the theater such as Jeremy Collier's *A Short View of the Immorality and Profaneness of the English Stage* (1698) and those of the Societies for the Reformation of Manners. Responding to the changing cultural climate, playwrights abandoned the satiric mode of libertine comedy and adopted one that has been described variously as pathetic, moral, sentimental, exemplary, bourgeois, or humane—exemplified by dramatists such as Cibber and Centlivre and culminating in the popularity of Steele's *The Conscious Lovers*.[9] With this play and with his work for the periodical press—notably *The Tatler* (1709–1711), *The Spectator* (1711–1712), and *The Theatre* (1720)—Steele deserves much of the credit for prompting the dwindling appeal of the Restoration stage rake. His famous assault in *The Spectator* no. 65 on *The Man of Mode* is one of many instances throughout his career when Steele castigates Restoration libertine drama.[10] Such work did not go unnoticed among his contemporaries. With the accession of George I, there developed a renewed interest in royal patronage of the stage.[11] One of the king's first acts in this regard was to authorize a theater patent that granted Steele, as a reward for his pro-Hanoverian loyalties, joint managerial control of Drury Lane along with the actors Colley Cibber, Barton Booth, and Robert Wilks. Steele was known for his staunch Whig politics, his moral essays, and his self-appointed title as "Censor of Great Britain" and so was an obvious choice to govern the stage back into respectability.[12]

Denunciations of Restoration drama are often read strictly in terms of the rise of sentimental or moral comedy.[13] But the alleged decline of libertine drama also coincided with the revolution in manners and sociability advanced in the 1710s by Whig moralists from the 3rd Earl of Shaftesbury to Addison and Steele. Derived from an older courtly tradition but newly theorized for an eighteenth-century audience suspicious of absolutist government, sociability or politeness, as Lawrence Klein has extensively documented, embraced the idea of the English subject's liberty while simultaneously calling for "the submission of the self to the disciplines of social interaction."[14] Shaftesbury in particular fashioned a link between the modes of genteel sociability and freedom from arbitrary rule, arguing directly that that "all politeness is owing to liberty."[15] His political philosophy relied on a model Athenian polity that eschewed what he labeled as the "Gothic" values of civic humanist writers—fierce economic and political freedom based in landed property and military arms, stoic virtue, and cultural simplicity—and emphasized instead the necessity of the cultivation of the liberal arts, the exchange of ideas and feelings in polite rational conversation, and complementary social relations (at least among the educated elite) to the stability of anti-despotic governments.[16] In effect, sociability could realize a kind of civil society dreamed of by the late seventeenth-century Whig jurists, the promise of liberty and social cohesion. It would do so not through juridical force, however, but through a disciplinary regime of behavioral and cultural production.

Addison and Steele, most notably in *The Tatler* and *The Spectator*, extended the reach of Shaftesbury's Whiggish cultural politics to a wider social base, disseminating ideals of gentility, sociability, and new cultural-aesthetic norms through urban and urbane public spaces occupied increasingly by the middling classes.[17] But, as Steele's work for the stage particularly indicates, the print-centric Habermasian public sphere is not the only paradigm imaginable for the forging of a civil subject. For Steele, the theatrical repertory and the repertoire of behaviors repeated within it on a daily basis also constitute a system by which the value of sociable relations is inculcated into a populace without the use of coercive authority. "It is a Matter of the highest Consideration," he declares in *The Spectator* no. 370, "what Manners and Customs are transfused from the Stage to the World."[18] Resembling Foucault's theory of governmentality, Steele's idea of transfusion recognizes a microphysics of power by which the "Manners" of theatrical representation permeate, circulate, and change from within the "Manners" of society. That the regulation of bodies onstage will instantiate a civil social order is the logic behind *The Conscious Lovers*; it is Steele's hope, articulated in the play's preface, that his new brand of comedy "may have some Effect upon the *Goths* and *Vandals* that frequent the Theatres."[19] As his Shaftesburian language discloses, Steele's program of hegemonic socialization is correlated with a Whiggish political agenda that advances the value of polite participatory culture as a means of training aesthetically refined, politically free subjects.

That the Restoration rake is, in these terms, a "Gothic" individual—hierarchical, antisocial, absolutist—and thus dangerous to the liberal politics housed in codes of civility accounts for Steele's repeated appeals for the character's dismissal from the repertory. His particular fixation on *The Man of Mode* originates, as he claims in *The Spectator* no. 65, from its reception as a "Pattern of Gentile Comedy."[20] Whereas critics interested in the succession from satiric to sentimental genres latch onto the word "Comedy" here, Steele emphasizes just as much a problem of gentility. He begins this essay with another allusion to theater's power in producing subjects and controlling bodies: "The Application of Wit in the Theatre has as strong an Effect upon the Manners of our Gentlemen, as the Taste of it has upon the Writings of our Authors."[21] In his reading, *The Man of Mode* and its libertine hero threaten to confuse true sociability with the hypocritical manipulation of polite social bonds. Steele suggests as much in his analysis of Dorimant's behavior as a witty "fine gentleman" in relation with his "friend" Young Bellair:

> I will take for granted, that a fine Gentleman should be honest in his Action, and refined in his Language. Instead of this, our Hero [Dorimant], in this piece, is a direct Knave in his Designs, and a Clown in his Language. *Bellair* is his Admirer and Friend, in return for which, because he is forsooth a greater Wit than his said friend, he thinks it reasonable to perswade him to Marry a young Lady [Emilia], whose Virtue, he thinks, will last no longer than 'till she is a Wife, and then she cannot but fall to his Share, as he is an irresistible Fine Gentleman.[22]

Dorimant's danger—as much for eighteenth-century audiences as for Young Bellair and Emilia—lies in his appeal as a "Wit" and an "irresistible Fine Gentleman" while violating the codes of genteel sociability for his own sexual self-interest. A true "Fine Gentleman," as Steele writes shortly later in *The Guardian* (1713), must be "compleatly qualify'd as well for the Service and Good, as for the Ornament and Delight, of Society."[23] Steele's condemnation of Dorimant and his frequent opposition of the Restoration rake to the "fine gentleman" in his journalism and in *The Conscious Lovers*—whose hero, Bevil Jr., reverses Dorimant's manner, staying faithful to his lover, Indiana, and to his hot-tempered friend, Myrtle—emerge in part from the vital role that sociability plays in sustaining a Shaftesburian vision of the sociopolitical "Good": creating free subjects whose autonomy is nonetheless restrained in their submission to the polite behaviors that make possible civil life.

Steele's censure of *The Man of Mode* persisted after his accession to the Drury Lane management in 1715; but it was notably following his assumption of this role of state-sanctioned cultural arbiter that Steele's program of theatrical governance became problematically entangled with the revival of both the Restoration rake and his associations with Stuart absolutist sovereignty. That Dorimant's wit and irresistibility as a "fine gentleman" bear worryingly not just on the control of individual bodies, but on the state of the nation is an argument Steele renews in an epilogue written for a failed production of *Measure for Measure* at Lincoln's Inn Fields in 1721. Never actually used, the epilogue was later published by the poet Leonard Welsted, who added a preface interpreting its motives. Steele, Welsted writes, "formerly attempted with much vigor to bring into disrepute the writings of Etherege, doubtless, because they had, in his judgement, a tendency to corrupt the chastity of manners, and introduce a wrong taste. Whatever the success of his labours then was, he seems to be of opinion, that there still wants a finishing stroke. This is what gave birth to the Epilogue. . . . Dorimant is the great Giant, with whom he is at war."[24] Roused by the fact that in January 1721 Lincoln's Inn Fields' *Measure for Measure* had twice competed unsuccessfully on the same nights as Drury Lane's production of *The Man of Mode*, Steele is here represented as attempting to finalize the rake's cultural demise, to produce the "finishing stroke" that would turn Dorimant's threateningly powerful "Giant" body into an inanimate corpse.

The epilogue itself reveals Steele's "war" with Dorimant to extend to a defense of Shakespeare as a means of safeguarding British bodies from this "Giant":

> This is the taste our sad experience shews;
> This is the taste of Belles as well as Beaux:
> Else say, in Britain why it should be heard
> That Etherege to Shakespeare is preferr'd;
> Whilst Dorimant to crowded audience wenches,
> Our Angelo repeat[s] to empty benches.[25]

As Angelo's words receive only lackluster attention and Dorimant's libertine performance draws in crowds, Steele reveals the Restoration rake's affective power in revival inappropriately to outdo even that of Shakespeare. This rejection of Shakespeare's play about social governance through surveillance and discipline, however, is emblematic of a larger threat to Britain's values:

> The perjur'd Dorimant the Beaux admire;
> Gay perjur'd Dorimant the Belles desire:
> With fellow-feeling, and with conscious gust,
> Each sex applauds inexorable lust.
> . . . .
> Love, glory, friendship, languishing must stand,
> While sense and appetite have sole command;
> Give men sometimes some force in the dispute;
> Be sometimes rational, though oftener brute.
> Believe it, Sirs, if fit for us to say,
> Or if our Epilogue may suit our Play;
> 'Tis time, 'tis time, ye should be more severe;
> And what less guilty nations suffer, fear;
> Be men, or hope not heaven will long secure ye
> From quicker pestilence than that round Drury.[26]

The continued valuation of the "perjur'd Dorimant" institutes a loss of British self-mastery, an enslavement to the absolutist "sole command" of brute appetite. It is as if the daily presence of Dorimant's body onstage poses a threat to actual British bodies, upsetting the post-1688 values of liberty and sociability, enervating the nation, and making it susceptible to providential retribution in the form of the plague that was, in 1721, ravaging parts of France.[27] Steele's attack thus targets the disciplinary effect of a theatrical repertory that revives characters and behaviors from the Restoration past. As Mackie suggests, Steele's program of social reform builds on hegemonic tactics that operate "through the individual internalization of normative standards" and that simultaneously contribute to a "model of modern bourgeois subjectivity" that "foregrounds autonomy, independence, and self-regulation."[28] Unlike Collier or the other early reformers, Steele does not cite church or state as the bulwark of English liberty. He rather represents the theatrical repertory itself as a tactic of governmentality, a site through which Whig cultural authorities may diffusely inculcate the qualities of sociable "love" and "friendship" and manly, if "severe," restraint and self-mastery against the persistence of the antisocial behaviors of "sense" and "appetite" associated with Stuart libertine culture.

But the very fact that Dorimant "wants a finishing stroke" in 1721, according to Welsted, suggests another story about Steele's progressively modern view of cultural authority. Libertine comedy may have been no longer written, but it was constantly under production in the early eighteenth-century London theaters. When looking at the statistics, theater historians typically consider the endurance of plays over the *longue durée*; when doing so, Restoration libertine comedy tends not to register very highly.[29] A closer look at the Drury Lane repertory under Steele's

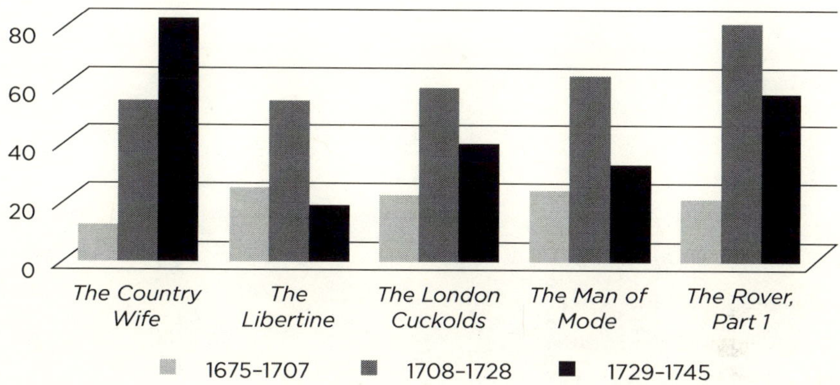

Figure 2.1: Total number of known performances of select libertine plays, 1675–1745. All calculations based on *The London Stage, 1660–1800: A Calendar of Plays, Entertainments, and Afterpieces*, ed. William Van Lennep, Emmett L. Avery, Arthur H. Scouten, George Winchester Stone Jr., and Charles Beecher Hogan, 5 parts in 11 vols. (Carbondale: Southern Illinois University Press, 1960–1968).

management, however, reveals that Dorimant is more of a "Giant" than ever (see figure 2.1 and table 2.1).[30] Culturally recognizable successes such as *The Man of Mode* and *The Rover* had been revived only sporadically after their initial run in the 1670s. After 1708, however, most of them thrived as repertory staples and were revived two to three times a year until the 1740s. While their success in the long term does not match that of Gay or George Farquhar, these libertine comedies have a salient afterlife in Hanoverian England. Steele's various assaults on Restoration comedy from 1709 until the 1720s are thus incredibly timely. But it is more striking that such plays actually experienced a dramatic increase in popularity under Steele's own management of Drury Lane. Quite often, we assume the reverse is true.

Other factors may certainly account for these statistics: the incompleteness of *The London Stage*'s records in the Restoration, the economic necessities of a repertory theater, or the fact that the actor-managers had a much larger role in determining Drury Lane's daily offerings than did Steele.[31] Nevertheless, these trends in early Hanoverian play production did not go unnoticed by reform-minded writers, and it was Steele, as cultural authority, who was represented as tacitly condoning such a repertory. In the popular pamphlet *Fears of the Pretender turn'd into the Fears of Debauchery* (1715)—attributed to Daniel Defoe—the new Whig culture industry spearheaded by Steele becomes a site in which a particularly Stuart idiom is restored to power. The tract's title succinctly sums up its message. Having

TABLE 2.1. Total number of known performances of select libertine plays in the years before and during Steele's tenure as active manager at Drury Lane Theater

	1675–1713 (38 years)		*1714–1720 (7 years)*	
	Number of performances	*Average per year*	*Number of performances*	*Average per year*
George Etherege, *The Man of Mode*	35	<1	20	3.0
Aphra Behn, *The Rover, Part 1*	39	1	18	2.5
Thomas Shadwell, *The Libertine*	39	1	14	2.0
William Wycherley, *The Country Wife*	12	<1	23	3.0

Note: All calculations based on *The London Stage, 1660–1800: A Calendar of Plays, Entertainments, and Afterpieces*, ed. William Van Lennep, Emmett L. Avery, Arthur H. Scouten, George Winchester Stone Jr., and Charles Beecher Hogan, 5 parts in 11 vols. (Carbondale: Southern Illinois University Press, 1960–1968).

prevented a second Stuart restoration in 1714 and thus undergone the "greatest Deliverance that has been wrought for the Nation since the late Revolution," the English have nonetheless been subsumed by a deluge of vice—gambling, masquerading, libertinism—as if "nothing but national Immorality [could] keep out the *Pretender*."[32] The alarmism echoes Samuel Butler's more tongue-in-cheek explanation of the social excesses that followed 1660:

> [The nation] had no other Way but Sin and Vice
> To be restor'd again to *Paradise*.[33]

Defoe's tract pursues similar logic but turns almost immediately from relief over the succession to an association of immorality with the Stuarts' imminent return. The new popularity of upper-class vice, Defoe suggests, is merely history repeating itself: "Those who remember the Days of King *Charles* II when the Iniquity of the Court seem'd to be come to a height, and their Cup to be full, cannot but see Things running the same Way."[34] In particular, the theater merits special attention as an insidious medium for restoring the Stuart past: "The Play-Houses [have] arriv'd to a greater degree of Grandeur and Worth, than ever they were in King *Charles* IId's Time! To what a height will these Men come in a few Years more! and how shall we see Play-Houses, Booths, itinerate Comedians, spread themselves over the whole Nation, as it was in King *Charles* II Time."[35] While with one hand Defoe's tract disavows fears of the political threat posed by James II's Catholic and absolutist heirs, with the other he instills the fear that libertinism may reinstate a Stuart ethos just the same.

While Defoe's antitheatricalism speaks to his puritan proclivities, it is also tied to his steadfast adherence to the "revolution principles" of the post-Restoration political settlements.[36] The rake figure, as he writes later in his career, is one that thinks himself "a King, an Emperor, Monarch of himself, and knows no-body, and values no-body. . . . He is above all Masters."[37] It is a character that crosses the line between the Lockean liberal subject—having the rights and capabilities to possess his person and property—and the social absolutist who maintains his personal liberty at expense of other selves and sociable ethics. Enablers of libertinism, the theaters produce this outcome: "The Play-Houses are the Receptacles of the Scandalous, the Nests of Rakes, Bullies, &c. that Fightings, Whorings, Murthers, are the common Practice of these Places; that the Plays grow Lewd in spight of Laws and Regulations, the Players scandalous and Lawless." Offering nothing more than "a Liberty so fatal to themselves," the theater encourages its audiences in behaviors of antisocial self-aggrandizement and lawlessness that are associated with a restoration of the values, if not the politics, of the Stuarts.[38]

Even more alarming for Defoe in *Fears of the Pretender* is the fact that Whig culture is responsible for perpetuating this form of mass entertainment. As cultural authority, Steele is the targeted scapegoat. While commending *The Tatler* and *The Spectator*'s work toward correcting "the Absurdities of Speech, of Gesture, of Behaviour" that had become "Legitimated by Custom" throughout Britain, Defoe decries Steele's support for the stage: "It can never be forgiven [Steele], either by God, or Man, till he Repents of, and Reforms it; that he did more by recommending the Play-Houses, to promote the present Madness of the Age, in running up the Humour of following Plays to such an Extream, as we now see it, than all the Agents of Hell ever employed before."[39] Not only has Steele's insistence on the stage as part of his program of social reform "assisted to Debauch the Morals of the People," but it also proves self-defeating, Defoe argues, as a method of governance: "For the *Spectator* to give a good Word to a Play, was to fill the House. In process of Time, his Name was put to the Prologue and Epilogue, to push a Play into the World; and for a grave Person, in an Antick Dress, with a Comick Gravity, to sit in a Box, and suppos'd, tho' but in Banter, to be the *Spectator*, was sufficient to draw the whole Town to the Theatre."[40] Scholars have long recognized Mr. Spectator's invisibility and disembodiment in print as the crucial detail that allows the periodical to function as a hegemonic device.[41] Defoe imagines the reverse. Mr. Spectator's role may be appropriated by any self-interested individual looking to promote himself, his agenda, or his play, thus undermining Steele's cultural authority.

If Defoe sees the theater as a space of restored Stuart libertine behavior, then other writers imagine Steele himself, as manager, to reembody the role of Stuart absolutist. In *The State of the Case . . . Restated* (1720)—a response to Steele's impassioned defense of his right to run Drury Lane, prompted by the temporary revocation of his managerial role by the current Lord Chamberlain, Thomas Pelham-Holles, the Duke of Newcastle—one anonymous critic complained that Steele had not made "one Step towards those glorious Ends propos'd by his *Majesty*" in the patent.[42] Drury Lane still suffered from a barrage of libertinism:

> The same Leud Plays being Acted and Reviv'd without any material Alteration, which gave occasion for that universal Complaint against the *English Stage*, of Leudness and Debauchery, from all the Sober and Religious Part of the Nation, the whole Business of *Comedy* continuing all [Steele's] time to be the Criminal Intrigues of Fornication and Adultery, ridiculing of Marriage, Virtue and Integrity, the giving of a favourable Turn to vicious Characters, and instructing loose People how to carry on their Leud Designs with Plausibility and Success, thus among other *Plays*, they have revived *The Country Wife*; *Sir Fopling Flutter*; *The Rover*; *The Libertine destroy'd*; and several others.[43]

Pointing directly toward the unaltered persistence of Restoration libertine drama in the repertory, the anonymous author brands Steele as a hypocrite. But he also implies that Steele has violated the conditions of the patent and thus the conditions of his authority. "Why may not the King," asks the anonymous author, "upon Information of the Continuance of these Disorders of the *Theatre*, take out of your Hands this *whole* and *sole* Government, after six Years Tryal of your Incapacity[?]"[44] In failing to fulfill the conditions set by George I in the patent—namely, stage reform—Steele's power is illegal, a challenge to the rule and law of the king.

In Steele's justification of his right to the managerial position, he cited his "*sole* Government and Authority" at Drury Lane, asserting that the patent was his property by contract and that the Lord Chamberlain's impositions threatened to undermine the liberty of the postrevolutionary subject.[45] Revoking the patent was akin to having "dispossessed" Steele of his "Freehold" and "deprived" him of his "Property by Violence," and thus Newcastle had committed an "Outrage upon the King's Authority, and the Subject's Property."[46] The author of *State of the Case . . . Restated* gets the greatest traction in attacking Steele on this point of personal property, replying, "*Sole* Governor is no more here than Director in those things mention'd before in the Patent; there is no Character or Patent that I know of, that gives any such despotick Power, or Rules, so beyond all Controul, that there is no Appeal from it. . . . [Steele] would be Judge in his own Cause, and do what Injustice, and commit what Insults he pleases."[47] Steele's defense of personal property is represented as an excessive bid for "despotick Power" by an overmighty subject, an extreme case of Michael McKeon's concept of the devolution of absolutism. Moreover, as his performance of cultural authority is made to appear absolutist, it restores the behavior of the stage rakes that Steele otherwise condemns—their exercise of personal will self-licensed as authority.[48] Alive in the repertory, the Restoration libertine's behaviors are also revived in the actions of the very Whig cultural arbiters who claim to circumscribe and resist them. Despite the culture of reform that grew up around the 1714 succession, the revival of Restoration libertine drama in the national repertories kept the question of Stuart personal rule alive in the performances of the moralists themselves.

DEBATING DORIMANT II: DENNIS

No fan of Steele's—for reasons that we will see shortly—John Dennis developed the connection between Steele and Stuart authority most bluntly, calling him "the greatest Pretender but one, of the Age in which he lives."[49] In his various replies to Steele's self-promotional campaign in *The Theatre* and to his devaluation of Dorimant from *The Spectator* to *The Conscious Lovers*, no critic was more vocal about the Drury Lane manager's poor treatment of Etherege's comedies. As with Steele, however, most scholarship treats Dennis's contributions to the exchange—*A Defence of Sir Fopling Flutter* (1722) and *Remarks on a Play call'd the Conscious Lovers* (1723)—only in terms of comedic genre, emphasizing either his defense of nonexemplary characters on the stage or his attack on sentimental comedy for its violations of the neoclassical rules. Notably, Brian Corman takes a different approach, arguing that Dennis's defense of Dorimant in particular stems from the critic's historicism: Dennis refutes Steele's argument that *The Man of Mode* is not genteel comedy as simply ahistorical by showing that notions of gentility are dependent on context. Dorimant, Corman posits, actually is a version of "the Restoration courtier Dennis takes him to be."[50] Corman's thesis is refreshing, but he does not reconstruct all the motives that underlie Dennis's historicist defense of the Restoration gentleman specifically at this time. Aesthetic value alone hardly explains Dennis's interest in Etherege's comedies. In order to understand his idiosyncratic defense of the rake amid the early Hanoverian culture of reform, I propose to read his aesthetic theories in the sociopolitical contexts of liberal subjectivity, absolute rule, and cultural authority.[51] Dorimant is not, for Dennis, the epitome of Stuart excess but rather the embodiment of liberty, self-possession, and heroic independence—in politics and in poetry—which England has sadly fallen away from in its turn to partisanship and commerce following Charles II's reign. Having nothing to do with libertine sexuality, Dennis's appreciative revival of the rake in his criticism focuses on the character's autonomy and its ability to resist the type of absolutist excesses that he imagines authorities such as Steele and Cibber to have inherited from Stuart politics and transposed to the cultural realm of the commercial theater. His attempt to resignify the role of gentlemanly authority in the name of proper taste and English liberty accounts for both his stance on Dorimant and his marginalization from mainstream critical discourse in the early eighteenth century.

Though Dennis is a major figure in the professionalization of imaginative literature and criticism, he is more often remembered for his irascible personality and as a parodic butt for some of the early eighteenth century's most adept satirists.[52] His career is usually segregated into two distinct periods; early on, he produced serious literary critical treatises on Milton, the sublime, and the role of the passions in poetry, but after Pope's mockery of him in *An Essay on Criticism* (1711), he spent much of his time vindictively attacking his detractors in print and trying to salvage his own reputation.[53] It is during this inauspicious second half of Dennis's career that he first engaged with Steele over the specific question of Restoration theater. After the Drury Lane managers postponed the production of Dennis's *Invader of His Country* in the 1718–1719 season and instead revived Dryden's *All for Love* (1677), Dennis sent a bitter public letter to Steele denouncing the decision in terms of the political memory surrounding the latter play. Otherwise a fan of Dryden, here Dennis represents him as a mere timeserver to despotic Stuart rule: "Was ever any thing so pernicious, so immoral, so criminal, as the Design of that Play? . . . Certainly never could the Design of an Author square more exactly with the Design of White-Hall, at the time when it was written, which was by debauching the People absolutely to enslave them" (2:163). For Dennis, *All for Love* is "criminal" not only for its tolerance of libertinism, but also for the way in which such tolerance may have been politically motivated. Dryden portrays Antony's illicit passion for a foreign queen sympathetically in an era when Charles II's affairs with the French—political and sexual—encouraged allegations of his support for French-Catholic absolute rule. Dennis's anti-Stuart stance, when it came to politics, was firm. His own play—an adaptation of *Coriolanus*—contained anti-Jacobite sentiments at a time when the nation was still wary of a repeat of the 1715 rebellion. In his view, Steele's fashioning of the repertory ignores the dangerous political associations of such pro-Stuart revivals at a moment when questions of the dynasty's legitimacy and popularity were still quite relevant.

Steele and the actor-managers, according to Dennis, thus act improperly as cultural arbiters. As Paul D. Cannan has shown, Dennis's whole critical program depended on an elitist system in which educated critical authorities upheld and disseminated the standards of good literary taste, which were to be followed by imaginative writers and imbibed by audiences less capable of discrimination.[54] Such critical dictums could not be arbitrary; their real goal, as Dennis argued in *The Grounds of Criticism in Poetry* (1704), was to help literature shape the world: "The End of Poetry [is] to instruct and reform the World, that is, to bring Mankind from Irregularity, Extravagance, and Confusion, to Rule and Order. . . . The great Design of Arts is to restore the Decays that happen'd to human Nature by the Fall, by restoring Order" (1:335–336). Though he often appears an overzealous neoclassicist, Dennis's desire for order and authority is not surprising given the historical context of his writing in a nation still reeling from the political and religious upheavals of the seventeenth century. That ordered poetry will help maintain an ordered sociopolitical system is a major part of Dennis's creed that, as Cannan puts it, "poets and critics should be patriots and write for the well-being of the public."[55] The theater in particular was a site in which writers were expected to exert such patriotism. As Dennis concludes in the preface to his play *Liberty Asserted* (1704), "When I say, that the Publick ought to receive Advantage from the Entertainments of our Theatres, I mean, that it ought to do so immediately, and that the Instructions which we receive from the Stage ought to be for the Benefit of the lawful establish'd Government" (1:320).

Dennis's ultimate goal is thus not to smear Steele as a Jacobite, but to indicate how his activity as a cultural arbiter fails to uphold the responsibilities of such authority. In deciding to revive *All for Love*, Steele is not necessarily a political agitator, but he does evince a lack of the necessary "publick spirit" (1:320) required to dictate taste and he participates in the general debasement of culture that Dennis continually bemoans, from his *Large Account of the Taste in Poetry* (1702) to his unpublished *Causes of the Decay and Defects of Dramatick Poetry* (1725). This lack of disinterested taste manifests itself both in the rise of theater as a commercial venture and in the greed that Dennis ascribes to Steele and the actors, one of his favorite targets. Brean Hammond and others have noted that the professionalization of literature in the late seventeenth century contributed to the playhouses' role in a new commodity culture, and Dennis regarded this transformation as a deplorable shift from "a Reign of Poetry and of Pleasure" to "a Reign of Politicks and of Business" (1:290).[56] As he comments—with characteristic spite—in *Decay and Defects*, it is the "illiterate, unthinking, unjust, ungratefull, and sordid" actor-managers such as Steele, Booth, and Cibber who "fancy themselves plac'd [in the theater] for their extraordinary merits, and for no other end but to accumulate Pelf, and bring Dishonour upon the Reign of the Best of Kings by sacrifising the British genius to their Insatiable avarice; who reject the Best plays and Receive the worst, if the Blockheads who writt them, are but Sycophants enough to cringe and to fawn upon Half the Town, and by that means engage whole crowds of Fools to applaud a senselesse Performance" (2:277). While Dennis was certainly bitter about the constant failure of his own plays, he has a larger point to make: political self-advancement and moneymaking have become reasons to engage in the theater, supplanting the proper reordering of society as the all-important focus of cultural authorities.

It is not so much commerce itself that Dennis objects to, but the ways in which the literary marketplace allows social absolutists to trump both the public good and the individual's ability for self-possession, which forms the bulwark of English liberty. In *The Characters and Conduct of Sir John Edgar, call'd by Himself Sole Monarch of the Stage in Drury-Lane* (1720)—an attack on Steele and the actor-managers—Dennis reads the self-interest of his opponents as the restoration of absolutist behavior transferred to the realm of commercialized culture. Rather than improving the stage, Steele has only improved his "own Privy-Purse" by granting control of the repertory to actors like Cibber: "What Interest can he, who centers wholly in himself, have to be Loyal to a good and gracious King? He must be for Absolute Power in his Heart; and would do his Business best in an Arbitrary Reign" (2:182, 189). The qualities of and an affinity for an absolute king are displaced onto Steele and Cibber, demonized for an excessive obsession with self and personal profit. Indeed, Dennis sees them as instituting a type of personal sovereignty in the theater itself as they manipulate the work of serious playwrights for their own gain. While adhering to his belief that "a Man [has] absolute Property in his Thoughts and Inventions alone," Dennis accuses Steele of making it "the Business of his Life to seize on them, and usurp them" (2:191–192). Applying John Locke's theory of personal self-possession from *The Second Treatise* to the literary marketplace, Dennis offers not only an early instance of a defense of literary property but also the implication that absolute rule has moved from the sphere of high politics to the everyday interactions of writers. Reviving coercive Stuart rule as a means to commercial gain in the playhouse, Steele and the managers are imagined to violate the English liberties ostensibly protected by the political settlements of 1688 and 1714.

The *Defence of Sir Fopling Flutter*, I want to suggest, must be read in the context of these other literary engagements. Dennis's initial motive for writing his defense of Dorimant is not to promulgate his disinterested views on comedy but to attack Steele for the "scandalous Methods" used to puff his upcoming production of *The Conscious Lovers* (2:241). Railing against the self-interest behind Steele's advertisements, Dennis again takes aim at the Drury Lane management:

> These are some of the Methods which the present Managers of the Stage have us'd to ruine the Dramas, and with it all other Human Learning, which is in some Measure dependent on it. For since Cabal and Trick, and the Favour and Interest of three or four sordid Wretches, have been found necessary for the obtaining Success; every one who is duly qualify'd to write for the *Stage*, has either with a just Disdain refus'd it, or has undertaken it with extream Reluctancy. The *Drama* therefore is like to be lost, and all the Arts dependent on it; therefore every one who is concern'd for the Honour of his Country, ought to do his utmost Endeavour to prevent a Calamity which will be so great a Disgrace to it. (2:242)

Writing for the stage under Steele's management, Dennis argues, involves an inherent loss of self-possession in the need to acquiesce to the pressures of "Cabal," pressures that have also caused those more disinterested cultural arbiters to flee the scene. In its opening pages, the *Defence* outlines a problem of absolute rule inherited and performed by the current directors of the Drury Lane repertory. Letting their self-possession grow excessive and avaricious, Steele and his cronies subordinate the interests of the nation for their own gain: "For whose Interest could it be but theirs, to endeavour to impose upon the World?" (2:241). The personal rule that Dennis finds here is not in the interest of an absolute king, but in the individual interests of overmighty cultural arbiters who impinge on the liberties of the nation. Dennis's argument does not lack for personal malice; but when read in the contexts of the early eighteenth-century stage that we have seen, he voices a pervasive concern about cultural absolutism spread through the inherent commercialism of ventures such as Steele's program of sociability.[57]

Dennis's defense of Dorimant is part of his response to this perceived rise of cultural absolutism. He does not excuse Dorimant's libertine sexuality—especially his "Perfidiousness" toward his various mistresses—but he does reserve the bulk of his ridicule for the characters of Mrs. Loveit and Sir Fopling (2:249). When he speaks of Dorimant, he is more inclined to remark that the character "pass'd for a fine Gentleman with the Court of King *Charles* the Second" and that there was an implicit association between Etherege's hero and the historical wits, such as the Earl of Rochester, who formed the playwright's circle of literary acquaintance (2:244). Dennis reminds the reader that "all the World was charm'd with *Dorimont*" much in the same way it was charmed with Rochester (2:248). Dennis ascribes to the polished Dorimant none of the brutality or tyranny apparent in other Restoration rakes—Shadwell's Don John or Nathaniel Lee's Nemours, for instance—who were also considered avatars of the court wits.

This characterization of Etherege's most infamous rake thus seems at odds with the legacy appointed him by other Whig reformers at the time. Yet when read in light of Dennis's comments on the Restoration past in his other works, we can begin to see that his treatment of Dorimant is as a stage avatar of a group of genteel wits who maintained independence and self-possession in the face of an increasingly absolutist state and who were able to direct literary tastes for the benefit of the commonwealth. Some scholars note that Dennis evinced admiration for the Restoration court of Charles II throughout his career, but this odd nostalgia remains largely unexplained.[58] For Dennis, Charles II's reign was a golden age for imaginative writing: it was "an age of Pleasure, and not of Business," in which the populace had the leisure to study "Poetry and Eloquence" and "cultivated at once their Imaginations and Judgments" (1:294, 292). This utopian vision extended to literary criticism as well, as the period produced genteel and considerate judges of taste unaffected by political or commercial gain: "At the Restoration the Theatres were in the Hands of Gentlemen . . . who were peculiarly qualifyd for the Discharge of that Important Trust. They had Honour, learning, breeding, Discernment, Integrity, Impartiality and generosity. Their chief aim was to see that the Town was well entertaind and The Drama improvd" (2:278). Unwilling to raise the specter of faction that haunted the Restoration stage, Dennis instead uses the period as a foil to the corruption he finds under George I.

But more importantly for Dennis, the Restoration court was also the site of independent gentlemen who were willing to resist any use of theatrical culture to subvert either the standards of good taste or English liberty. Specifically, he cites Rochester, Buckingham, and their circle—the models for Dorimant—as the center of this resistance:

> Then there were several extraordinary men at Court who wanted neither Zeal nor Capacity, nor Authority to sett [the people] right again. There was Villiers Duke of Buckingham, Wilmot Earl of Rochester, the late Earl of Dorsett, the Earl of Mulgrave who was afterwards Duke of Buckinghamshire, Mr. Savil, Mr. Buckley, Sir John Denham, Mr. Waller &c. When these or the Majority of them Declard themselves upon any new Dramatick performance, the Town fell Immediately in with them. . . . When the Town too lightly gave their applause, to Half a Dozen Romantick, Ryming, whining Blustring Tragedies, allurd by their novelty and by their glare, then Villiers Duke of Buckingham writt the *Rehearsall*, which in a little Time opend their eyes, and taught them to Despise what before they rashly admird. And when upon the first representations of the *Plain Dealer*, the Town, as the Authour has often told me, appeard Doubtfull what Judgment to Form of it; the forementioned gentlemen by their loud approbation of it, gave it both a sudden and lasting reputation. (2:277)

While Matthew Kinservik rightly suggests that Dennis looked to state authorities—such as the Lord Chamberlain—to regulate the repertory, Dennis also celebrates the power of high-profile, elite amateurs such as the Restoration court wits to keep the stage in line.[59] Unlike the "Town," Rochester and Buckingham are not seduced by the "novelty" and "glare" of the heroic drama's bombastic aesthetics; they rather break the allure that such spectacles have over credulous audiences. They not only propagate good taste by promoting the genteel comedies of Etherege and Wycherley, but also represent the value of self-possessed independence from political or economic interests. Dennis ascribes to the court wits the same allure that Steele recognizes and bemoans in Dorimant. The difference for Dennis is that such rakes use their charisma—unavailable to the participants of an enervating and corrupt bourgeois commercial and sociable sphere—to resist excess rather than to induce sexual or social misconduct.

Such resistance bears a political as well as an aesthetic motivation, and Dennis finds in the Restoration rake an additional role—that of the performance of personal liberty in the face of absolutism. Rochester's mock-heroic, antimonarchist poems partake of the skeptical attack on Stuart politics through aesthetic form, and Buckingham's deflation of the heroic play in *The Rehearsal*—staged during his period of marginalization from Charles II's court in the early 1670s—simultaneously critiques Stuart political ideology as engendering arbitrary rule.[60] As James Turner has shown, the excessive behaviors of Restoration libertinism were often directed against the imagined embodiments of despotic Stuart rule, a defense of the liberties of the subject that battled too much government with no government at all.[61] But the wits' attachment to liberty was not expressed in libertinism alone. Dennis's admiration for Buckingham in particular is matched by other accounts recalling the duke not for his sexual transgressions but for his resistance to arbitrary government and his support of dissent and religious toleration in the 1670s.[62] The opposition poet Andrew Marvell made him into a hero of English liberty in *An Account of the Growth of Popery and Arbitrary Government* (1677) and *The Rehearsal Transpros'd* (1672), and in Dennis's time, Buckingham's political performances were kept fresh in memory by the frequent republication of *An Account of a Conference between His Grace George, late Duke of Buckingham, and Father Fitzgerald an Irish Priest* (1704), a satiric dialogue in which the aging duke resists the unconstitutional and non-Protestant impositions of the Stuart kings.

In light of the Restoration wits' pose as defenders of the liberty of the subject against political and cultural impositions, we can read Dennis as desirous to cultivate a similar self-image with his own criticism. If Steele and Cibber restore bad Stuart behavior, Dennis imagines himself as the heir to opposition politics in the form of an independent, genteel cultural authority that traces its roots back to the likes of Buckingham or Rochester. Dorimant, though not an unqualified pattern for imitation, affords Dennis nonetheless a repertoire of behaviors that may be crucially resignified in the battle against self-interested corrupters of culture. In the *Defence*, Dennis admires Dorimant's "Wit" and "Spirit"—unleashed in *The Man of Mode* against rule-bound codes of civil society—as indispensable to the genteel critic's assertion of autonomy (2:248). A member of Dryden's circle at Will's coffeehouse in the 1690s, Dennis had participated in a culture where, as we saw in chapter 1, wit served as the stylistic counterpart to and sign of gentlemanly privilege, antithetical to the campaign for moral reform led by Blackmore and other Williamite writers. For Dennis and his circle, wit was a stylistic tactic opposed to the agenda of a sovereign court that fostered codes of propriety as a means of curbing the freedom of the subject, especially that of traditional aristocratic independence. Whereas Blackmore and Steele view the perpetuation of Restoration libertine wit as representative of cultural decay, Dennis sees in both of their reformist programs a dangerous suppression of individual freedom. Opposed to the restraint inherent in modern models of gentility, Dennis promotes the Restoration rake's extravagant wit because it is a sign of the autonomy and genteel privilege that proper authorities must exercise in their service to national culture.[63]

Revived along with Dorimant's wit and autonomy, however, is the rake's anticivility. As Anna Bryson has shown, the various modes of anticivility—from indecent language to street violence—performed by Charles II's wits functioned as a rearguard affirmation of their privileged status in the face of eroding social divisions. New socioeconomic arrangements at the close of the seventeenth century allowed the middling ranks to challenge the gentry for the right to partake in and direct fashionable culture; libertine anticivility was a reactionary response to the ascendency of the lower orders into polite society.[64] The familiar battle of libertine wit versus pedestrian but often wealthy "cit" in Restoration comedy arises in part from the disintegration of the former's social and economic prerogatives. Like the rake, Dennis too reacts to a perceived misplacement of cultural power in "those upstarts . . . meanly born, and more meanly educated, and who had beyond their own expectation acquird pelf enough . . . to assist in Bringing the Diversions of Smithfield to which they had been usd from their Infancy to be Theatricall entertainments" (2:276). Aggressively plainspoken, his critical voice levels its assault at the infiltration of the commercial classes into the echelons of cultural authority traditionally reserved for the elite.

Scholars have long recognized, however, that the heroic, authoritative poses of Rochester and his peers are always ironically self-deflating, their emphatic claim to liberty betraying an often impotent desire for personal absolutism.[65] The criticism leveled at Dennis—often more memorable than his own writing—is so successful in marginalizing him because it parodies the petty tyranny inherent in his rhetoric. Pope dubbed him the tyrant Appius in *An Essay on Criticism*, an association that the Scriblerian collaborators of *Three Hours after Marriage* (1717) would extend in the character of the bombastic literary critic Sir Tremendous Longinus, "a Gentleman who can instruct the Town to dislike what has pleased them, and to be pleased with what they disliked."[66] Rather than the hero of liberal autonomy, Dennis was perceived as a coercive critic, his elitist insistence on the neoclassical rules leaving him open to accusations of personal rule. Just as he and the author of *The State of the Case . . . Restated* interpret Steele's defense of his own managerial liberties as absolutist, so too is Dennis's pose as public-spirited critic interpreted to harbor an underlying desire for sovereignty.

DORIMANT IN THE POLITE PUBLIC SPHERE

What Dennis's revival of the rake's cultural politics reveals is that, in the aftermath of Stuart monarchical rule, absolutism is neither the opposite of nor the chronological predecessor to liberal forms of governmentality and subjecthood. It is a pose, rather, born out of a response to cultural formations such as the commercial repertory by which the public is governed along new disciplinary lines. A formation that foregrounds this intricate nexus of the absolute pose and disciplinarity is the polite public sphere. Following Jürgen Habermas's classic account of the public sphere's emergence as a discursive site of citizen-subjects whose rational, critical authority may be opposed to the state, a generation of eighteenth-century scholars has found in the public sphere a heuristic device for exploring the chronological and ideological distinction between Stuart monarchical absolutism and new forms of liberal governance and identity. The idea of the public sphere is thought to preclude the sovereign in favor of rational and sociable collectivity.[67] As I argue in this section, however, the reappearance of the Stuart libertine within the realm of public-sphere criticism upsets the straightforward teleology of such a distinction. Dennis's defense of Dorimant is not idiosyncratic. In the wake of his and Steele's exchange over the "fine gentleman," Dorimant is adopted as the voice of a largely Whiggish response to the production of disciplinary forms of cultural authority. Extending into the theater criticism of the later 1720s, the Dorimant debate reveals how the performance of cultural governance becomes entangled with the concept of a polite public sphere that inherits rather than dispels a repertoire of behaviors from the Restoration libertine stage.

Steele and Dennis's debate over *The Man of Mode* and *The Conscious Lovers* occasioned a small paper war, polarizing their contemporaries largely across already-entrenched party lines. Whigs such as Benjamin Victor and writers for *The Whitehall Journal* and *The St. James's Journal* sided with Steele, and a number of Tory newspapers—notably *The Freeholder's Journal* and Nathaniel Mist's *Weekly Journal*—sided, if not with Dennis, then certainly against the Drury Lane manager. While some theater historians read in the journalistic controversy the seeds of modern dramatic and literary criticism, much of this writing is fixated on the politics of Steele's and Dennis's performances as cultural arbiters.[68] Those opposed to Dennis tended to censure his anticivility, finding it especially inappropriate in a public critic. Victor, for instance, contrasts the sociable Bevil Jr. not only with Dorimant, but with Dennis himself, associating his "scurrilous Language" with a lack of true gentility: "I can but wonder . . . at the Behaviour of this Critic, to treat so many Gentlemen [Steele and the actor-managers] with such ill Manners."[69] Dennis's fault lay not simply in his outdated critical program, but in his mannerisms—his diction, his address, his style—the performance of which violated the codes of sociability that dominated the literary public sphere. Critics of Steele, conversely, mocked this obsession with politeness; *The Freeholder's Journal* critiqued *The Conscious Lovers* for "annexing the Idea of [politeness] to Weeping" and satirically proposed that Steele export the play to "regulate and refine" the "unciviliz'd Nation" of Russia.[70]

Reactions such as Victor's and the *Freeholder*'s express the real divisiveness of Steele's theatrical model for sociable reform within debates about the constitution of the public's power of critical authority. On the one hand, for defenders of *The Conscious Lovers*, politeness could, as Steele had hoped, turn affective social bonds to good political purpose. The play's prologue encouraged audiences to think in this way, asking them to "Judge" the play "Politely for your Countrey's Fame."[71] Impolite critical judgment, it is here implied, is nationally undesirable because opposed to the ideally sociable authority vested in the liberal subject and civil society. For Steele's proponents, then, Dennis's public "ill Manners" identify him as "Gothic" in this sense, lacking in personal etiquette and, like Locke's tyrant, actually dangerous to the norms that undergird the Hanoverian sociopolitical order.[72] On the other hand, the *Freeholder* rejects this ideal of politeness for the very same reasons. Affiliating politeness with sentiment has only "cut off a very numerous Part of the World, of both Sexes, and of all Ranks and Orders, from the least Pretensions to Politeness, that in other Respects might be entitled to the Character." Chiefly excluded are those who, "notwithstanding the indispensible Duty of Crying," want only to "burst into Laughter" at Steele's play.[73] The *Freeholder* exposes Steele's idea of politeness as a partisan tactic that, driven by Whig ideology, regulates certain bodily responses as "Duty" and others as inappropriate; as such, it produces social exclusion and discord rather than affective mutuality and, in banning "Laughter," precludes true critical disagreement and independence in favor of a dangerous uniformity. Underneath arguments about literary merit, then, the public controversy sparked by Steele and Dennis's exchange is one of the disciplinary forces of culture.

The most fascinating intervention into this controversy comes from Dorimant himself. On November 22, 1722, *The St. James's Journal*—a short-lived pro-ministry newspaper—printed a letter to the editor responding to previous attacks on Dennis's poor manners:

> I observ'd in your last Paper, one of your Correspondents, in the Title of his Letter, promis'd us a short Defence of the *Conscious Lovers*; but it seems afterwards utterly forgot it, and diverted us with his Severities upon the *Old Critick*, and his Panegyricks upon his good Friends (as I suppose 'em) *the Triumvirate*. Now, Sir, you are to understand I am a Person above all that, and as I have thought myself concern'd to see a Representation of this Comedy more than once, I present your Readers, under your favour, with the following Account of it.[74]

Dismissing partisan backbiting in favor of a firsthand critical analysis of the play, the writer here takes a neutral stance between the conflicting parties of "the *Old Critick*" (Dennis) and "*the Triumvirate*" (the actor-managers). Writing from Button's coffeehouse, he claims to be impartial—"a Person above all that"—and suggests that his interests lie strictly in the dramatic poetry itself. His brief self-characterization supports this; he describes himself as one of the "Idle People" of society who follow the dictates of "Pleasure" rather than "Affairs of Politicks" and states concisely, "I profess *Poetry*."[75] In the rest of the letter, he acts as disinterested literary critic, discussing the play in terms of its form, characterization, and sentiments without reverting to personal or political invective. The correspondent signed the letter "Dorimant."

In this letter and in a following one printed in the same journal on December 8, it is clear that "Dorimant" finds more merit in Steele's sentimental comedy than otherwise, making his assumption of the name of Etherege's hero largely ironic.[76] He ultimately favors Steele, approving of the playwright's representation of the "fine gentleman" that would make his own Restoration version of libertine gentility obsolete. But the more important irony, I suggest, lies in how the *St. James's Journal* "Dorimant" corresponds closely to Dennis's ideal vision of the Restoration rake as cultural arbiter. Etherege's hero is appropriated by a persona who founds his authority on moderation and impartiality. "Dorimant" is precisely the kind of cultural arbiter that Dennis alleged the elite Restoration wits to be: rational, autonomous, and out for the public good against self-interested and absolutist forms of authority. The cleverness of the *St. James's Journal* correspondent's entry into this controversy inheres in how he accords value to certain behaviors from the Stuart rake's repertoire within Steele's program of postrevolutionary social reform rather than opposing such behaviors as contradictory to it.

One such behavior is Dorimant's critical aloofness. *The Man of Mode* is replete with scenes of Dorimant watching and judging the other characters as if they were onstage: Dorimant and the others at Lady Townley's judge Sir Fopling's outlandish taste, Dorimant and Harriet critique Lady Woodvil's displays of antiquated civility, Dorimant arranges and judges the performances of Mrs. Loveit and Sir Fopling at the play's end.[77] To many readers, Dorimant appears among his more sensual libertine peers as a "cold calculator," critically distanced from feeling and action.[78] The *St. James's Journal* writer is able to co-opt Dorimant so effectively by recoding the character's menacing libertine frigidity as an essential ingredient of the public-sphere critic. À la Mr. Spectator—a more familiar embodiment of the concept of public-sphere authority—"Dorimant" alleges a lack of personal interest even in Steele and Dennis's debate, which is, as we have seen, very much about himself. Oddly enough, the voice of the self-centric Stuart rake here emerges from the supposedly decentered, depersonalized, antiabsolutist polite public sphere. Whereas Dorimant's voice is originally one of dangerous allure—as Lady Woodvil notes with some trepidation, "He has a tongue, they say, would tempt the angels to a second fall"—"Dorimant" discusses his culture with polite yet dispassionate rationality, thus projecting a greater claim to serve as critical arbiter in his representation of the general public interest.[79]

That "Dorimant" dates his letters from Button's coffeehouse both affirms his affiliation with the polite public sphere and troubles it. According to Habermas, the early eighteenth-century coffeehouse offered a venue for the exchange of critical ideas and for the emergence of a self-governing, rational public whose authority could challenge that of the sovereign or state.[80] Writing from Button's may reinforce "Dorimant's" claim as objective cultural arbiter. But, from its establishment in 1712 to well into the 1720s, Button's was also the headquarters of Addison's "little Senate," a partisan coterie of Whig wits that included Steele, Cibber, and their Drury Lane associates.[81] If this appears to weaken "Dorimant's" disinterested stance, in a later letter to *The St. James's Journal*, upon criticizing a failed production of John Fletcher's *Philaster* at Drury Lane, "Dorimant" distances himself from the crowd at Button's over the very question of the constitution of the polite public sphere. "I hear several People have thought fit to quarrel with me for my Opinion of *Philaster*," "Dorimant" writes: "Several of my gloomy Brethren of this Coffee-House are not able to comprehend whether I am a Friend or an Enemy; whether I am heartily in the interests of the Theatre, or else am secretly growling over some old Grudge. . . . That the Reputation of my Understanding ought to rise or fall at *Button's* Coffee-House, just as my Subject happens to lead me to censure or commend the Transactions of the Neighbouring Stage, is certainly very unjust."[82] With Button's very much partial to Drury Lane interests, the frank analysis of *Philaster*'s failure made "Dorimant" seem disloyal. His remonstrance to this charge underscores his commitment to the performance of disinterested cultural criticism, the right—guaranteed in the very constitution of the polite public sphere—for subjects to gather and exchange ideas without partisan coercion.

"Dorimant" emphasizes the Buttonians' betrayal of their own principles of politeness by capping his letter with a pirated version of Pope's lines on "Atticus"—a satire on Addison as the despot of London literary culture, first composed in the 1710s and later incorporated into the *Epistle to Arbuthnot* (1735):

> But were there one whom better Stars conspire,
> To form a *Bard*, or raise his Genius higher;
> Blest with each Talent, and each Art to please,
> And born to write, converse, and live with Ease;
> Should such a Man, too fond to reign alone,
> Bear, like the *Turk*, no Brother to the Throne;
> . . . .
> Like *Cato* gives his little Senate Laws,
> And sits attentive to his own Applause;
> . . . .
> Who but must grieve if such a Man there be?
> Who would not weep if *Ad—n* were he![83]

With Pope's lines, "Dorimant" alludes to Button's as a site in which a liberal form of cultural rule has been corrupted by a reanimated sovereignty—an enervated "little Senate" that does not support politeness as the bulwark of a free participatory culture but revives politeness's courtly past in bowing to the law of a self-centric absolutist. The disciplinary power of the polite public sphere that Whig theorists imagine can be harnessed benevolently to shape subjects fit for civil society here opens a space for the performance of Stuart-style absolutism. Subjection not only replaces subjectivation, it problematically emerges from it.

The idea of Button's as synonymous with cultural absolutism was popular, especially among Tory authors at this time. Writing to James Craggs on July 15, 1715, Pope derisively calls Addison an "absolute Lord," the "Grand Monarch" of the "small Court faction at Button's," which in happier times had been the site of nonpartisan wit. Tory newspapers utilized similar imagery to criticize Steele's ascendancy there in the early 1720s. *Applebee's Original Weekly Journal* questioned "what Right *Button's Coffee-House* has to the decision of Wit and good Sense, tho Sir *John Edgar* and *Cyberini* [Cibber] be Chairmen," and *The Freeholder's Journal* mocked Button's pretensions to politeness as part of its attack on *The Conscious Lovers*.[84] Unlike these oppositional satirists, however, and unlike the anticivil Dennis, "Dorimant" does not renounce politeness in the face of its corruption by Whig cultural arbiters. He rather reasserts the Shaftesburian ideal of politeness-as-liberty from which he perceives the wits at Button's to have defected. His short defense of his "Opinion" of the Drury Lane repertory and his exposure of absolutism at Button's, voiced rationally and civilly, are not simply promotions of his personal views, but a defense of the very right—guaranteed by the polite public sphere—of citizens to critique authority. "Dorimant" recuperates the liberty of the subject not by putting it in competition with politeness, but by deriving it from politeness, defending the postrevolutionary subject through a defense of the public structure that gives him a voice.

Other writers adopted Etherege's hero less ironically than *The St. James's Journal*. From 1726 into the 1730s—during the rise to power of Robert Walpole's court Whig party and the formation of a literary-political opposition to it—a new "Dorimant" became a regular correspondent in James Read's "violently whiggish" *Weekly Journal, or the British Gazetteer*, a vehicle through which he polices culture in the interests of the ministry.[85] This "Dorimant" contributes to the journal in a variety of roles: as a retailer of poetry, as a critic of London's literary and theatrical life, as a writer of moralistic cultural essays in the tradition of *The Tatler* and *The Spectator*. Like the "Dorimant" of *The St. James's Journal*, he proposes to speak with the unbiased voice of the literary public sphere. "I would aim at the Character of an impartial Writer," he asserts in one essay; and in a later set of verses on the literary war between the Scriblerian wits and the ministry dunces, he declares himself a "neutral Bard" in the "Civil Discords [that] rend *Apollo's* State," one "who nor with *Th—d* [Theobald] Leagues, nor fawns on *P*— [Pope]."[86] But despite such claims, much of "Dorimant's" work in Read's *Weekly Journal* exposes an uncompromising pro-ministry stance, not so much in direct political argument, but in a politicized cultural criticism. For instance, he often attacks writers of the oppositional periodical press such as Mist and the authors of *The Craftsman* as Grub Street scandal mongers intent on debasing the rules of polite journalism. He is also a staunch supporter of Drury Lane, a theater with ties to Walpole and one that was thus increasingly the target of Scriblerian satire.[87]

Given the afterlife of the Restoration rake that we have traced so far, it may seem odd that Dorimant could be seriously appropriated as a voice of the mainstream Whig ministry. It seems less odd, I suggest, if we recall the tactics by which pro-ministerial writers articulated their claims to cultural authority. As Bertrand

Goldgar notes, Walpole's writers often borrowed a discourse of "the decay of taste and the decline of letters" from their Scriblerian opponents and turned it against them.[88] As Pope, in *Peri Bathous* (1727) and *The Dunciad* (1729), attacked pro-ministry writers as corrupt dunces, so too did ministry writers accuse Pope, Swift, Gay, and Bolingbroke of encouraging a "low Humour" and retarding "polite Learning" with, as one pro-Walpole author put it, their "numerous Swarms of Mock-Epicks, Mock-Operas, [and] mock every Thing."[89] For the ministry, this argument bore a temporal component. In a reversal of Steele's attitude toward the Restoration past, but much in line with Dennis, anti-Scriblerian Whig satires such as *The Twickenham Hotch-Potch* (1728) and *A View of the Town; or, Memoirs of London* (1731) favorably compared Charles II's culture to England's current state of literary decline; the former even quotes Dennis, appropriating one of his tributes to the Restoration wits as part of an attack on the degeneracy of *The Beggar's Opera*.[90] The *Weekly Journal*'s use of "Dorimant" is fitting when read within the ministry's broader recourse to the Restoration past as an imagined time of cultural refinement prior to the spread of Scriblerian tastelessness. "Dorimant" is revived here not for his critical aloofness, as he was in *The St. James's Journal*, but for his pose as the elitist "fine gentleman," one capable of reliably discriminating between the high and the low and thus encouraging a political affiliation through an aesthetic one.

"Dorimant's" critique of *The Beggar's Opera*—published on March 30, 1728—functions in just this way to attribute refinement to Whig centers of cultural governance and lowness to their competitors. Shortly after its premiere at Lincoln's Inn Fields on January 29, 1728, Gay's comedy became a dangerous weapon in the arsenal of patriot opposition members, who were able to interpret its dizzyingly supple satire to their own anti-Walpole ends.[91] "Dorimant," like many of his pro-ministry peers, grounds his response in the aesthetic but also bares the consequences of a low taste to traditional British values. Skeptical of the "universal Admiration" that audiences have accorded Lavinia Fenton—the actress who created the role of Polly Peachum—"Dorimant" suggests that her success is due less to actual talent than to the resemblance she bears to her character, a thief-taker's daughter: "The Lowness of the Character [Fenton] represents, is, as I take it, the most material advantageous Circumstance in her Favour." This essential "lowness" of Gay's star, "Dorimant" continues, has the more damaging effect of eclipsing the real thespian talents of Drury Lane's Anne Oldfield:

> If the over Zeal of [Fenton's] Advocates and Applauders had not led them into a very ungenerous Treatment of the Merits of another of the same Sex [Oldfield], I might probably have continu'd entirely silent. . . . Yet

> I cannot but think it both the Business and Duty of every Person, to whom the preserving the *British* Theatre in its true Dignity, is a Matter of the least Moment, to interest his Resentment, when the Name of Mrs. *Oldfield*, who is a greater Ornament to it, than any Actress, that ever yet appear'd on the Stage, is made ungrateful mention of, to offer ridiculous Incense to so mean and inconsiderable a Competitor as *Polly Peachum*.[92]

"Dorimant" ties Oldfield—who had been at Drury Lane since 1711; had recently starred as Lady Townly in *The Beggar's Opera*'s most serious competitor, Cibber's *The Provoked Husband* (1728); and had become a status symbol for Whig ideology—to the "Dignity" and heritage of the British stage itself; her displacement by a "mean and inconsiderable" upstart such as Fenton suggests that "lowness" is not just aesthetically displeasing but actually dangerous to the nation's cultural traditions.[93]

Underneath the obvious partisanship of this critique, however, lies a fundamental problem of the transformation of the public sphere's utility for Whig cultural authority. "Dorimant's" appeal to "every Person" to make it his or her "Business and Duty" to support high theatrical culture, embodied in Oldfield, makes it appear that he is one with the public. But, in reality, he is its antagonist: "I am very sensible, that he undertakes a very hazardous and disrelishing Subject, who will have the Hardiness to offer his own private Judgment in Opposition to any prevailing Humour, Fashion, or Caprice of the Publick." For "Dorimant," it is the "Stupidity of the Kingdom," not that of the Scriblerian political opposition, that has occasioned "the prodigious Applause and Encouragement given to the *Beggar's Opera*."[94] The "Publick" has become its own authoritative judge of what is culturally worthwhile, its critical voice dissociated from the ministry's arbitration and thus degenerate. This antagonism is not so much born out of the public's resistance to the Whig project of fashioning culture as it is ultimately an effect of that project. As Jonathan Kramnick has shown, the early eighteenth-century Whiggish scheme of egalitarian refinement of taste was, by midcentury, perceived as paradoxically contributing to the emergence of tasteless mass culture, as the social diffusion and commercialization of the products of polite society negated their distinction from the "low."[95] "Dorimant" registers a related worry that the opening up of the polite public sphere has actually consolidated a public that is too free, hence resistant to the disciplinary forces of the Whig periodical press and theatrical repertory. The latent conflict of the coercive and the consensual, the sovereign and the disciplinary, that scholars have recognized in the early Whig reformist project becomes an overt one for ministry Whiggism.[96]

Compared to Addison and Steele's optimism about recovering Britain "out of that desperate State of Vice and Folly into which the Age has fallen," "Dorimant" sees in the popularity of *The Beggar's Opera* an example of the public's fixed coarseness: "The People of *England*, in my humble Opinion, have shewn, by their extravagant Fondness for [*The Beggar's Opera*], that the Degeneracy of Taste, with which they have been justly reproach'd for some Years past, is a Malady, not to be cured at once by the noble Medicine of Performances truly rational and sublime, but such an one, as must be sooth'd, like Bodily Ailments, by the Prescriptions of old Women, whose highest Successes never reach'd farther than to leave the Distemper just as they found it, or turn it to another."[97] The simile of incurable disease reveals the foibles of taste to be a permanent fixture of the public, leaving politeness and refinement to the elite arbiters of culture who may stand over against them. "Dorimant" sounds very much like Dennis here, with the important exception that his attack on the "Degeneracy of Taste" is not directed at avaricious arbiters who willfully mislead the public, but at a public that has itself been constituted by a post-1688 disciplinary Whig reformist project. Faced with the erosion of his own authority by the very polite public sphere that his Whig colleagues helped to consolidate, "Dorimant's" response is a pose of sovereign elitism that attaches him more firmly to his rakish Stuart namesake, a performance, that is, concerned primarily with securing his and the Walpole ministry's own right to rule in the cultural melee accompanying the shifts in power within Whig politics.

In different ways, then, "Dorimant" is a role useful to a Whiggish cultural criticism that would reform and govern British society in line with postrevolutionary values. For *The St. James's Journal*, Dorimant becomes a guardian of a polite public sphere whose courtly roots threaten to overrun its liberal promise; in Read's *Weekly Journal*, Dorimant is transformed into a conservative, elitist watchdog for a Whig ministry looking to secure a grip on cultural authority against a rising mass public. The ultimate Restoration "fine gentleman" that Steele initially tried to oust from the theatrical repertory and fashionable society returns in the aftermath of *The Conscious Lovers*—not as a straw man for Whig ideology, but as a pose by which writers could enact their visions of cultural authority. Far from expelled from the polite public sphere, the Restoration dramatic libertine stood at the very center of it.

Dorimant's transformation from absolutist anticivil Whig bugbear to spokesman for Walpole's ministry was not unmet by resistance. In the final section of this chapter, I turn to the literary opposition's response to Walpole's government in two texts, *The Beggar's Opera* and the anonymous *Memoirs Concerning the Life and Manners of Captain Mackheath* (1728), reading them as extensions of the debate over competing forms of cultural and political authority that Steele and Dennis inaugurated. An irreverent Tory ballad opera glamorizing the low life of highwaymen and prostitutes, *The Beggar's Opera* also takes an interest in the afterlife of the Restoration rake, specifically the character's unlikely persistence within the program of early eighteenth-century Whig reform. Following the pioneering readings of Isaac Kramnick and William Empson, many scholars recognize the play as a satire on a bourgeois political economy largely associated with the corrupt Walpole Whigs and the rise of finance capitalism.[98] Turning in detail to the play's rakish highwayman hero, Captain Macheath—who, like Dorimant, is described with varying levels of irony as a "fine gentleman" and "as fine as a lord"—I suggest that *The Beggar's Opera* and the opposition writers who capitalize on its success satirize not only the Whig commercialization of social relations but also the various cultural modes through which Whig power is established and enacted in the 1720s, including their appropriation of the Restoration rake as a figure of gentlemanly cultural authority.[99]

DORIMANT IN OPPOSITION

If with *The Conscious Lovers* Steele attempts to dethrone Restoration comedy and its rake-heroes from the repertory, Gay has been thought to do quite the opposite with his "Newgate pastoral."[100] A debonair outlaw who enjoys the fashionable vices of drinking and gambling and whose inexorable sexuality has saddled him with numerous "wives"—including the play's two female leads, Polly Peachum and Lucy Lockit—Macheath is heir to a variety of traditions of Restoration libertinism, including Stuart cavalier masculinity and the dangerous glamour of a Rochester. He has likewise been read more specifically as a reincarnation of individual rakes: Dryden's Antony, Shadwell's Don John, Wycherley's Horner, and the "gay perjur'd" Dorimant himself.[101]

Eighteenth-century readers recognized such similarities, drawing moral and political conclusions from them. In the wake of *The Beggar's Opera*'s popularity, London exploded with an assortment of publications purporting to document the "lives" of the play's characters. In the fictionalized criminal biography *Memoirs Concerning the Life and Manners of Captain Mackheath*, the author worries about the "popular Applause" that Gay's hero has drawn from an impressionable theatergoing public. To emphasize the moral stakes, he sketches a parallel to Etherege's seducer: "[Mackheath] is a perfect, polite, modern fine Gentleman, and *Dorimant* in Sir *Fopling*; tho a Person of equal Morals, is not a more accomplished Rake. He commits his Robberies with an Air of Authority and Gallantry, the common People mistake his Vices for Virtues."[102] The comparison here is not so much between Macheath and Dorimant as it is between Macheath and the idea of Dorimant that had taken hold of writers' imaginations in the 1720s. Rehashing the language of the decade's earlier Dorimant debate, the memoirist shows the danger in the pose of the "polite, modern fine Gentleman," how its skillful performance obscures the rake's actual threat to the populace. For Dennis and his fellow Whig journalists, Dorimant's autonomy and polite gentility—his "Authority and Gallantry"—were what made him so capable of dictating cultural norms to his audiences; for Macheath's biographer, these same qualities are what make him so good at picking their pockets.

The *Memoirs* thus announces itself as a moral tale, critical of Gay's representation of vice as all too "polite." As Bertrand Goldgar notes, moral denunciations of *The Beggar's Opera* were often exploited to political purpose by ministry writers.[103] But this moral discourse was also adopted by opposition writers looking either to caricature the views of their political enemies or to target Walpole through a critique of characters in the play thought to represent him, notably Macheath.[104] Such tactics are a particular favorite of the chief opposition periodical, *The Craftsman*. In the issue for May 18, 1728, Caleb D'Anvers, the editorial persona, includes a lengthy puff for the *Memoirs*, promising it to be "very agreeable Entertainment" and stating that it "comes from an Hand that hath often appeared in this Paper, and never without Success."[105] The association with *The Craftsman* indicates that the *Memoirs* is not a moral critique of Gay's play per se, but a satire on Walpole-as-Macheath, on Walpole as a robber of the public, and ultimately on the Whig project of cultural reform that operates through the leadership of the polite yet rakish "fine gentleman."

This reading emerges as the memoirist narrates the life story of his version of Macheath (whom he styles "Mackheath"), based loosely on Walpole's rise to power. Mackheath's career as a highwayman begins in the aftermath of the Hanoverian succession and the defeat of the French-Jacobite threat. À la *Fears of the Pretender*, the memoirist describes an English society, recently delivered from political turmoil, in the throes of debauchery and corruption. There arose in the people at this time an "uncommon Desire of Money" and an "extraordinary Appetite for Power," which led the nation to "Rapine, Injustice, [and] a general Dissolution of Morals; and in each Man was found a Desire after the Goods of his Neighbour, and the Rich oppress'd the Poor without Modesty or Moderation" (10–11, 12). Though Mackheath is "dissolute" himself, he witnesses these results and aspires to social change:

> He contemn'd those Laws, and that Society, who could only punish those who broke the Laws, not those who *broke thro* them; and by virtue

> of which, the Poor had very little Protection against the Oppressions of the Rich. . . . He saw no Reason why Property should be so unfairly distributed. . . . These Considerations had determin'd him to excommune himself, to leap over the Pale of the Society, to run wild again, and remit himself to the Original State where all Men had a Right to all Things; and this Way of Proceeding, he flatter'd himself was Honourable and Just. . . . But this Project of running wild soon vanish'd, and made way for what he conceiv'd to be much more commode and natural. He began to imagine, very unjustly, as Men who suffer their Reason to stray are soon lost, that not only the whole Community, but any Part of it, had a Right to dissolve it self and to erect another; and to form such Regulations or Laws for the Society as they should think proper. (16–18)

Mackheath's rationalizing parodies the recognizable tenets of early eighteenth-century Whig political theory, interpreted from Locke's *Second Treatise*: equality in a state of nature, the distribution of property, the right to resist unjust government. Pondering and rejecting a straightforwardly Hobbesian "wild," "Original State," he opts to establish a "Confederacy of Thieves" on the reformed Whiggish principles of liberty and property (19, 33–36). Underneath his pose as a Lockean Robin Hood, however, Mackheath never relinquishes his initial acquisitive Hobbesian dream: as the gang's "Captain," he possesses "great Authority; he has the whole Body intirely under the Menage" (26). In Walpole-Mackheath's agenda of sociopolitical reform, liberal postrevolutionary values are exposed to have an underbelly of self-centric sovereign autonomy and possessive individualism.

Included in the *Memoirs*' parody is the Whig ideology of politeness. Mackheath's gang follows his genteel lead: "It must be confess'd by all who have had the Honour to be robb'd by them, that they collected in a very Gentleman-like manner" (44). If Dorimant's suavity in *The Man of Mode* masks a deeper anticivility, then so too does the performance of politeness serve as a handy guise for the arbitrary lawlessness of the Walpole Whigs. As it will be later in Henry Fielding's *Shamela* (1741)—a spoof of both Walpole and the reformed rake narrative, popularized anew by Samuel Richardson's *Pamela* (1740)—in the *Memoirs* the reforming ideals of politeness are converted into "poluteness," a corruption that not so much betrays the Lockean tenets of liberty and property as reveals them to be coextensive with, rather than opposed to, the sociopolitical aggrandizement of absolutist individuals.[106] Through the figure of a rake that a decade of Whig writers adopted as their own—polite, autonomous, distanced from the interests of a corrupt court or the degenerate public—the *Memoirs* indicts an entire history of Whig political and cultural governance that has led to Walpole's reign.

The Beggar's Opera itself does not cultivate the sustained one-to-one allegorization of Macheath/Walpole that we find in subsequent opposition propaganda such as *The Craftsman* or the *Memoirs*.[107] Nevertheless, with the exposure of contraries in its protagonist—genteel allure and bourgeois corruption, Restoration rake and ministry figurehead, lawless autonomy and Lockean principles—the *Memoirs* extends a satire on Whiggish cultural authority already embedded within Gay's text. As the Beggar reminds us, "throughout the whole piece . . . it is difficult to determine whether (in the fashionable vices) the fine gentlemen imitate the gentlemen of the road, or the gentlemen of the road the fine gentlemen" (121). The collapsing together of the gentleman and the criminal, the high and the low, is a Scriblerian motif that drives Gay's criticism of social injustice. But the play also presents a partisan critique of the "fine gentleman"—figure of Whiggish cultural authority in the 1720s—as the reembodiment of the politically suspect behaviors of the Stuart rake.

As with Dennis or the Dorimants of the public journals, Gay's "fine gentlemen" adopt a performance of sociability and autonomy politically opposed to courtly self-interest and commercial corruption. In the self-congratulatory conversation that opens act 2, Macheath's gang establishes this pose:

> JEMMY TWITCHER. Why are the laws levelled at us? Are we more dishonest than the rest of mankind? What we win, gentlemen, is our own by the law of arms, and the right of conquest. . . .
>
> WAT DREARY. Sound men, and true!
>
> ROBIN OF BAGSHOT. Of tried courage, and indefatigable industry!
>
> NIMMING NED. Who is there here that would not die for his friend?
>
> HARRY PADDINGTON. Who is there here that would betray him for his interest?
>
> MATT OF THE MINT. Show me a gang of courtiers that can say as much.
>
> BEN BUDGE. We are for a just partition of the world, for every man hath a right to enjoy life. (68–69)

The gang rejects the false politeness of the "courtier" in favor of an older model of aristocratic gentility: independent, sociable, honorable, capable of dictating the terms of an equitable society. As with the Mackheath of the *Memoirs*, however, the rhetoric of "a just partition of the world" and the "right" of every man to liberty and property elides but does not erase a far less pastoral vision of a state of nature governed by a "law of arms." As liberal as the gang's appeal to "right" appears, it cannot expunge Jemmy Twitcher's association of the word with conquest, a kind of sovereign individualism that acknowledges no power outside of the self's desires. The fact that it is Jemmy who will betray Macheath at the close of the play only confirms the skepticism toward the Shaftesburian language of sociability and liberty evinced by the jailor Lockit: "Of all animals of prey, man is the only sociable one. Every one of us preys upon his neighbour, and yet we herd together" (98–99). Toying with Whig language throughout, Gay reduces the ideal of the sociable "fine gentleman" as the bedrock of a reformed polity to a form of opportunism under which absolutist individuals may more easily exploit weaker members of the "herd."

As chief "fine gentleman," Macheath embodies similar disparities. Blithely proclaiming that "the town" is "obliged" to his libertine sexuality for the production of "free-hearted ladies," Macheath partakes in the gang's rhetoric of free circulation, opposed to the hoarding tendencies of the bourgeois villains Peachum and Lockit (72). Noting Macheath's "largess" with both money and his own sexualized body, some scholars accept him as representative of "sexual and economic freedom."[108] But whatever liberality he does possess is belied by his self-centric desire, inherited from his Restoration predecessors. As he reveals in soliloquy, "a man who loves money, might as well by contented with one guinea, as I with one woman" (72). Three scenes earlier, he compares Polly—his alleged true love—to a "shilling" coveted by a "miser," and subsequently, he regales himself in a tavern with prostitutes like a king in a harem (67). The tavern scenes are also ones of intensely burlesqued gentility, filled with "fine ladies," formal French dances, and a discourse of politeness that only thinly veils the characters' sensual and monetary desires (74). In the end, Gay implies, the Whiggish polite "fine gentleman" may be no better than the self-centric absolutist Stuart rake he was designed to combat.

The play's famous denouement, in which Macheath's execution is averted, complements Gay's critique of the politics of politeness with an ironic jab at a related facet of Whig culture: the death or reform of the Restoration libertine. Because "an opera must end happily," the Player explains to the Beggar, and "to comply with the taste of the town," Macheath is let off and is "brought back to his wives in triumph" (121). In reprieving his hero, Gay reverses the typical eighteenth-century trajectory of the rake's progress toward cultural obsolescence, but it is equally important that this reversal occurs through a deus ex machina in the form of aesthetic discrimination, "taste." Both Michael Denning and J. Douglas Canfield read the forced happy ending as Gay's self-reflexive wink at the inevitably complicit role of the author in modern commercial mass culture; like the Beggar, Gay must concede to an audience that is capitalistic, bourgeois, low.[109]

The thrust of the satire, however, points not just to the "rabble" but to their "taste," which, as Canfield notes, demands "a wish-fulfillment ending": the reform, marriage, and socialization of the rake (121).[110] It is a taste, in other words, in line with the Whig program of cultural and sociopolitical reform itself. But it is also a taste that ultimately allows the libertine to "triumph." Macheath agrees to "have a wife at last" and even acknowledges Polly as that wife, thus fulfilling the initial romantic premise. But his closing aria suggests the fleeting nature of this arrangement:

> Thus I stand like the Turk, with his doxies around;
> From all sides their glances his passion confound;
> For black, brown, and fair, his inconstancy burns,
> And the different beauties subdue him by turns:
> Each calls forth her charms, to provoke his desires:
> Though willing to all; but with one he retires.
> But think of this maxim, and put off your sorrow,
> The wretch of today, may be happy tomorrow. (121–122)

The rake's "inconstancy" has not been put conclusively to rest. This final aria, during which Macheath dances with his "wives," undoes the capitalistic bourgeois logic of marriage—which Gay has throughout critiqued as linked to a corrupt system of Whiggish possessive individualism—and renders ineffective the cultivation of the town's "taste" for the purposes of a Whig sociopolitical program. In other words, Gay suggests, instead of reforming and appropriating the Restoration rake, the Whig cultural arbiters should have killed him when they had the chance.

Nor is Macheath's "triumph" simply a straightforward political victory over a corrupt bourgeois system. In demanding a reformist ending, the "taste of the town" saves the polite "fine gentleman" who is revealed to be merely a "Turk," an absolutist, self-centric, criminal individual who will—as a pirate in the New World setting of Gay's suppressed sequel, *Polly* (1729)—go on to plunder again. It is a taste that produces not liberty but highway robbery on an international scale. In this, Gay's satire is leveled directly at the Whig cultural arbiters for whom the developing, reforming, and refining of taste in the "Goths and Vandals" of the theatergoing public carried such sociopolitical weight and for whom a reformed or reappropriated Dorimant served as model. If *The Weekly Journal*'s "Dorimant" sees the public's applause for Macheath as a revolt against the rightful reign of ministry Whig cultural arbiters such as himself, Gay wittily suggests that applauding Macheath is precisely what such Whig cultural arbiters have trained the public to do. Such applause both undermines the Whig program of reform and reveals it to be self-serving in its underlying desire to co-opt the absolutist power of the rake. The political effects of the libertine's persistence are, ironically, produced by the Whig cultural-aesthetic program: the socializing of the nation's taste leads to a reempowerment of the sovereign rake. If Macheath's execution in *Polly* is a straightforward attack on the Walpole Whigs, so too, paradoxically, is his reprieve in *The Beggar's Opera*.

With *The Beggar's Opera*, then, Gay rewrites the "rake's progress" as open-ended. Rather than delivering "a finishing stroke" to the Restoration libertine as Steele intended, Gay shows how the very project of Whig cultural reform forestalls the libertine's death. The critique of the Walpole Whigs for betraying their party's own revolutionary principles was to become a popular tactic for the patriot opposition in the 1730s, voiced most powerfully in Bolingbroke's *Dissertation upon Parties* (1733–1734). In a sense, Gay anticipates this argument, not as a politician but as a playwright. *The Beggar's Opera* gestures to a constant theme, as we have seen, in the debates about the Restoration rake in the 1720s: behind the rhetoric of purging a theatrical past associated with Stuart sovereignty from polite civil society, Whig cultural reform harbors the rake and appropriates his behaviors for its own devices in governing the public.

Of course, Macheath remained enduringly popular with audiences for reasons beyond his role in a partisan satire of recent Whig history. For a host of scholars who disagree on just about everything else regarding *The Beggar's Opera*, Macheath stands acknowledged as a figure of nostalgia or anachronism, with no real place in modern bourgeois Whig society.[111] What such readings miss, I suggest, is how Gay attunes us to the fact that the pose of the sovereign libertine is neither politically nor chronologically antecedent to a new Whig order, but actually an effect of it. While propagandists such as Bolingbroke, *The Craftsman*, or the author of the *Memoirs* made much anti-Walpole hay out of the notable irony of a liberal public robber, Macheath's sovereign pose channels a latent desire of the postrevolutionary British subject, a desire for absolute authority of the free individual under the restrictive conditions of a disciplinary Whig regime. The rise of new Whig mechanisms of power—cultural, political, and economic—did not kill off or make anachronistic the Restoration libertine; it created the conditions under which the subject could, in the first place, desire to restore the libertine's performance of liberty, autonomy, and sovereignty as a mode of post-1688 liberty. Macheath's unprecedented attractiveness as a role model for eighteenth-century audiences and readers, as Joseph Roach has documented, lies in his purchase on an ineffable charisma that partakes of both the forbidden and the alluring.[112] I would add that his charismatic power proceeds from his offering of a dream of liberty to the sovereign absolute subject, even if this type of liberty often (perhaps always) fails to be effectively realized as it devolves into absolutism. Macheath's pose, in other words, may be so enduringly popular for the very way it makes uncomfortable the chronological succession—in political and theatrical history—from the stage of the sovereign Stuart rake to the stage of the postrevolutionary subject.

3

STUARTS WITHOUT END

By MIDCENTURY, ONE'S CHANCES OF SEEING *The Man of Mode*—or indeed, most Restoration libertine plays—on the London stages had significantly lessened. Hester Thrale, writing in the margins of her copy of *The Spectator* no. 65, remarked on the play's disappearance: "Tis banish'd from the Stage now; I fancy by Garrick."[1] As we will see further on, Thrale's attribution of Etherege's exile to the iconic actor-manager David Garrick was well founded; it is during Garrick's long tenure as cultural arbiter at Drury Lane between the 1740s and 1770s that Restoration libertine drama, at least in its unadulterated form, slips from the repertory.[2] This period, in fact, witnessed a striking reversal of Defoe's 1715 pronouncement that the spread of licentious Stuart drama had replaced the invasion of Jacobite forces: at the midcentury, the Restoration Stuarts are off the stage, but the Jacobites (real and imagined) are up in arms. In the latter half of 1745, Charles Edward Stuart, the Young Pretender, marched across Scotland and northern England in a failed attempt to retake the throne that produced both national panic and a renewed sense of Hanoverian patriotism, but at the same time ensured the romanticization of the Stuarts as a fixture of the British cultural imaginary. At George III's 1760 accession, the new king's approach to executive power and ministerial choices stoked fears that a restoration of Stuart principles, if not Jacobite personae, had been effected at the heart of the Hanoverian dynasty itself. As the oppositionist poet Charles Churchill lamented in *The Prophecy of Famine* (1763), Britain appeared to be cursed by "Stuarts without end."[3]

This chapter explores the basis of Churchill's complaint as it relates to the ongoingness of Restoration libertine drama at its supposed midcentury moment of demise. Resurgent Stuart absolutism—in the forms of Jacobitism and Georgian state authoritarianism—was countered not only by Whig militarism and statecraft, but also by a Whiggish cultural politics. In the theaters, this amounted to a deluge of plays, new and revived, that scrutinized, parodied, or otherwise exploited the Jacobite furor by staging topically relevant scenes of rebellion, invasion, and monarchical pretendership.[4] The Restoration rake also achieved renewed anti-Stuart significance in this moment due to his iconicity as sociopolitical renegade, sexual usurper, and tyrant. Samuel Richardson's *Clarissa* (1747–1748) has been the best-documented example of this phenomenon. As is noted in most studies of *Clarissa,* Lovelace's lineage descends from Restoration drama. His epistolary self-fashioning consciously literary, he owes a debt, on the one hand, to Restoration tragedies by Dryden, Otway, and Lee in which bombastic libertine antagonists exert their absolutist sway in political and sexual arenas and, on the other, to the aristocratic and highly theatricalized performances of the Stuart court wits and their representatives in Restoration sex comedy. In thus molding Lovelace, the novel makes him appear outmoded, behind the times of modernity's respect for law and property. His death at the end of the novel offers a repudiation of mid-century Jacobitism's threat to the (Whiggish and Hanoverian) social and political order in the annihilation of the aesthetic figure inextricably linked to Restoration culture: the witty, charismatic, heroic, but ultimately criminal libertine.[5]

My goal in what follows is not to contest the many readings that trace anti-Stuart motivations in the dismissal of the Restoration rake hero at the midcentury. Elaine McGirr's memorably succinct argument about *Clarissa* remains quite convincing: from Richardson's political vantage, "Lovelace must die."[6] What I want to suggest, however, is that the canonization of Richardson's representation of the libertine's fate has overshadowed alternative ways that this figure and his Restoration dramatic heritage functioned in these decades of Stuart political reanimation. If banished from the theaters and demonized within the culture of the novel, the Restoration stage rake nonetheless lingers as an emulative model in the everyday performances of eighteenth-century individuals for whom the figure's purchase on the language of freedom and anti-authoritarianism was mobilized against the threats of foreign and domestic absolutism. Writing of *Clarissa*'s central conflict between the libertine-aristocrat and the modern forces of bourgeois governance, Denis Diderot claimed that most readers "would prefer to die Lovelace, at the hand of Colonel Morden, than to live Solmes."[7] The appeal of the Restoration rake that I trace supports Diderot's assumption that sovereign desire was alive and well in the midcentury subject's imagination of personal and political liberty.

In the rest of this chapter, I turn to Restoration libertine drama's lingering appeal as it is manifested in a broad but interconnecting set of real-life personalities who adopt the poses of figures such as Lothario, Macheath, and Sir John Brute and whose enactments engender a debate about the proximity of liberal Whig values to transgressive lawlessness. In the histrionic style of David Garrick in the late

1740s and in the out-of-doors politicking of John Wilkes and his radical adherents in the early 1760s, these Restoration literary descendants' aristocratic performances of freedom from social norms and economic strictures, along with their antimonarchism, are repurposed as tools to defend the promise of popular sovereignty. As such versions of popular sovereignty are predicated on sovereign popularity (the flashy displays of privilege and prerogative that account for the extravagant self-licensed libertine's appeal), however, for skeptical observers, adapting the rake in this fashion only implicated his emulators in the disciplinary mechanisms that they purported to resist. I conclude the chapter with an exploration of how this debate over sovereign popularity's relation to Stuart absolutism and postrevolutionary liberty manifests itself in the performances of the Scotsman James Boswell in London in 1762–1763, for whom desire for the sovereign privilege of the individual and disgust at its self-consuming license operate in tandem in the construction of (one possible version of) midcentury subjectivity. The internalization of Restoration libertine drama in everyday styles and behaviors at once reveals its legacy at the midcentury as more than an ideological stand-in for the exiled Stuarts and becomes a historical site that exposes the contradictions and conflicts inherent in the changing relation of sovereignty to liberty. I begin this exploration with a return to the stage history of Rowe's Lothario.

LOTHARIO REDUX

If the success of *Clarissa* hangs on the textual finality of the libertine's death, that of *The Fair Penitent* depends on his life or, more specifically, on the animating features of the theatrical event: his ontic liveness and his nightly revival under the standard practice of the repertory stage. Echoing Samuel Johnson's anxiety over spectators' continuing "kindness" toward Lothario's libertine qualities (discussed in my introduction), theatrical anecdotalists across the eighteenth century confirm Lothario's liveness as the source of both his popularity and his challenge to the play's social utility. Lothario, one contemporary writer notes, if "properly disposed, might have had a due effect, by creating a necessary abhorrence of the blemishes that stain [his appealing character]," but the consensus of reviewers is that the play's ontic register forestalls this outcome.[8] In a review of a 1766 revival of the play, for example, *The Whitehall Evening Post* warned that Lothario's "licentious and immoral tendency" is made worse "as he is represented in a pleasing point of light" in the production and is "considered as a model for imitation" by "injudicious" viewers; Francis Gentleman interprets Lothario as a "licentious gallant [who] gilds his pernicious principles with very delusive qualifications" that have particularly dire ramifications during the "representation of this piece" onstage; and Elizabeth Inchbald similarly cautioned against an "immoral tendency . . . deduced from the influence of beholding so enchanting a personage as Lothario."[9] The anxiety voiced in such accounts is not that reading Rowe's text will produce detrimental effects on the public but that *seeing* staged representations of Lothario has almost certainly already done so.

As with Lovelace, Lothario's threat is political as well as moral. Fielding, in *The Champion* (1740), claims to have witnessed Lothario's effects firsthand in female playgoers "whose voice hath no inconsiderable Weight in our constitution": "I have observed in our Theatres, that the Intrepidity of Lothario and Morat, gained Mr Booth no small Number of fair Admirers, notwithstanding all the Vices with which those Characters are drawn."[10] His diction at once distinguishes Lothario's performance onstage from the moral intent of how he is "drawn" in print and emphasizes the danger that such a radical divergence poses to the "constitution" of the British public. This word bears a distinct politics, as Fielding links Lothario to his Restoration lineage through Morat, the rake tyrant of Dryden's *Aureng-Zebe* (1675); the "constitution" of the Hanoverian nation is endangered as Lothario's inappropriately appealing embodiment restores Stuart tyranny to power within the theatrical space, a privileged site of governmentality. The Stuarts' reign, Fielding implies, may be over, but their ethos lives on in the attractions of Lothario's libertine body, inflecting the behavior of a populace who, following 1688, now stand as representative of national and cultural values.

As Fielding's nod to the actor Barton Booth suggests, the danger of a new Stuart succession in the form of the exiled dynasty's stage avatars comes distinctly from a key element of ontic signification: the embodiment and interpretation of literary character. It is only from the second third of the eighteenth century onward that Lothario came to elicit the appeal that these reviewers lament, and this shift can be explained with reference to the string of actors whose star power kept the role in constant demand.[11] As we saw in chapter 1, in the text Calista remains drawn to Lothario's élan. According to reviewers such as Fielding, Gentleman, and Inchbald, audiences in London's theaters responded in kind. For them, the popularity of *The Fair Penitent* rested not on the morally and politically appropriate pleasures of witnessing the Stuart rake's death, but on this figure's charismatic and disquieting returns to life in celebrity portrayals.

Garrick's history with Lothario offers a rich example of this phenomenon, particularly as his popularization of the role coincides with an attempted Stuart restoration in the '45. Garrick's acting career began at Henry Giffard's theater at Goodman's Fields in 1741, but his meteoric rise to fame immediately propelled him onto the main stages at Drury Lane and Covent Garden. As contemporaries noted and scholars continue to affirm, his appearance on the theatrical scene constituted a revolution, the roots of which lay in his overturning many of the older conventions informing English histrionic style. Earlier popular acting theories had privileged vocal declamation over expressive action, the virtuosic exhibition of universally conceived passions over characterological intricacy. In contrast, Garrick's "natural" style put the control of the passions in the service of a more empirical and particularized approach to character. By utilizing dynamic and nuanced body movements and by staying consistently in character, Garrick allowed his roles to come alive not as stock types, but as idiosyncratic individuals.[12] Early on, his fame in this mode derived from his performances of stage villains, one of the most enduring of which was Lothario. As Peter Thomson suggests, such presentations of humanized villainy in the "natural" style proved "irresistibly charming" to audiences but were also fraught with "moral ambiguity," justifying the fears of theatrical commentators regarding the power of the ontic register to foil didactic purposes.[13]

Lothario's place in a genealogy of Restoration stage libertines makes him unique among the villain parts that Garrick took up. His affinity for the role runs counter to the narrative of dismissal that informs how we usually view Garrick's relationship to the Restoration theatrical past. Thrale's attribution of the repertory disappearance of *The Man of Mode* to Garrick's tenure as cultural arbiter is only one example. As actor, manager, and author, Garrick encouraged a declining national taste for Restoration drama at the midcentury. He discontinued the tradition of annually producing Ravenscroft's *The London Cuckolds* (1681) on the Lord Mayor's Day; he approved expurgations in Restoration revivals such as Wycherley's *The Plain Dealer* (1676) and Vanbrugh's *The Provoked Wife* (1697); and his own work as dramatist, notably in *The Male Coquette* (1757) and *The Country Girl* (1766), took both satirical and moralizing swipes at the traditions of high Carolean comedy.[14] In anesthetizing this theatrical heritage, Garrick is firmly in the realm of the moral reviewers who called for the dispelling of Lothario's dangerous ontic allure.

Moreover, as an avatar of Stuart absolutism, Lothario seems antithetical to Garrick's own loyalties. Arthur Murphy, one of Garrick's early biographers, makes it clear that while Garrick avoided partisan quarrels between Whig and Tory, he was "true to his King and the Constitution," his politics staunchly Hanoverian.[15] Beyond the anti-Jacobitism found in his personal correspondence in the years surrounding the '45, his political principles were largely expressed through disputes over style. Both Murphy and Thomas Davies record an exchange between Garrick and James Quin—soon after the former's rise to celebrity—that played out in these terms. Quin—an older actor who performed in the declamatory style of the Restoration—had mockingly likened Garrick to the Methodist preacher George Whitefield, whose performative sermonizing Quin viewed as a fad: "he said, 'That Garrick was a new religion; Whitfield was followed for a time; but they would all come to church again.'" Garrick's reply came in an impromptu poetic rebuttal:

> Pope Quin, who damns all churches but his own,
> Complains that heresy infects the town;
> That Whitfield-Garrick has misled the age,
> And taints the sound religion of the stage:
> Schism, he cries, has turn'd the nation's brain;
> But eyes will open, and to church again!
> Though great infallible, forbear to roar,
> Thy bulls and errors are rever'd no more;
> When doctrines meet with gen'ral approbation,
> It is not heresy, but reformation.[16]

Allying himself with a Protestant "reformation" and Quin with Catholicism, Garrick mobilizes a history of England's religious contentions in order to demonize Quin as both politically and stylistically outmoded. Catholicism was aligned with the Stuart absolutism that supposedly inhered in the contemporary Jacobite cause. Quin's "roar[ing]" and his "great[ness]" refer satirically to his stoic heavyset stage presence and his penchant for declamation, styles of acting that Garrick's histrionic revolution were making obsolete. Absolutism, intolerance, and theatrical ranting, Garrick suggests, are all part of a Stuart past that his own Hanoverian-tinged reforms—which possess the "gen'ral approbation" of the English people—promise to dispel.

Lothario embodies the litany of dangers that loyalist authors marshaled in their anti-Jacobite propaganda in the 1740s and would thus seem fair game for dismissive treatment by Garrick. Yet the extant accounts do not mark his portrayal of Rowe's villain as analogous to those of the Jacobite rebels, and they do not emphasize the rake's death as the triumph of Hanoverian modernity. Instead, they recognize in Garrick's performance as Lothario an ability to dissociate Stuart theater from Stuart politics and, indeed, even to co-opt the Restoration theatrical rake for the forces of modern English liberty in the ideological battle against Jacobitism.

This effect is especially evident in the 1746 revival of *The Fair Penitent*, in which Garrick (as Lothario) appeared opposite Quin (as Horatio) at Covent Garden. Arranged by John Rich, the market-savvy Covent Garden manager, this pairing capitalized on the two actors' earlier rivalry, reenacting a contest between the old-fashioned and the revolutionary at a time when such terms carried loaded political weight. Anecdotal accounts of the event focus primarily on Lothario and Horatio's second-act encounter, which, as I discussed in chapter 1, served as a set-piece expression of Rowe's politics via a cultural clash between bourgeois moral virtue and aristocratic license. This scene continued to be recognized as such at the midcentury; as Arthur Murphy saw it, Quin was particularly suited to perform the "emphasis and dignity" of "moral sentiments" and Garrick to the part of "the gay young man of intrigue."[17] But when overlaid, in the ontic register, with the pair's competing histrionic styles, the outcome of their encounter was far from a settled bourgeois-moral victory. As Davies describes it,

> The town had often wished to see these great actors fairly matched in two characters of almost equal importance. The Fair Penitent presented an opportunity to display their several merits; though it must be owned, that the balance was as much in favour of Quin, as the advocate of virtue is superior in argument to the defender of libertinism. . . . Notwithstanding the evident disparity arising from one actor's pleading the cause of truth and virtue, and the other being engaged on the side of licentiousness and profligacy, Mr. Quin was, in the opinion of the best judges, fairly defeated.

Davies goes on to suggest that Quin's ponderous declamatory style—"the strong emphasis which he stamped on almost every word in a line"—was responsible for this production's reversal of the expected and politically correct defeat of libertine values.[18] Against a declining national taste for Stuart theatrical culture, Garrick's performance as Lothario is here thought by the "best judges" to outdo Quin's performance as the champion of morality and virtue.

Richard Cumberland's recollection of this revival of *The Fair Penitent* offers an even more politically charged representation of the actors' stylistic differences. For Cumberland, Garrick's appearance in the second act was a revelation:

> Heavens, what a transition!—it seemed as if a whole century had been stept over in the transition of a single scene; old things were done away, and a new order at once brought forward, bright and luminous, and clearly destined to dispel the barbarisms and bigotry of a tasteless age, too long attached to the prejudices of custom, and superstitiously devoted to the illusions of imposing declamation. This heaven-born actor was then struggling to emancipate his audience from the slavery they were resigned to, and though at times he succeeded in throwing in some gleams of new born light upon them, yet in general they seemed to *love darkness better than light*, and in the dialogue of altercation between Horatio and

> Lothario bestowed far greater *show of hands* upon the master of the old school than upon the founder of the new.[19]

This passage is often cited as evidence of the contemporary recognition of Garrick's novelty, but far less attention has been paid to its political valence. Though Cumberland was writing at a significant remove from the concerns of the 1740s—he was a teenager when he saw Garrick and Quin perform, and his memoirs were published in 1806—he nevertheless marshals a set of anti-Jacobite tropes to depict the outmodedness of Quin's style. He imagines the older actor's popularity as an effect of "the prejudices of custom" and superstition, evidence of a barbaric and intolerant national taste and features often associated with the Catholic Stuarts. For Cumberland, English audiences are currently enslaved to the reign of "imposing declamation," a cultural bondage analogous to the effects that Stuart tyranny had on the nation during the Restoration and that, according to Hanoverian loyalists, were in danger of recurring in the Jacobite scare. If Quin here, as "master of the old school," is the cultural embodiment of the Stuart absolutist past, then Garrick represents the nation's emancipatory future, the bringer of enlightenment and liberty to a people still enthralled (as their recent flirtation with Jacobitism and their applause for Quin attest) to this Stuart idiom.

There is, then, an anti-Jacobite politics to Garrick's theatrical revolution, as his revival of *The Fair Penitent* deposes not only declamation, but also the authoritarian Stuart past that such an acting style conjures. The political thrust of his performance is effected not through the mimetic death of Lothario at the hands of the play's morally and politically righteous men, but through his ontic enlivening of the stage rake as a figure of enlightened freedom. Known as a reformer of licentious Restoration drama, Garrick in this early instance enacts the theatrical reform of the stage rake in quite a different sense, transforming Lothario into a figure of opposition to Stuart insurrection and defeating the principles of absolutism that inhere in a past—embodied by Quin's style and the '45—that refuses to be over.

The accounts of Cumberland and others reveal that Garrick's power as cultural liberator lies in his enactment of the Restoration rake's traditional élan—not only the figure's charisma but also, in a more literal sense, his "emphatic vivacity."[20] Compared to the "heavy-paced" Quin, who epitomized a wooden formality, speaking "with very little variation of cadence" and moving with "a sawing kind of action, which had more of the senate than the stage in it," Garrick's Lothario exudes vitality: he "bound[s]" across the stage, "young and light and alive in every muscle and in every feature."[21] Cumberland is able to position Garrick as a convincing representative of modern English liberty against outmoded Jacobite slavery because his "natural" acting style exemplifies a physical freeing of the body, in terms of its vigorous mobility and its loosening of the restraints of older histrionic conventions. As Garrick's technique yokes acting "natural" with liberty and puts both terms in conflict with the tyranny of convention, it revises a fundamental strategy of the Restoration rake's defense of his personal rule. In *The Fair Penitent*, the Stuart rake's claim of following the dictates of "nature" against the constraints of social and moral convention marks the foundation of his specious assertions of the liberty of the subject. In his Lothario, Garrick mobilizes this libertine claim on nature to parallel but politically divergent ends: the assertion of the bodily freedom of the subject against the (Jacobite) slavery of convention. If the Stuart élan is what other moralists deplore in staged representations of Restoration rakes such as Lothario, Garrick's performance reverses its supposedly deleterious effects, repurposing the "natural" vitality of the libertine in the service of Hanoverian values.

Accounts such as Cumberland's indicate that the popularity of Rowe's play rested on the persistent attraction of the aristocratic Stuart rake, generated by the idiosyncrasies of interpretive embodiments. Rowe and Richardson attempt in their respective texts to reform Restoration libertine drama through Lothario/Lovelace's death; Garrick reforms the stage, however, through Lothario's revival, his ontic variations promoting the anti-Jacobite politics that underpin his theatrical revolution. If the death of the aristocratic Stuart rake has been perceived as thematically central to the forging of bourgeois and Hanoverian culture, then Garrick offers a distinctive way of rereading such moments of historical transition as he exploits the heritage of Restoration libertine drama in the name of these very causes, revealing the Hanoverian cultural present to emerge not out of its distance from, but out of its recycling of the Stuart past. The performance of Lothario in 1746–1747 that solidified his career as a theatrical revolutionary and Hanoverian loyalist is predicated on the long-running Restoration, the refusal of the Stuart rake to vanish from the theatrical or national scene.

SOVEREIGN POPULARITY I: THE WILKITES

After the 1740s, the pose of the Restoration theatrical libertine turned to the account of the liberty of the people is nowhere more apparent than in the career of the radical politician John Wilkes. A distiller's son with rakish appetites and gentlemanly aspirations, Wilkes rose to prominence in the early 1760s as a Member of Parliament and polemicist affiliated with the out-of-power Whig oligarchs William Pitt and the Earl of Temple, oppositionists to the ministry of the recently crowned George III. Wilkes's weekly periodical, *The North Briton* (1762–1763), written with the poet Charles Churchill, hurled scurrilous xenophobic satire at the policies and personnel of the new Tory administration, particularly their leader, John Stuart, the 3rd Earl of Bute, whose surname and Scottish heritage made him an easy target. Having overstepped in *The North Briton* no. 45, published on April 23, 1763, Wilkes was arrested, charged with libeling the king and blasphemy, and outlawed, only to return to England in 1768 and eventually to attain the office of London's Lord Mayor in the mid-1770s. A savvy self-promoter, over this decade Wilkes and his adherents ensured his celebrity status, fashioning his image into that of the hero of the constitutional rights and popular sovereignty of the English people, a phenomenon encapsulated in the cry of "Wilkes and Liberty" voiced by his followers.[22]

For many scholars, however, Wilkes's set of conflicting roles—an outlaw and a parliamentarian, a champion of freedom and a chauvinistic nationalist, a populist and an aspiring aristocrat—necessitate a reevaluation of his seemingly straightforward relation to liberty and liberal politics. In this section, I turn to how contemporary accounts of Wilkes relied on libertine figures of Stuart dramatic descent to explore the paradoxes inherent in his personification of liberty. In this writing, Wilkes's pose as the Restoration rake is a fundamental point of political debate, as this figure's performance of personal rule comes both to stand against and to serve as representative of a corrupted rule of law. But more broadly, Wilkes's provocations reveal how a fantasy of absolutism endures at the heart of the midcentury subject's imagination of collective sovereignty and constitutional rights. Indeed, these Wilkite debates, through their play with the memory of Restoration drama, suggest how popular sovereignty may be predicated on sovereign popularity.

Wilkes's rise to fame as the personification of English liberty was conditioned by, and helped to fuel, a national fear of "Stuarts without end." If in the 1740s this phrase might have signaled the external threat of resurgent Jacobitism, in the early 1760s it registered a worry that Stuart principles had been internalized by the Hanoverian regime itself, a feeling initially encouraged by George III's approach to monarchy. The new king—having witnessed his grandfather's ability to rule constrained by overmighty Whig politicians—asserted the monarch's personal role in government, particularly his prerogative in staffing his cabinet.[23] Notoriously, this included his appointment of the unpopular Lord Bute, who, along with being a Scot and with having what was deemed an inappropriately intimate relationship with the royal family, organized a press campaign that, as John Brewer claims, "condemned any conduct on the part of politicians, both in and out of power, which could be construed as curbing the powers of the Crown as head of the executive."[24] From Philip Francis's controversial pamphlet *A Letter from the Cocoa Tree to the Country Gentlemen* (1762) to the weekly news sheets of Tobias Smollett and Arthur Murphy, *The Briton* and *The Auditor*, the ministerial press stoutly endorsed the "prerogative of the crown" and the king's "indubitable right to chuse his ministers."[25] For many readers, such emphasis on monarchical power rather than constitutional rights smacked of Stuart rather than Hanoverian values, and allegations that the court's measures amounted to a "revival of Tory-Maxims" from the Restoration, such as passive obedience and personal government, became the standard fare of the Whig opposition.[26]

While historians have deemed the claim that restored Stuart Tory behavior had infiltrated 1760s Hanoverian high politics an unreliable gauge of political realities—neither George III nor his ministers harbored absolutist designs but simply desired to break the long-standing Whig hegemony—it was a popular rhetorical strategy of opposition politics. As Kathleen Wilson has shown, Wilkes and Churchill's work in *The North Briton* established the standard tropes for the decade's out-of-doors radicalism by conjuring historical parallels between the seventeenth-century Stuarts and the personalities at the head of the present government: as foreign (Jacobite, Scottish, and French) interlopers, as autocratic and unconstitutional, and as sexually deviant.[27] As Wilkite rhetoric attempted to delegitimize ministers such as Bute, reading them as the embodiment of the "new-revived power" of Charles II, James II, and their Tory-Jacobite adherents, it also claimed a legacy of seventeenth-century revolution as its own.[28] It did so by updating what were in the eighteenth century often considered disreputable ideas from the Whig past—populism and resistance—in service of an argument for the sovereignty of the (expressly English) people, making these ideas palatable to those whom Wilkes publicly celebrated as its bedrock, "the middling and inferior" classes.[29]

Wilkes's special status within the radical discourse that came to bear his name lies in his gift not only for popularizing historicist analogy in print culture but also for performing it in live reenactment. In the wake of the scandal over *The North Briton* no. 45, Wilkes abandoned his role as satirical ventriloquist of Tory values and transformed himself into a living emblem of the private citizen suffering under Stuart persecution. During his initial arrest in 1763, the ministry had searched Wilkes's house and confiscated a number of his personal papers—including the *Essay on Woman*, an unpublished irreligious and vulgar parody of Pope's *Essay on Man*—documents that ultimately led to his conviction. In a series of public letters in response, Wilkes accuses Lords Egremont and Halifax, the secretaries of state in charge of the prosecution, of having "robbed" his house; he declares their actions tantamount to having "violated, in the highest and most offensive manner, the liberties of all the commons in England" and promises, "I will assert the security of my own house, the liberty of my person, and every right of the people, not so much for my own sake, as for the sake of every one of my English fellow-subjects."[30] Eliding his "house" with his personal freedom, and his personal freedom with that of the nation, Wilkes invokes "the commons" as a collective whose rights are secured by their possession of private property and the theft as proof of the threat that "Stuarts without end" pose to revolution principles. In his *Letter to the Electors of Aylesbury* (1764), he casts the whole affair as a familiar Restoration political drama stuck on replay: "This is, I believe, the most daring violation of the rights of Englishmen, which has been committed by any judge since the time of Jeffreys. . . . In this infamous manner did government get possession of this new subject of accusation; and, except in the case of Algernon Sydney, of this new species of crime: for a Stuart only could make the refinement in tyranny, of ransacking and robbing the recesses of closets and studies, in order to convert private amusements into state crimes."[31] Posing as the Whig martyr Sidney—whose unpublished *Discourses concerning Government* contributed to his 1683 conviction and execution for treason by the notoriously brutal and biased Lord Chief Justice George Jeffries—Wilkes engages here in a version of historical reenactment. It is a resemblance he courts in performance, citing Sidney's personal circumstances and even his readiness "to give [his] life a willing sacrifice to [his] native country" as a role model for his own behavior as English patriot.[32]

Though falling short of Sidney's martyrdom, Wilkes attempts to stage convincingly the effects of a Stuart revival on the 1760s subject. The secondariness of his staging (he is a second Sidney) should not deceive us, as Rebecca Schneider warns in regard to historical reenactment more broadly, into thinking that Wilkes engages in "mere" theatrical play.[33] Despite the clearly rhetorical nature of his historical paralleling, and despite the temporally linear historical consciousness that conditions modern historians to see it only as such, Wilkes's pose as Sidney reveals how the Stuart past inheres "in" the 1760s present, 1683 in 1763. It is an idea recognizable to Wilkes's contemporaries. Writing to Lord Hardwicke, the Duke of Newcastle (the Lord Chamberlain and Steele's managerial antagonist from chapter 2) claimed that, in the Wilkite controversy, he could "see the end of Charles the Second's reign coming on very fast."[34] Referring to the so-called Tory Reaction—the final years of Charles II's rule that witnessed the state repression of Whig radicals such as Sidney—Newcastle belies the "overness" of the Stuart past, seeing rather a performative endlessness to the "end of Charles the Second's reign." What he understands in Wilkes's resistance to Stuart absolutism is the status of history as theatrical revival, the past's "coming on" in the present as akin to a player's entrance onstage. More than analogy, the lines of historical kinship that 1760s politics ubiquitously draw point to the long-running nature of the Restoration's political fixations, something the Wilkite moment reveals about the Restoration's dramatic corpus as well.

Pro-Wilkite writers were eager to perpetuate their hero's role as Sidney.[35] But for some, Wilkes's performances as private citizen resonated less with the Whig martyr and more with the Stuart stage rake—and not always in ways that upset his anti-Stuart politics. Wilkes's libertine habits are well documented. He was a philanderer, a spendthrift, and a religious skeptic, one who reveled in phallic and anticlerical posturing among his inner circle of friends. Enamored of aristocratic license, he was often dismissive of the values of the middling classes that he claimed to defend, encouraging and partaking in a number of cit-cuckolding exploits.[36] Yet far from tarnishing his reputation, such traits advanced Wilkes's agenda in the early 1760s, particularly, Marilyn Morris suggests, as his libertinism "became symbolic of political liberty and manly independence, held up in contrast to the sodomitical dependency and submission that he claimed characterized the ethos of the royal court and its debauched aristocrats."[37] Wilkite radicalism conflated liberal political citizenship with a masculinist heterosexual subject position, one whose anti-authoritarianism could be deemed legitimate rather than revolutionary because of the perceived provenance of individual liberty and social order in "naturalness" of heterosexual desire (an idea codified by new Enlightenment theories of sexuality) and because of its impulse to resist and demarcate as "unnatural" and repressive any opposing religious and political ideologies.[38] Bearing such a lineage, Wilkes's personal libertinism did not necessarily stand as a liability to his public cause.

But if modern scholarship recognizes Wilkite libertinism as grounded in gender and religious politics that are distinctly of an Enlightenment or eighteenth-century Whig cast, contemporaries nonetheless read it as a stage in the history of Restoration libertine drama. Worried about the political consequences of *The North Briton*'s ad hominem scurrility, in a letter to Wilkes, Lord Temple encourages his protégé to turn his wit to the more respectable channels of parliamentary debate and draws on *The Fair Penitent*'s famous rake as a model: "Parce puer stimulis et fortiùs utere loris; give yourself up to parliamentary labours, and let applauding senates give testimony to the excellent talents of the gallant gay Lothario."[39] Applying Apollo's advice to Phaeton from Ovid's *Metamorphoses*—"Spare the lash, boy, and use the reins more strongly"—Temple urges the restraint and redirection of Wilkes's linguistic facilities but also claims his "excellent talents" of persuasion as the heritage of the Restoration libertine.[40] Wilkes's likeness to Lothario in his seductive powers is, for Temple, what may allow him to strike a figure in the realms of representative government, to redeem the rake's self-centric eloquence and make it speak for the people. Rather than the heterosexual potency of the midcentury libertine, it is the linguistic potency of the Restoration libertine that permits the rake's progress to end not in death but in the "applauding" halls of Parliament.

Temple would likely not have agreed (he was always wary of Wilkes's publicity), but for other Wilkites, it was specifically their leader's pose as the *gay* Lothario that defined his political appeal. As Horace Walpole's commentary suggests, Wilkes's desire for carefree pleasure was perceived to dictate the course of his ambition: "Wantonness, rather than ambition or vengeance, guided his hand; and though he became the martyr of the best cause, there was nothing in his principles or morals that led him to care under what government he lived. To laugh and riot and scatter firebrands, with him was liberty—despotism will ever reproach freedom with the profligacy of such a saint."[41] What Wilkes shares with Lothario is not only a desire to "indulge" in "gayer thoughts and let laughter loose," but also the conflation of such actions with the pursuit of liberty. For critics such as Walpole, this is a disingenuous equation that degrades liberty into licentiousness. But for sympathetic writers, Wilkes proved an example of how libertine mirth might be transformed into a legitimate defense of the liberty of the subject. Much Wilkite literature, in fact, acknowledged the political value of laughter. The title page of the popular *Wilkes's Jest Book; or, The Merry Patriot* (1769), for example, promised a "Collection of all the Choicest Bon-Mots, Puns, Epigrams, Drolleries, Songs, and other Witticisms, said or written from the Year 1764, to the present Time," and its epigraph claimed pleasure as the territory of a specifically Whiggish liberty and loyalty:

> While you read our Patriot's Page,
> Scorn the Tory's Idle Rage;
> And with Loyal Whigs combine
> To read, and smile at ev'ry Line.
> Sons of Freedom laugh away;
> Honest Hearts are always Gay.[42]

Opposed to the "Idle" malice of the lone Tory figure, reading jests, smiling, and laughing are encouraged as a communal means of furthering a postrevolutionary Whig agenda. A similar collection of Wilkite songs, *The Patriot's Jubilee* (1770), affiliated patriotism with mirthful activity, enjoining its readers to celebrate their hero's release from prison after his return from exile in 1770 and announcing its mission with an opening quote from *The Fair Penitent* itself (albeit from Sciolto): "Let Mirth go on! let Pleasure know no Pause, / But fill up ev'ry Minute of this Day."[43] That such literature should entangle the Wilkite political cause with Wilkite jollity makes sense given the purported terms of the former: the vindication of the rights of "all the commons in England." As these texts included songs and catches, anecdotes and jokes ready-made for oral transmission, and a stress on public celebration, they render pleasure as a communal and openly participatory mode of extraparliamentary engagement.

Together with a vindication of present pleasure, the Restoration stage libertine's habitual antipathy to economic prudence also worked to Wilkite ideological advantage in the postwar climate of national financing. To compensate for the expenses of the Seven Years' War, Bute's administration began to pedal a governmental policy of economizing that included the passing of new taxes such as the unpopular excise on cider. Such procedures were parsed by the opposition as an arbitrary attack on the property of the subject, a drain on the working and middle classes that only served to enrich an oppressive patrician state. In his *Epistle to William Hogarth* (1763), for example, Churchill proclaimed that "Wretched Liberty expiring lies / Beneath the fatal burthen of Excise," while Wilkes, in *The North Briton*, further interpreted the rhetoric of national frugality as a pretext for the "unbounded prodigality" and "unjustifiable profusion" of corrupt ministers, a mask covering their real desire to enrich themselves at the expense of the commons.[44] Most significant, however, is the way in which Wilkes develops such accusations in terms that recall the Restoration stage cuckold: it is "the monster of Excise" in *The North Briton* no. 42 and "the most abhorred monster that ever sprung from arbitrary power" in his *Letter to the Electors of Aylesbury*.[45] Often referred to as a "monster" in the canon of Restoration libertine drama, the cuckold is not only a figure of sexual incapacity but also, as in the case of *The Country Wife*'s Pinchwife, regularly one of avaricious parsimony, exaggeratedly possessive in relation to both wives and wealth. More often than not, such plays gauge the cuckold's stinginess as an unnatural abuse of his social power, evidence of a stifling and "arbitrary" rule that elicits the rake's sexual intervention as a form of liberation. As a "monster" in this sense, the excise and, by extension, the ministers who support it become the perpetuators of an absolutist economic policy that damages the free circulation of property and power among the nation's rightful rulers, its citizens. The force of Wilkes's reliance on the Restoration cuckold is thus to assert the unnatural and self-serving foundation of Bute's idea of economy: its unproductiveness.[46]

If Wilkes's writing does not press this analogy to Restoration libertine drama any further, that of a number of his supporters does, touting their hero's lifestyle of spendthrift pleasure as a counter to the government's hypocritical economizing. The figure most often mobilized in this endeavor was another descendant of the Stuart stage rake, John Gay's Macheath. Allusions to *The Beggar's Opera* became popular in the aftermath of Wilkes's prosecution for printing the *Essay on Woman*, an event precipitated by the Earl of Sandwich—Wilkes's onetime friend and a member of his libertine coterie—who first brought the poem to the attention of the House of Lords. According to Walpole, the theatergoing public was quick to analogize this act of disloyalty to Macheath's betrayal by his fellow outlaw Jemmy Twitcher, and "Twitcher" became popular shorthand in the Wilkite mythos not only for Sandwich himself but also for the inherent duplicity of Parliament in its treatment of private citizens.[47]

The Beggar's Opera analogy also implicitly renders Wilkes as Macheath, attaching him to a set of ideals that Gay's highwayman embodies and that the Wilkite cause sought to adopt as its own. In the play, Macheath's gang represents its criminal activity as honorable in that it ensures a "just partition of the world" and every man's "right to enjoy life" by circulating money outside the hands of a corrupt elite. "We retrench the superfluities of mankind," Matt of the Mint explains, "The world is avaricious, and I hate avarice. A covetous fellow, like a jackdaw, steals what he was never made to enjoy, for the sake of hiding it. These are the robbers of mankind, for money was made for the free-hearted and generous."[48] Matt's interpretation of their actions corresponds with Lawrence Stone's assessment of a broad eighteenth-century shift in the social economics of desire, wherein the pursuit of egotistical gratifications may be made "synonymous with public good."[49] Highway robbery here becomes an act of liberality, a freeing up of capital from the play's villains, Peachum and Lockit—representations of a corrupt legal-political system—and a redistribution of it to a populace who understands its use value. Twitcher's betrayal thus assails the entire ethos of the libertine-outlaw company's "free-hearted and generous" civic productiveness, an ethos that Wilkites were eager to embrace in opposition to the British state's self-serving "avarice." Although we saw in chapter 2 that *The Beggar's Opera* proceeds to make statements such as Matt's deeply ironic, the usefulness of the play for Wilkites nevertheless lies in how the gang's pose can be handled straightforwardly, not just to demonize Sandwich but more broadly to attribute a set of populist socioeconomic values to themselves.

Macheath proved an expedient role for Wilkites to conjure in turning their leader's less desirable qualities to political purpose. In *The Beggar's Opera*, Macheath's economic freedoms are self-destructive. Intent on living for the enjoyment of the present moment, he gambles and otherwise spends his capital liberally on wine and women, but this cavalier attitude prompts his downfall—he is initially arrested in a tavern while cavorting with prostitutes and singing the *carpe diem* song "Youth's the season," and as Peachum predicts, "Marylebone and the chocolate-houses," sites of gaming, prove to be his "undoing," as he is eventually recaptured by being traced in these locales.[50] Wilkes's libertine lifestyle led him to similar economic extravagances as Gay's rake, but Wilkite literature turns such resemblance to advantage.[51] *A New Form of Prayer, and Thanksgiving for the Happy Deliverance of John Wilkes* (1768), for instance, invokes *The Beggar's Opera* in its plea for Wilkes's release from the prison sentence he faced upon his return from exile: "Be merry O my countrymen, let your hearts be filled with gladness, and chear up your souls with a song. Be ye sure that [Wilkes] shall [be] released: it is he that defendeth us, and not our Twitchers."[52] Wilkes's status here as a jailed outlaw mirrors that of Macheath; both are imprisoned for their rakish indulgences and their violations of the law. However, the passage indicates that this shared narrative does not constitute Wilkes's ruin but serves rather to confirm his role as national savior and should thus be the cause for merriment. Revived in Wilkes, Macheath's self-indulgent, self-destructive performances are transformed into acts of self-sacrifice for the greater civic good, at once setting Wilkes apart from the avaricious Twitchers and binding subjects together in the type of communal mirth that plays such a large part in other pro-Wilkite writing. Whereas Wilkes favored the pose of the Whig martyr Sidney and others saw in him the gaiety of the cavalier rake, with Macheath, *A New Form of Prayer* conflates the two, spinning Wilkes's sexual and economic excesses as an indication of his good nature, in contrast to the self-enriching measures of the ministry.

That Wilkites could find allusions to Gay's outlaw so effective also follows from Wilkes's depiction of the current state of English law in *The North Briton* no. 45:

> In vain will [Bute], or the foul dregs of his power, the tools of corruption and despotism, preach up in *the speech that spirit of concord, and that obedience to the laws, which is essential to good order*. They have sent the *spirit of discord* through the land, and I will prophecy, that it will never be extinguished, but by the extinction of their power. Is the *spirit of concord* to go hand in hand with the Peace and Excise, through this nation? Is it to be expected between an insolent Exciseman, and a *peer, gentleman, freeholder, or farmer*, whose private houses are now made liable to be entered and searched at pleasure? . . . A nation as sensible as the *English*, will see that a *spirit of concord* when they are oppressed, means a tame submission to injury, and that a *spirit of liberty* ought then to arise.[53]

The North Briton's stance against the legalization of the excise—with its extensive powers of search and seizure—mobilizes some predictable facets of Whig resistance theory. As violations of private property are codified in parliamentary law, the Lockean rationale of political society—the assurance of individual liberty via the protection of property—is upended. More remarkable, however, is Wilkes's figuration of the "justifiable resistance" for which this situation calls:

> The *prerogative* of the crown is to exert the constitutional powers entrusted to it in a way not of blind favour and partiality, but of wisdom and judgment. This is the spirit of our constitution. The people too have their *prerogative*, and I hope the fine words of Dryden will be engraven on our hearts.
>
> Freedom *Is the English Subject's* Prerogative.[54]

Contemporaries and modern scholars alike have construed aspects of Wilkes's radicalism as resonant of monarchical culture, but here *The North Briton* shapes liberal subjectivity itself in terms of royal sovereignty.[55] According to William Blackstone, as the executive's privilege to rule in special cases outside the jurisdiction of ordinary law, "prerogative" is distinctly not a property of the commons.[56] *The North Briton* reimagines it otherwise. In merging a principally Whiggish idea of freedom with sovereign extralegality, the passage extends to the people a right to liberty that exceeds constitutional law only, in the end, in order to reassert it, enabling them to defend their legal rights in moments when the law itself is understood to have placed those rights in jeopardy. For Wilkites, what Macheath offers is a dramatic manifestation of this concept of the liberty of the subject, his lawless stance against civil society capable of being rethought as a defense of property and freedom of the sovereign self under conditions in which legal-political institutions have been corrupted by absolutist lawlessness. With his inheritances from the Stuart rake, Macheath is useful to pro-Wilkite politics because of how the character embodies the conjuncture of liberty and prerogative that *The North Briton* initially formulated as its model for the rights-bearing subject.

Wilkes's redefinition of the subject relies on his (slightly misquoted) citation of Dryden's verse, and this detail points to what I have been tracing more broadly in my reading of the Stuart stage rake in the Wilkite repertoire: the production of postrevolutionary politics as an effect of the long-running Restoration. The line on prerogative appears first in *Threnodia Augustalis* (1685), Dryden's funereal poem for Charles II, in which the poet thanks the dead king for the nation's fortunes that succeeded the Restoration:

> For numerous Blessings yearly shour'd,
> And Property with Plenty crown'd;
> For Freedom, still maintain'd alive,
> Freedom which in no other Land will thrive,
> Freedom an *English* Subject's sole Prerogative.
>
> . . . .
>
> Posterity is charg'd the more,
> Because the large abounding store
> To them and to their Heirs, is still entail'd by thee.[57]

The English exceptionalism of these lines is certainly apropos to Wilkes's nationalist bigotry, but otherwise his co-opting of a royalist panegyric that credits Charles II with "entail[ing]" liberty and property on future generations seems odd. During the Tory reaction—a time of absolutist persecution that, for the political opposition, was being revived in the 1760s—Charles had ruled largely without Parliament. Dryden slyly acknowledges his master's close associations with monarchical prerogative in his deployment of the word here, as if to give the foundation of the subject's liberty (traditional purview of the Whigs) a royalist twist through imagining the people's freedoms as offspring to those of their king. If Wilkes ignores Dryden's context, it haunts his borrowing of this line nonetheless, revealing a genealogy in which Wilkes's formulation of popular sovereignty is as much rooted in Stuart absolutism as it more obviously is in Whig revolution principles.

A poem on the end Charles's reign, *Threnodia Augustalis* bears an afterlife in *The North Briton* no. 45 that belies any such finality of the Restoration. As Wilkes's use of it exposes popular sovereignty to share traits with the prerogative of Charles, it accords with how the libertine's assertions of sovereign independence are co-opted as a pose, in the literature of his supporters, through which antiministerial resistance might be enacted. Instances of the long-running nature of the Restoration, both tactics recuperate rather than dispel the provocations of Stuart royalty and the Stuart stage in the name of the English people's contest against arbitrary political and legal institutions.

SOVEREIGN POPULARITY II: THE ANTI-WILKITES

The irony of *The North Briton* eliding the people's rights with Charles II's prerogative did not escape Wilkes's censurers. Much criticism of Wilkes's cause objected to its populism—its tendering of ancient English liberties to the "middling and inferior" sorts, its physical manifestation in riots, crowds, and other forms of street theater—and was often expressed in terms that played on the propertied classes' fear of mob rule.[58] Such antipathy to Wilkite out-of-doors politicking was accompanied by ancillary attacks on its figurehead's celebrity. *An Epistle from Col. John Lilburn, In the Shades, to John Wilkes* (1765) mocked not only Wilkes's radicalism but also the way his alleged "desire of popularity" impeded the success of popular sovereignty. Another tract berated the Wilkite "mobility" for "danc[ing] round their hobby-horse Jack of Aylesbury, as the whores in the *Beggars Opera* do round Captain Macheath."[59] Such gibes, of course, label Wilkes as politically unsound—affiliating him variously with Levellers and Stuart cavaliers—and reread his ideological celebration of communal pleasures as low libertine vulgarity. But in imagining how his popularity elevates him as a kind of sovereign center among the commons—Macheath among his prostitutes—they also register a different anxiety regarding Wilkes's distinction: his distance from the English people whom he represents. If Wilkes was, in John Brewer's apt term, a "lord of misrule," his role as "lord" proved as irksome as his role as fomenter of "misrule."[60]

The anxiety that a fantasy of sovereignty was hardwired into Wilkes's peculiar brand of political agency finds voice even among more measured observers, those not necessarily hostile to Wilkes's partisan politics but nonetheless wary of his methods. In the *Narrative of the Proceedings against John Wilkes, Esq.* (1768), an even-handed recounting of the scandal of *The North Briton* no. 45, the author makes special note of the fact that Wilkes was released from the Tower on the "privilege of parliament," the immunity from arrest that Members of Parliament like himself had in certain civil cases: "Beyond all measure was the popular party elated by this success. Mobs attended the prisoner with praises and acclamations wherever he went. With very moderate sufferings he was considered as the martyr of liberty; and his discharge on account of privilege, was supposed a point gained to the freedom of every individual."[61] The *Narrative* pointedly reminds its readers that "the freedom of every individual" is not the same as Wilkes's privileged exemption from jail; it was only "supposed" to be so by his adherents after the fact. Calling into question the suitability of Wilkes's personification of the liberties of the average subject, the *Narrative* draws attention to the way, as we have seen, Wilkite ideology muddles the lines between liberty and privilege, rights and prerogative. This confusion, it implies, is the foundation of an inappropriate understanding of liberty that extends sovereign prerogative as a template for political subjectivity available to any private citizen. The *Narrative*'s skepticism is grounded in the possibility of taking *The North Briton*'s analogy of royal prerogative and the people's rights all too seriously, perpetuating a notion of liberty as license outside the norms of law and infusing the egalitarian politics of popular sovereignty with an antithetical idea of exclusive privilege.

For one piece of anti-Wilkite literature—the poetic satire *Rodondo; or, The State Jugglers* (1763–1770) by the Scottish advocate Hugh Dalrymple—criticism of the troubling conflation of prerogative and liberty assumed the form of a revived Restoration libertine drama. Published in three cantos over the course of the decade, the pro-Scots poem is a topical, bawdy send-up of opposition politicians and writers.[62] In the first two cantos, the satire principally targets William Pitt, for whom the titular character acts as a stand-in. In the final canto, Dalrymple shifts the focus onto Wilkes, Churchill, and their friend the wine merchant Humphrey Cotes as heirs to Pitt's legacy, introducing them as

Three first rate English Patriots.
All *three* inspir'd with equal zeal,
To drink about for England's weal;
To make a trial, whether Ale,
Or Wine, could best inspire to rail:
Whether, in Claret there might be
Some salve, for wounded Liberty.[63]

An ad hominem attack on his heroes—Dalrymple underscores their socioeconomically "low" connections within the liquor trade, as well as their notoriously debauched lifestyles—this ascription of their "zeal" for English patriotism to drunkenness overtly mocks the ideological Wilkite pairing of pleasure and liberty. In the episode that follows, the trio engages in a bout of drinking and boasting of their personal and political freedoms; it quickly devolves into a scatological extended metaphor comparing opposition polemic to flatulence and implying the emptiness of the Wilkite politics of pleasure. Beyond the poem's perfunctory savaging of Wilkes's libertine habits, however, *Rodondo* explores the fate of the Whiggish ideals of liberty and property in Wilkes's hands, ultimately assuming the form of a revived Restoration libertine drama to mark and condemn his political appropriation of the rake as belonging to a Stuart political genealogy he wishes to resist. The alcoholic frolicking of Wilkes, Churchill, and Cotes that features centrally in canto 3 specifically restages that of another triumvirate of drunks: Sir John Brute, Lord Rake, and Colonel Bully in John Vanbrugh's *The Provoked Wife*.

The Provoked Wife explores the force, and the limits, of moral and social restraints on individual desire through the popular 1690s form of marriage comedy, thematically testing the premise of Constant, one of its leading libertine seducers, that "where laws dispense with equity, equity should dispense with laws."[64] Its main plot turns on the domestic discord of Sir John and Lady Brute, juxtaposing the former's debauched riot against social decorum, religious authority, and the law with the latter's moral dilemma over whether to pursue an intrigue with Constant or remain bound to her failing marriage. As the couple's struggle for self-licensed authority intensifies, the end of act 3 finds Sir John, Lord Rake, and Colonel Bully in a tavern, toasting to "Confusion to all order" and to "liberty of conscience" just as Lord Rake bursts into a song that explains such an incongruous pairing. Referring to recent controversy over religious toleration, the song derides "the king and the state" for making "a pother of late" over "setting our consciences free," flaunting instead the power of the "bottle" to procure liberty: "When my head's full of wine, / I o'erflow with design, / And know no penal laws that can curb me / . . . / And religion ne'er dares to disturb me" (*The Provoked Wife*, 197–198). The rakes' reliance on political allusion to describe their exploits continues shortly thereafter; when Lord Rake proposes that the company sally forth to "beat up" the town's citizens, Sir John assents with boasts of his "privileges" as "a free-born Englishman": "I am within a hair's breadth as absolute by my privileges as the King of France is by his prerogative. He by his prerogative takes money where it is not his due; I by my privilege refuse paying it, where I owe it. Liberty and property and old England, huzza!" (198–199). The scene inherits much from earlier Restoration dramatic episodes of libertine revelry; but in dispensing so completely with law and order, the behavior of Sir John and his friends accords with Erin Mackie's reading of the eighteenth-century rake's license as fundamentally criminal, a point only strengthened later as the trio marauds through Covent Garden assaulting the town's citizens until Sir John is arrested by the watch.[65]

Most disturbing about this scene, politically, is how Brute and his companions validate their libertine violence with Whiggish dictums of the subject's rights. Lord Rake's appreciative toast to religious toleration and his accompanying song convert the liberal value of "liberty of conscience"—defended by Locke in *A Letter Concerning Toleration* (1689) as a "Foundation of . . . Liberty" and "every mans natural Right"—into an invitation to freethinking that denies religious and civil authority altogether.[66] Likewise for Sir John, the corollary of the 1688 rallying cry of "Liberty and Property" is the production of an absolutist individual who refuses to be "curb[ed]" by law. His elision of this Whig motto with both anarchic "confusion" and French-style absolute rule exposes his bluster, for Brean Hammond, as "meaningless" and, for Michael Cordner, as "ideologically muddled," thus making him subject to the play's irony.[67] Characterological analysis aside, however, what Brute's pose as a liberty-loving Englishman intimates is the possibility of a collapsing together of liberal and absolutist subjectivity—the way an attractive fantasy of extrajudicial sovereign "prerogative" is embedded in and engendered by the Whig values of freedom from domination and self-ownership that propose themselves as absolutism's opposite. In Brute's slippage between Whig and Stuart forms of rule as metaphors for his personal rights, the play bears out the later quip of Heartfree, Constant's libertine companion: "All revolutions run into extremes" (233).

The ironies of the creed of Vanbrugh's libertines are what *Rodondo* exploits for its critique of Wilkite radicalism. Dalrymple does not draw exact parallels between *The Provoked Wife*'s individual rakes and his own, but replicates more broadly the scene of three inebriated braggadocios in a tavern asserting their rights, beginning with a rebellious toast by Cotes that echoes Lord Rake's opening salvo against social order:

> Quoth Humphry, after rueful pause,
> "Here goes: Confusion to all Laws!

> Curse them, they force a man to pay
> His debts; or, d—m me, run away!"
> Quoth [Churchill], "That's a trimmer,
> I'll pledge you, Humphry, in a brimmer;
> For whether human, or divine,
> By G—d, they are no friends of mine." (*Rodondo*, 15)

Cotes and Churchill's anarchic desire to evade the reach of both natural and positive law leads the trio to fall out over whose libertinism is preeminent, with Wilkes claiming that his political performances outdo the others' inferior antics:

> "You, d—m your bodies, talk of Law?
> What! think ye your escapes from *Bums*,
> Your beating Bawds, and bilking *Strums*?
> Think ye your Poxes and Bepoxings,
> Your Ale-house Riotings and Boxings;
> . . . .
> Can raise you to the rank, which I
> As Freedom's Champion enjoy!" (15)

As does its setup, the progression of Dalrymple's scene follows that of Vanbrugh's. The rakes' initial defiance of law concludes with one member of the group—Wilkes/Brute—strenuously articulating his privileged lawlessness as an extension of his purchase on the constitutional rights of the subject. Wilkes's self-identification as "Freedom's Champion" resonates with the ironies of Sir John's cry of "Liberty and property." Couched in Whig idioms, both attestations are boasts of libertine disorder. For the knighted Sir John, the "privileges" of the "free-born Englishman" do not denote the constitutional rights of the commons but his special socioeconomic license to lord it over fellow subjects. For Wilkes, the "rank" of "Freedom's Champion" is merely a higher stage in a competitive hierarchy of rakish performances; his efforts as political celebrity, the poem implies, may be different in degree from the brutish brawling, cheating, and whoring of his companions but not in kind.

Specifically in the way it recalls the treatment by Vanbrugh's rakes of the Lockean idea of property, *Rodondo* describes Wilkes's definition of liberty as the subject's "prerogative" as criminal. In *The Provoked Wife*, Brute's "frolic" culminates in the theft of a parson's gown from a "dissenting journeyman tailor," an act that highlights both Sir John's abuse of the disparity of freedoms that exists within the social order and his ultimate reliance on the stability of that very same social order that his drunken toasts purport to confound (*The Provoked Wife*, 178, 204). Indeed, earlier in the tavern, he is able to claim robbery of a different sort—not paying his debts—as his right because of the way he pictures the liberties of the subject in terms of monarchical prerogative. For Brute, the fundamental Lockean principle of property ownership does not drive popular sovereignty but rather sanctions the already empowered propertied elite to enact their freedom at the expense of other socially inferior subjects. Dalrymple's Wilkites treat property in much the same way, confounding laws because "they force a man to pay / His debts." Wilkes's financial troubles and debtor's status were well-known, as John Sainsbury has shown; despite making property rights central to his rhetoric, he relied on a notion of gentlemanly privilege—like Brute and the Restoration rake more broadly—to arbitrarily bilk "the middling and inferior" trading classes that he claimed to represent.[68]

Through the Brute parallel, moreover, *Rodondo* suggests that Wilkes's Lockean call for the protection of private property from state interference invites the ascendancy of the privileged absolutist subject. The first of the enjambed lines on debt quoted earlier equate "force" and law so as to evoke the familiar Wilkite argument about the ministry's legal-political coercions. But as the final line of the couplet reveals that Cotes is being forced merely to pay what he owes—not to the state even, but to fellow citizens—it upends Whig political theory. Wilkites, *Rodondo* implies, perversely interpret the legal and communal responsibility of paying one's debts as a breach of the constitutional rights of the subject to keep one's property inviolate from arbitrary incursion, and in doing so they delimit the rule of the people to the rule of the privileged elite. Read through Brute's union of class privilege and theft, Wilkes's pose as "Freedom's Champion" is ultimately an exclusionary one as it dispossesses other subjects of the property that forms the bulwark of political agency. As Cotes suggests later in the episode, the rise of Wilkite radicalism has little to do with any political reality beyond the interests of propertied selves:

> "While I could my liquor sell,
> The state affairs went very well;
> But with my cash, and credit, spent,
> Old England's independence went.
> . . . .
> Where nothing's to be got,
> What man would be a patriot?" (*Rodondo*, 19)

As the Wilkite movement is exposed as based on nothing but possessive individualism, its Lockean defense of private property as the foundation of "England's weal" is made to be, at best, a refusal of true inclusivity of the commons and, at worst, tantamount to the criminal activity of the privileged classes. Wilkes's grounding of his populist cause in a Whiggish emphasis on property paradoxically becomes the self-same mechanism by which the popular sovereignty of the commons is hollowed out.

Rodondo's reliance on *The Provoked Wife*'s tavern scene stretches the indictment of Wilkes as criminal so far as to implicate his patriotic activity as the revival of the Stuart absolutism that it sought to contain. With Brute, Dalrymple's Wilkes shares an understanding of liberty that derives from French absolute rule; he "learn[ed] the Principles of Freedom" only when he "scamper'd off to *France*" during his exile (*Rodondo*, 11).[69] Beneath his English nationalism, the poem suggests, lie the Stuart political principles that Wilkes persistently attributed to the foreign (usually Scots) other. But the danger for Dalrymple inheres less in Wilkes as representative of a dynastic threat to English values and more in how the performance of Stuart absolutism is devolved in the activities of the radical libertine subject. The parallel to Brute is again important here. Vanbrugh sets the revelry of his rakes in London's real-life Blue Posts Tavern, which was a known Jacobite haunt and the staging ground for the 1696 assassination attempt on William III.[70] *Rodondo*'s reference to a scene with such Jacobite allusions furthers the poem's ironic affiliation of "Wilkes and liberty" with foreign absolutism; but it also activates a scenario of sedition against a legitimately constituted government. As Wilkes is made heir to a Restoration rake who both covets the power of one king and inhabits a space of treason against another king, he is labeled with the stigma of Stuart insurgency. This is the true confusion of law and order that Dalrymple's use of *The Provoked Wife* points to: the potential for criminal usurpation that resides at the heart of Wilkite political carnivalesque. Failing so ironically in defending the English subject against a corrupt patrician state, Wilkes's pose as the lawless Restoration rake instead perpetuates a desire of the propertied English subject for absolute power that upsets the workings of the balanced constitution.

For *Rodondo*, then, it is the radical Wilkite subject and not the state that houses Stuart absolutism. The poem's critique relies on extrapolating the consequences of *The North Briton*'s own conflation of liberty and prerogative in the name of Whig political resistance. The Wilkite imagining of every subject as a sovereign, endowed with a kind of extrajudicial privilege that may infringe on fellow subjects' property rights when it comes to securing one's own, reinscribes absolutism within the egalitarian ideal of the rule of the people. In this way, "Stuarts without end" becomes an accusation that redounds on the heads of Wilkes and Churchill; indicated in how it so readily replays the political muddle of Restoration dramatic libertines like Sir John Brute, Dalrymple suggests, it is the Wilkite pose that revives Stuart absolutism as a model for Hanoverian political agency, its particular handling of the traditional Whig values of "liberty and property" responsible for their very undoing.

The fact that Restoration libertine drama was so prevalent in Wilkite debates qualifies the narrative of its midcentury disappearance. In this moment, one of the Restoration rake's defining paradoxes—how his rhetoric of freedom is always coupled with his hierarchical power and sovereign privilege—materializes within Whig liberalism's incipient working out of the extent and basis of political rights, the way they encompass postrevolutionary values such as property ownership that conflict with the ideals of popular sovereignty as often as they do sustain them. Restoration libertine drama is thus far from "over," as radical Wilkites and their antagonists rely on the contradictions of its central characters to test and contest the possibilities and problems of political agency under George III. In other words, the "pose" of the Restoration rake functions as one of its etymological derivations would suggest: presenting difficult questions about the heritage and self-identity of liberal Whig principles. What the genealogical connection between Wilkite radicalism and the Stuart libertine reveals is the long-running nature of the desire for sovereign absolutism, the persistence of its fantasy at the heart of the liberal political subject.

Perhaps, however, the most damning aspect of *Rodondo*'s activation of *The Provoked Wife* is not its allegation of treason lodged in the heart of the Wilkite subject but rather its suggestion of that subject's failure to ever fully inhabit such a fantasy. For Sir John is, the play reminds us, only a pretender to the libertinism he professes. Replying to Constant's and Heartfree's queries about his hatred of Lady Brute, he informs them that he married her only "because [he] had a mind to lie with her" and because he was fearful of "hedg[ing] [him]self into forty quarrels with her relations" should he "ravish" her. "But more than all that," he adds, "I was afraid of being damned in those days, for I kept sneaking cowardly company, fellows that went to church, said grace to their meat, and had not the least tincture of quality about 'em" (*The Provoked Wife*, 177–178). Defined in his past by religious squeamishness, cowardice, and a non-genteel social network, and ending the play in drunken dissoluteness and resignation over his potential cuckoldry, Sir John shares literary roots with Restoration drama's host of new-titled knights and boorish would-be's, figures who often seek but never achieve entry into the ranks of the Lotharios, Dorimants, and Lord Rakes as a means of self-assertion.[71] *Rodondo*'s association of Wilkes with Brute renders its hero as thus twice removed from an authentic purchase on the sovereign absolutist subject through his libertinism: he is merely posing (in our modern sense of "faking") as a man posing as a self-licensed rake.

In the final section, I turn to the way in which the terms of such Wilkite debates regarding the Restoration rake's status as powerful sovereign subject or debased pretender are internalized in the psychic operations of a particular eighteenth-century gentleman, the Scotsman James Boswell. Occupying the same temporal and physical space as Wilkes's early political provocations, 1762–1763, Boswell's diurnal account of his visit to London as a pleasure-seeking twenty-two-year-old (retroactively titled the *London Journal* by scholars) offers an instance of a midcentury subject living day-to-day in the long-running Restoration, his private life shaped by the cultural conventions of the Stuart past. In particular, *The Provoked Wife* and its portrayal of Sir John Brute as a reflection on the Restoration libertine's contests with and appropriations of authority emerge in the journal as dramatic templates through which Boswell grapples with the entanglements of the liberty of the subject and the fantasy of monarchical prerogative. As a documentation of Boswell's stylized testing out of the possibilities and failures of the Restoration libertine as a figure for self-rule, the journal demonstrates the attractions and anxieties of the Stuart sovereign subject to be not only ideological and targeted but also actual and widespread in Hanoverian Britain, enacted on Garrick's and Wilkes's grand stages of national theater and high-profile politics and at the local level of London's streets and in the personal realms of journalistic self-fashioning.

SOVEREIGN DISGUST: BOSWELL AND SIR JOHN BRUTE

Boswell kept a journal for most of his adult life, but the account of his second trip to London in 1762–1763 is remarkable in its sustained, often self-aware attention to the construction of identity. Portraying Boswell as performer, spectator, and anecdotalist in one, the *London Journal* documents a set of poses, much of the interest of which, for recent eighteenth-century scholars, lies in the way they reveal their actor/recorder's identity to be shaped by an intersection of sociocultural forms and practices: the performances of historical gendered, class, and national subject positions; the relation between theatricality/publicity and interiority/private feeling; the modes of novelistic fiction, life-writing, and drama.[72] Boswell's autobiographical endeavor was written in part for the amusement of his friend John Johnston of Grange and in part as a private account, and he conceived of it as a way not only to record his adventures in a city he adored but also to view his character in objective form, a tool by which to regulate a public persona that he worried to be immature and inconsistent. Authorship is, he tells Lord Kames, an act of self-control; it is "making another self, which can be present in many places and is not subject to the inconstancies of passion which the man himself is."[73] Beyond the *London Journal*'s uniquely detailed documentation of eighteenth-century life, its power abides in the literariness through which Boswell pursues these ends, the way in which the writing of his self in accordance with cultural conventions and role models both enables and troubles his quest for self-government.

Boswell's particular literary fantasies have been well documented. A "source book for stock masculine characters current in mid-eighteenth-century Britain," as Erin Mackie describes it, the journal archives the varied personae that Boswell adopts in his struggle for self-definition, from Gay's Macheath and Addison and Steele's Mr. Spectator and Cato to Captain Plume in George Farquhar's *The Recruiting Officer* (1706) and the Wrongheads in Colley Cibber's *The Provoked Husband* (1728).[74] One figure largely absent from the myriad scholarly accounts detailing Boswell's emulative identifications, however, is Vanbrugh's Sir John Brute. Boswell alludes to *The Provoked Wife* only once in the *London Journal*, but this paucity belies the real power of this avatar for him, his deep indebtedness to Restoration drama that shapes his time in the metropolis. On March 25, 1763—during his fifth month in London and after a day spent "saunter[ing] up & down the streets rather out of spirits" and discussing politics with Thomas Sheridan—Boswell gives in to sexual urges: "As I was coming home this night I felt carnal inclinations raging thro' my frame. I determined to gratify them. I went to St. James's Park & like Sir John Brute, picked up a Whore."[75] The scene to which he alludes follows directly from that which we examined in relation to *Rodondo*. Apprehended by a constable while drunkenly scouring the London streets, Sir John is taken before the justice of the peace and—due to his disguise as a clergyman—is ultimately released so as not to cause a scandal. As he leaves the justice's quarters unrepentant, he asks, "So—now, Mr. Constable, shall you and I go pick up a whore together?" (*The Provoked Wife*, 212).

This identification with Sir John's libertinism, announced in the encounter with the prostitute on March 25, is as multifaceted as that character's midcentury theatrical reception. Boswell's pose as Vanbrugh's knight can certainly be read as a self-loathing acknowledgment of his urges that mirrors the way he guiltily views his sexual slumming on London's streets as surrendering to "brutish appetite[s]" in similar moments (*London Journal*, 215). But beyond shorthand for a lapse into "carnal inclinations," Sir John also offers a theatrical template through which Boswell parses his personal history and his own desire—omnipresent in the journal—for social status and for what, importantly, comes with it: independence. The reference to Sir John highlights the complexity of the Restoration's theatrical heritage in Boswell's writing. A recognized aspect of his masculine agency and aspirations, Boswell's sexual libertinism has been read for its affiliations with the cultural iconography of the Stuart past. But his pose as a Stuart rake—what David Weed defines as his "cavalier masculinity"—is usually understood to be insufficient to the maintenance of his stature as self-controlled gentleman and replaced, by the conclusion of his time in London, with a character more in accord with a Hanoverian bourgeois model of sociable gentility.[76] I would suggest, however, that the reliance on Sir John Brute and on *The Provoked Wife*'s treatment of Restoration libertine culture more broadly complicates this reading of the *London Journal* as another instance of the Restoration rake's linear progress toward cultural obsolescence. Boswell's enactment of the absolutist libertine Brute is pervasive; its presence in the journal suggests how the Stuart absolutist rake does not precede the Hanoverian political subject only to be negated by him as a nostalgic or insufficient historical artifact but emerges in the performances and desires of the liberal subject's quest for autonomy from governing structures.

Boswell's past experiences and social aspirations mirror Sir John's in a number of ways. As we explored in the context of *Rodondo*, Sir John's identity in the play as a "free-born Englishman" seeking absolute self-rule has been conditioned by a need to distance himself from a history of religious apprehension and social inferiority. Raised under the austere principles of Scots Presbyterianism and under the tutelage of his Calvinist mother, Boswell identified early on with Sir John's fear of "being damned." He describes how in his youth, "The eternity of punishment was the first great idea I ever formed. How it made me shudder! . . . I was horrified because of the fear that I would sin and be damned."[77] Such "dreary tolboothkirk ideas," remnants of "the dismal hours of Apprehension, that [he] endured in [his] youth from narrow notions of Religion," punctuate the journal, though Boswell tends to attribute them, as does Sir John, to a past self: "I am surprised how I have got rid of these notions so entirely" (61).

As pressing as Boswell's religious anxieties was his contentious relationship with his father, Lord Auchinleck, whom Gordon Turnbull describes as "a kind of secular equivalent of the determinist Calvinist deity" in Boswell's life.[78] From the start of the journal, Boswell's theatrical self-fashioning is shaped by a need to escape the confines of paternal authority, imagined as a dramatic blocking agent. "The scene," he notes on November 15, the day he leaves Edinburgh for London, "of being a Son setting out from home for the wide world and the idea of being my own Master, pleased me much" (4). Over the journal's nine-month record, Boswell's recurring obsession is how to "be quite an independent Man," and his goal of self-determination is often expressed, as his new friend Samuel Johnson recognized, in terms of a conflict between a father's "power" and a son's desire for "Independency" (153, 269). The particulars of this contest involve Lord Auchinleck's ambitions for his son as familial and professional heir. What so often appeared as domineering to Boswell were his father's strict notions of the succeeding laird's filial responsibility to the family's estate and to its historical prominence in the Scottish legal profession. By the early 1760s, Lord Auchinleck's faith in Boswell on both accounts was dwindling. He viewed his son's fondness for theater, his ambitions of literary celebrity, and his graphic journalizing of his private life as damaging to his ability to serve in the public echelons of Scottish law and the landed gentry. Boswell, for his part, had little interest in becoming an advocate. The journal associates this profession with the authoritarian effect of his father on his freedom, repeatedly recording his fears of being "confined to live in my Father's family & and pressed to study law" (117–118).

The "rooted aversion" to the law that Boswell voices derives also from the socially inferior, cit-like qualities that he attributes to its professional persona (153). Despite admittedly knowing many advocates who were "very genteel people," he divulges, "I connected with that character low breeding & presbyterian stiffness" (152). Even in moments when the "law-scheme" seems to him more reasonable, Boswell does all he can to distinguish himself from his perceptions of an ordinary lawyer; if he were to enter the profession, he imagines in the entry for February 24, 1763, "I might show all the dull vulgar plodding young lawyers how easily superior parts can outstrip them" (152). Similar to Sir John's distaste for the "sneaking cowardly company"—possessed of "not the least tincture of quality"—of which he was formerly a part, Boswell's aversion to the law here is both psychic and social. It is a reaction to a past and future self-image that, read through a familiar stock type, is conceived as lowbred, and it reveals his pursuits in London as engaged in a competitive hierarchy of masculinity.

If Boswell and Sir John share comparable anxieties, they also share a comparable method of compensation: imitating the Restoration aristocratic rake. Acting the part of the Restoration libertine, for Sir John, comes in the form of joining in Lord Rake's frolics. With its flamboyant singing, toasting, and drinking in act 3's tavern scene and its violent brawling in act 4, the gang is *The Provoked Wife*'s representation of Charles II's court wits, a group who, as Anna Bryson and James Turner have extensively documented, gloried in emulating the riotous, often vulgar excesses of urban lower-class culture at once to prove their lawless exemption from the codes of civil society and to reinforce their superiority in the hierarchies of class and gender that structure it.[79] With such oxymoronic libertine gestures—the cultivation of "low" behavior to assert one's "high" status—Sir John attempts to dominate his sociocultural landscape and thus to abrogate the inferiority of his past identity. Boswell's efforts to establish his "quality" and "Independency" are fashioned as well out of the cultural memory of the Stuart court wit's public performances. He adopts the pose as a Restoration libertine self-consciously in his courtship of the Covent Garden actress "Louisa," his predominant sexual interest during his early months in London. Having occupied him from the entry on December 14, 1762 forward, the seduction of Louisa comes to a climax on January 12, when Boswell arranges a night's stay at an inn with her and they have sex. His self-satisfied return to the London streets on the following morning is rendered as a revival of the Restoration court wit: "I got up between nine & ten, and walked out, till Louisa should rise. I patroled up and down Fleet-street thinking on London, the seat of Parliament and the seat of pleasure, and seeming to myself one of the Wits in King Charles the Second's time" (94). The wit's draw in this episode does not come—as it does for Sir John—from its history of upper-class riots.[80] In Boswell's reading, rather, Charles II and his "merry gang" are men of fashion and good breeding, trendsetters in a tasteful beau monde. It is an image he revisits in his *Letters between the Honourable Andrew Erskine, and James Boswell, Esq.* (1763). Admitting to being "a little of a beau," he details dressing in a manner so as "witty Charles's tale to wake" in his spectators.[81] The Restoration wit here epitomizes urbane sophistication and aristocratic leisure, a historical iteration of the masculine gentility that Boswell is determined to adopt at the outset of his courtship of Louisa: "a young fellow of spirit & fashion, heir to a good fortune, enjoying the pleasures of London" (53).

Nonetheless, Boswell's polished ideal of the Restoration wit is still underwritten by an assertion of hierarchical male dominance that takes the form not of intellect or fashion but of physicality—in Boswell's case, sexual prowess. Before playing the self-congratulatory role of the wit, Boswell describes his night with Louisa in graphic details meant to distinguish him from the common man: "I felt myself animated with the strongest powers of love, and, from my dearest Creature's kindness had a most luscious feast. Proud of my godlike vigour I soon resumed the noble game. . . . A more voluptuous night, I never enjoyed. Five times was I fairly lost in supreme rapture. Louisa was madly fond of me; she declared I was a Prodigy, & and asked me if this was not extraordinary for human nature. . . . I surely may be stiled a Man of Pleasure" (93–94). Boswell reenacts the Restoration libertine's association—familiar in the sexual exploits of the court wits and in those of their stage avatars—of sexual potency with sociocultural supremacy and sovereign subjectivity, his "godlike vigour" indicating both his "extraordinary" and his "noble" status in the bedroom and beyond.[82] In this sense, the climax of the Louisa episode plays out like an internalization of Restoration drama's "wit versus cit" scenario within Boswell's psyche. His deliberate reenactment of Charles II's court libertines strutting the streets of London, conscious that their sexual audacity challenges the limits of ordinary men, is a performance of social preeminence. By putting his "superior parts" on display in this scene, Boswell-the-wit seeks to challenge the "vulgar" self-image of Boswell-the-lawyer.

Indeed, Boswell stage-manages the entire affair with Louisa to recall the plotting Restoration libertine rather than the "plodding" midcentury advocate. The journal renders the buildup to the moment of consummation on January 12 as highly theatrical, a series of beaux' stratagems and mishaps reminiscent of the tropes of Restoration sex comedy: Boswell recounts many of their early encounters in the form of theatrical dialogues, rife with suggestive banter and interspersed by escalating attempts to take physical "liberties" (72); an initial assignation on January 2 is interrupted by the untimely return of Louisa's landlady, which causes him to "invent some method by which we might meet in Security" (75); their meeting at the inn is arranged as an affair of high intrigue, pursued under assumed identities. In anticipating the sexual encounter, Boswell draws from the stage rake's repertoire of martial metaphors, feeling ready "undaunted to engage in the wars of the Paphian Queen" (90). In the encounter's immediate aftermath, he shifts to laying plots for future sexual conquests, admitting, "I could not help roving in fancy to the embraces of some other Ladies which my lively Imagination strongly pictured" (94). Imitating the stylized theatricality and the imagery of conquest and roving of the Restoration gentleman reveals that, as with Etherege's Dorimant or Wycherley's Horner, the securing of Boswell's reputation as an adroit competitor in the social field is the true endgame in his sexual adventuring. "The participation of genuine reciprocal amorous affection with an amiable Woman," he claims upon introducing Louisa in the journal, does allow for a "full indulgence of all the delicate feelings & pleasures both of Body & mind," but it moreover permits the male partner to "exult" in the "consciousness that he is the superior Person" (45). Boswell resembles the Restoration wit in that, for both, the seduction plot is all about asserting one's social standing, the woman not a figure to possess but to exploit in the competitive game of displaying one's "superior parts."[83]

Mitigating Boswell's anxieties of social inferiority, the pose as the Restoration wit also assures him of his ability to manage his self-image in public representation. Stability and regulation of character, the production of a "composed genteel" one rather than a "rattling uncultivated" one, are foremost concerns during his stay in London (9). While he begins the journal confident in his powers of self-control—"I have discovered," he boasts on November 21, 1762, "that we may be in some degree whatever character we chuse" (9)—his optimism in personal choice often wanes as he realizes that he is "obliged to deviate from [his chosen character], by a variety of circumstances" and frets about being "a character very different from what God intended me, and I myself chose," all of which signal him to be "a very inferior being" (22). If one ignores Restoration drama's ironic portrayal of the totalizing social power of its libertine heroes, the likes of Dorimant or Horner can be seen as masterful manipulators of their own self-image, stage managers who exert sovereign control over their character and the beau monde's perception of it in a way that Boswell desires. That Boswell misreads the Restoration libertine in such a way is signaled in how the entries for January 12 and 13 conjoin the cultural memory of Charles II's court with the "Man of Pleasure," a character type whom he understands in terms similar to those of Lord Chesterfield. Not a rake—which for Chesterfield signifies only "a beastly drunkard, an abandoned whoremaster, and a profligate swearer and curser," "a composition of all the lowest, most ignoble, degrading, and shameful vices"—the Man of Pleasure is defined by his "taste," decency," and "dignity."[84] The Man of Pleasure does not give up his passions but pursues them with a steadfast control over his public image that emphasizes his sovereign powers of self-possession; "Choose your pleasures for yourself," Chesterfield encourages his son, "do not let them be imposed upon you."[85] For Boswell too, the Man of Pleasure is a self-authorizing individual. In an earlier journal, he admiringly describes a family friend, Lord Galloway, as a "man of pleasure, that is to say, he has followed his own inclinations."[86] Control of one's image, freedom of choice, and freedom from domination are the foundational attributes of the Man of Pleasure, a masculine type historically embodied, for Boswell, in Charles II's wits. The Restoration wit is a role, then, that Boswell inhabits for its perceived ability to balance the sovereign self's indulgence in his "inclinations" with the government of his public character so as to negate the compromising associations, with regard to class and gender, that Enlightenment thought attributed to the passions.[87]

It is notable, in fact, how Boswell's posturing as the Restoration wit on January 13 is correlated with another image of self-government and self-display: Parliament. In the entry, London, his stage, is both "the seat of Parliament and the seat of pleasure." (94). Structurally, the passage draws a parallel between the self-authorizing Man of Pleasure and the institution that, historically opposed to the Stuart court, symbolizes the nation's representative government and its subjects' right to self-rule. On the one hand, it presents the Restoration wit and Parliament not as icons of competing ideologies but as partnered in their value for the liberty of the people to choose their own rulers. Despite Boswell's well-known Tory nostalgia, his self-fashioning here brings the Restoration wit's assertions of sovereignty into proximity with a Whiggish ideology of liberal political subjectivity as it parallels the history of the theatrical rake with the definitively 1688 value of choice.[88] On the other hand, its analogy of Man of Pleasure and Member of Parliament speaks more to the sovereignty of the self than it does to the representation of the nation's interests. To Boswell's mind, being a Member of Parliament was all about what Habermas calls "representative publicness," that is, showing off one's status.[89] As Frank Brady has documented, a seat in Parliament was Boswell's lifelong dream, an outlet for his ambition to reside in London (and thus to be freed from his father's will) and for his feelings of ancestral pride.[90] The articulation of this desire in the journal is revealing for the way it materializes in tandem with other role models of public exhibitionism such as the Guardsman. On January 20, 1763, for instance, Boswell admits in the journal to "indulg[ing] noble Reveries of having a Regiment, of getting into parliament, making a figure, and becoming a man of consequence in the state"; in a letter to his patron Lord Eglinton a few weeks later, he sketches his ideal future self as "a man of Genius," "a distinguished figure in parliament," and "one of the brightest Wits in the court of George the Third" (112, 132). In these contexts, his allusion to Parliament signals not just faith in constitutional rule but also the desire for the social standing, privileges, and independence that Boswell imagined to accompany political office.

That all of these Boswellian fantasies of individual liberty and social authority converge in the January 13 appearance of the Stuart wit suggests that Boswell's revived Restoration drama in the *London Journal* is a performance with which he tries to offset a personal history perceived to be lacking in self-determination. Boswell recycles the Restoration wit's public displays of sexual and theatrical superiority as a method for securing the subject's liberties and powers of self-ownership, seeing the pose as resistant to both the authoritarianism of his father and the "low" bourgeois and religious associations of his past. The journal reveals the persistent appeal of Restoration drama to lie in how its libertine heroes' performances of sovereign dominance in their social fields can serve as a figuration of the values of self-governance and freedom of choice against absolutist dictates. As it records how Boswell's fantasies of the public display of social privilege bleed into his desire for self-government, moreover, the journal articulates a propinquity reminiscent of Sir John Brute's muddle of the prerogatives of absolute rule and the subject's rights of liberty and property. If, for Vanbrugh, Sir John's confusion of political slogans unearths the troubling way that the foundations of Whig liberal thought resemble the absolutist assertions of the rake, the *London Journal*'s rehearsal of Restoration drama suggests the desire for the "superior parts" of the sovereign libertine to persist at the midcentury as a possible performative mode for the self-determining subject.

When Boswell poses as Sir John Brute on March 25, then, the allusion runs much deeper than the sexual encounter it is meant to gloss. Rather, it indexes a whole personal history that he shares with Vanbrugh's knight, visible throughout the *London Journal* in his struggle for independence and status and in his periodic recourse to the Restoration wit as a desirable mode of achieving these ends. But the moment of the pose also produces a self-parodying comment on this history of flirtations with the Stuart wit role. In the play, Brute's insistence on his personal sovereignty as a member of Lord Rake's gang is ultimately belied by the outcome of his imitative libertinism. His riots in act 4 result in his arrest, a capitulation to the law and order that he purports to affront. Upon his return home shortly later, his subjugation within a masculine social hierarchy is likewise confirmed as he discovers his wife on the verge of an assignation with Constant. While actual adultery never occurs, Sir John remains suspicious that it has, and he is only prevented from abusing Lady Brute for it after Constant intimidates him with a sword, icon of gentlemanly power. By the end, Sir John is, in the words of his servant Razor, a "cuckoldy drunken sot," one who has, by his own admission, become "governable" in a reversal of his earlier boasts of absolutist autonomy (*The Provoked Wife*, 96, 109). Not an actual cuckold sexually, he nonetheless succumbs to the Restoration dramatic cuckold's fate socially; he is left a loser in the competition for status, secure of neither independence nor the privileges of social authority and exposed as merely a pretender to the sovereign power of the libertine.

In this way, Sir John serves as a caricature of the reversals that, by the spring of 1763, attended Boswell's own emulation of the Stuart wit's pretensions to liberty and social authority. Not only had his relationship with Louisa ended poorly—leaving him with wounded pride and a venereal infection that kept him confined to his chambers for five weeks, thus "wholly unconnected" to "the variety of scenes going on in this Metropolis"—but in early March, his prospects of a commission in the Guards had also perceptibly diminished (*London Journal*, 128). Pursuing the "elegant scene[s] of gallantry" that he associated with the sexually potent Man of Pleasure ironically results in a lowering of status and inhibits the theatrical posturing on London's streets that he uses to confirm his genteel superiority (73). At this time, Lord Auchinleck's displeasure at his son's intransigent frivolity—never mentioned in the journal but exhibited in Boswell's correspondence—had reached such a height that he was threatening to sell the family's Ayrshire estate, a move that would have effectively stripped Boswell of his title as laird.[91] In these contexts, playing Sir John is a recognition that his pose as Restoration wit not only has failed to secure him a London life of cultured privilege but has actually jeopardized the very thing that grounds his capacity for gentlemanly independence: his lairdship. That his staging of Sir John happens in St. James's Park—the site, infamously, where Lord Rochester's poetic rambler suffers a similarly parodic loss of status as his displays of socio-sexual potency are readily appropriated by the lower classes—only further confirms this moment as a deflationary retrospective on the assurances of the Restoration wit's freedoms.[92]

Acting the part of Sir John, a failed imitator of the Restoration Man of Pleasure's claims to distinction, thus gestures toward Boswell's disillusionment with a role that had defined his first few months in London. The incident with the prostitute in St. James's Park is the first sexual encounter he pursues after his falling out with Louisa, and on the following day, his musings turn on how "venereal delight" and "the pleasures of love" would be "more refined & more valuable" if they were to be "permitted only to the Virtuous" (*London Journal*, 182–183). "At present," he concludes, "[sexual passion] is the common solace of the Virtuous and the Wicked. The man of taste & the man of Brutality" (183). The sexual potency of the Restoration wit here is no longer a feature that distinguishes his "refined" superiority and privileged independence from the masses but confounds class distinctions.[93] In this realization about the "man of taste," the journal again reveals itself to be haunted by *The Provoked Wife*. For the play's satire aims not just at Sir John as a would-be wit but at the whole emulative culture of the Restoration wits as always already failed, a system of performative pretense that only poorly masks its players' debasement. For Vanbrugh, the oxymoronic appropriation of low libertine debauchery that is meant to mark the Restoration wit's ascendant status in the social hierarchy only confirms this character to be merely what Sir John's surname denotes: a brute, an absolutist in the sense of a being still ensconced in a state of nature, controlled by his passions rather than in command of himself. In showing how Sir John's rakish exploits fail to grant him the distinguished personal sovereignty he craves, *The Provoked Wife* condemns the whole Restoration culture of libertine riot and emulative competition.

If Boswell's pose as Sir John serves similarly as a self-conscious critique of what the Restoration wit model had earlier signified to him in terms of gentility and independence, this realization does not necessarily induce the vanishing of this role.[94] For as much as Boswell increasingly attempts to enact a character defined by its *retenu*—a term that he frequently uses to denote polite self-control rather than the audacious self-displays of the wit—his moment of identification with Sir John triggers ensuing performances in the style of a more openly Brute-like Restoration rake. On June 4, "the King's Birth-night," for example, Boswell sallies forth on the London streets "resolved to be a Blackguard" (*London Journal*, 237). Dressed in dirty clothes, armed with an "old oaken stick," and claiming to spectators to be a variety of underclass characters (a barber, a soldier, a highwayman), he proceeds to accost a series of prostitutes, performing "most manfully" with one but physically "abus[ing]" another, who refuses to conform to his sexual wishes (237). The goal of this outing, Boswell suggests, is the gratification of his "Vanity" regarding his "superior parts": "Notwithstanding of my dress, I was allways taken for a Gentleman in disguise" (237). Boswell does not attribute his performance to the heritage of the Restoration wit, but it nevertheless clearly ghosts the abject behavior that Sir John and the Stuart court libertines use to stage their social supremacy. The violent scene is enacted for "a parcel of more Whores and Soldiers," who in Boswell's mind recognize in it his inherent gentility, and it operates as a troubling double of the episode with Louisa (237). While the former is stark in its aggression and the latter is couched in terms of romantic gallantry, the endgame of both is identical: the performative exploitation of the lower-class woman as a means of proving Boswell's own social status and gentlemanly license to an audience, whether it be on the London streets or in the journal's readership. The blackguard's performance of upper-class abusive privilege retrospectively casts the Restoration wit's performance of personal liberty as the actions of the bestial absolutist. The "man of taste" is indeed the "man of Brutality"—but unlike how Boswell catalogs this confusion on March 26, he here does not see this as detrimental to his status.

Boswell's blackguard scene reveals a lack of separation between genteel prerogative and criminal brutality, as Erin Mackie has suggested.[95] But in exposing unconsciously the Stuart wit in his true colors as an absolutist, the scene also evinces how this figure's repertoire of anticivility persists, however disturbingly, as a midcentury mode for the display of masculine aristocratic license. As the journal reveals Boswell continuing to act as Sir John Brute in bald-faced form, it does not so much chronicle a relinquishing of the Stuart libertine's fantasy of sovereign prerogative in the linear march forward to eighteenth-century sociability as it does expose that fantasy to haunt the midcentury subject's articulations of personal liberty. Boswell's psychic drama—structured both consciously and unconsciously around Sir John's muddle of "liberty and property" and absolute rule—rehearses the tension between desire for and disgust with the Stuart rake that drives *The Provoked Wife* and its meditation on the history of Restoration libertine drama. In doing so, the *London Journal* is a stage in the history of Restoration drama, but it is also a stage upon which that history presents itself as more than a dead artifact of the past. Reviving the dramatic Stuart wit and *The Provoked Wife*'s satire on him as part of Boswell's testing the bounds of personal liberty, the journal records the Restoration as a period not "over" but long-running, signaling the enduring power of its cultural corpus as a structuring mechanism for the exploration and representation of psychic and social impulses.

4

LIBERTINES AND LIBERALISM

BY THE EARLY NINETEENTH CENTURY, the vanishing of Restoration libertine drama from the British repertory theaters that had been urged by Collier and Steele and initiated by Garrick had come to fruition. To repeat, with a difference, one of the opening quotes of this book's introduction, Charles Lamb proclaimed this disappearance as fact in 1822: "The artificial Comedy, or Comedy of Manners, is quite extinct on our stage. Congreve and Farquhar show their heads once in seven years only, to be exploded and put down instantly. The times cannot bear them."[1] Lamb was seconded by William Hazlitt, who, in his *Lectures on the English Comic Writers* (1819), credited the Restoration as "the golden period of our comedy" from which the stage had since fallen away and who regretted that its plays had "become a dead letter" to Romantic theatergoers.[2] Extinction, loss, death: these keywords haunt accounts of the immediate post-1800 fate of Restoration libertine comedy. Unlike Lamb or Hazlitt, more recent theater historians refuse to associate Romantic theater with a narrative of dramatic decline, opting rather to uncover the "social and political changes [that] lie behind the banishment of certain dramatic characters and subjects from the stage," such as those of the Restoration.[3] Nevertheless, their recourse to keywords such as "banishment" to describe changes in cultural tastes and sociopolitical ideologies reiterates a linear contrast between one end of the long eighteenth century and the other that remains firmly planted in Lamb's conceptual universe.

If such studies primarily query *why* Restoration libertine drama vanished from the post-1800 scene, this chapter asks *if* it truly did so. My aim is neither to deny the workings of historical rupture—the idea that Romantic plays took new forms and that these forms are bound up with sociopolitical change—nor to contest the statistical decline of Restoration comedy. I would contest, rather, the pervasive assumption that the lack of Stuart-era revivals is identical to the banishment of a Restoration comedic heritage from the Romantic stages. In this case, as I have argued throughout this book, canonical claims of "overness" such as those of Lamb only occlude the working of reappearance and reenactment.

Chapter 3 revealed Restoration drama's migration to the everyday performances of mid-eighteenth-century theatrical, political, and social actors who test and contest the indistinction between the sovereign's prerogative and the subject's liberty. This chapter shows Restoration drama's "ongoingness" in the early nineteenth century to be located in staged historical reenactments of Restoration-era sovereigns and subjects themselves. As Allardyce Nicoll notes, this era was marked not only by an exhaustive purging of Restoration drama, but also by a desire to see the real-life Stuarts (for whom these libertines served as avatars) revived onstage. "It is noticeable," Nicoll writes, "that both dramatists and audiences, even if they would have nothing to do with Wycherley and his peers, seemed to take a sneaking interest in the affairs of the Restoration court. . . . A number of playwrights looked back with not unlonging eyes to the days of Charles II."[4] Particularly in the "age of Reform," the period following the end of the Napoleonic wars in 1815 and continuing into the 1830s, London's patent and minor theaters alike hosted a wave of pseudohistorical comedies starring Charles and his libertine court: William Thomas Moncrieff's *Rochester; or, Charles the Second's Merry Days* (1818), John Howard Payne's *Charles the Second; or, The Merry Monarch* (1824), Douglas Jerrold's *The Bride of Ludgate* (1831) and *Nell Gwynne; or, The Prologue* (1833), Henry Robert Addison's *The King's Word* (1835), and more. Devoid of Dorimants and Willmores, these plays nonetheless feature the personalities—the king, Lord Rochester, Sir Charles Sedley, the Duke of Buckingham—on whom such rakish characters were based, recounting tales both authentic and apocryphal of their libertine exploits in Restoration society.

The popularity of such seventeenth-century period pieces accords with a burgeoning fascination of Romantic theatergoers with historical reenactment and scenic realism. But when scholars have paused over this set of Charles II plays at all, they have tended to see their historical reenactments as merely apolitical comic diversion, a reading aligned with a broader narrative of the decline of the radical political satire that marked the Regency and of popular culture's consequent depoliticization in the 1820s and 1830s.[5] As Nicoll's language of "longing" suggests, his reading of these plays fits squarely with that of Lamb, for whom the world of Restoration comedy denoted a nostalgic "fairy-land," a "Utopia of gallantry, where pleasure is duty and the manners perfect freedom."[6] More recent interpretations as well concede these plays' uncomplicated frivolity. As Dorothea Flothow argues, their history is essentially "escapism": "They show the past as colourful and funny.

Except for a few short references, politics is avoided; instead the Merry Monarch is shown in pursuit of wine, women and pleasure."[7]

The twofold danger of such interpretations, however, lies in the segregation of libertine social and sexual behavior from questions of political subjectivity and in the construing of theatricality and reenactment as "a matter of playful, infelicitous farce," an ideological vantage that, as Rebecca Schneider warns, occludes the working of "queer time."[8] Ignoring these plays' broader contexts, Nicoll and Flothow miss the deeply liberal—and at times radical—drive of this theatrical trend. Most of the Charles II plays manufacture a similar pattern of events: seduction and reform. Each play turns on a plot of mistaken identities that allows for an attempted sexual coercion of middle- or lower-class women by royal or aristocratic rakes and the eventual reformation of the libertine protagonist. The thematic insistence on royal and aristocratic malfeasance and its ultimate reformation takes on political significance in light of historical conditions under which the plays were produced: the rise of a liberal movement to reform Parliament and London's theaters in the years leading up to 1832. Over the corpse of Restoration comedy arises a corpus of drama that revives the Restoration rake's sexual predation as part of a progressive sociopolitical agenda. Certainly fitting Bernard Shaw's description of "historical romance"—"mostly fiction with historical names attached to the stock characters of the stage"—these plays are better conceived as a set of repeated scenarios, Diana Taylor's term for "a paradigmatic setup that relies on supposedly live participants, structured around a schematic plot, with an intended (though adaptable) end."[9] Key here is the prospect of adaptability; as embodied acts, scenarios are "meaning-making paradigms that structure social environments" around shared cultural memories and values, but whose outwardly formulaic structures can be easily altered to suit the purposes of new players.[10] In these Charles II comedies, the Restoration rake's scenarios—the class politics of his seduction plots, his dual pose as tyrannical absolutist and liberty-loving rebel, his theatrical collapsing of the categories of high and low culture and behavior, his reform—index questions of the subject's liberty in the face of a perceived post-Waterloo resurgence of absolutist governance (in direction of both the state and the national stages) and imagine outcomes in line with the terms of liberal reform.

Thus, if these plays register a "longing" for the Restoration past, it is better read as an exploration of sovereign desire (primary feature of the long-running Restoration) than as nostalgia. The rest of this chapter explores how the libertine scenarios of these Restoration-era comedies mobilized different possibilities for what the reform of the British state and stage might look like and the place of the sovereign and the subject within it. For some of these liberal playwrights and activists, reactivating these scenarios is a tactic by which to banish the ghosts of Stuart absolutism and codify the future's separation from Britain's illiberal past in the ascendance of progressive middle-class values. For others, notably William Thomas Moncrieff, the rehearsal of a scenario of libertine misbehavior partakes in a critique of the current state of the body politic and theatrical government, but also radically adapts that scenario to underscore the absolutist exclusions and sociopolitical biases of liberal reform itself. Taken together, the plays' deployment of Restoration rake scenarios of tyranny and liberty, and seduction and reform, enact and resist the rise of hegemonic liberalism in politics and in the theater. I begin first with an overview of the role of the Stuarts and their drama in the historiographical construction of liberal reform and afterward turn to a reading of the plays' rendering of Restoration libertine personalities in this context.

SCENARIO I: TYRANNY AND LIBERTY

Despite the absence of Restoration comedy on the theatrical stage, Romantic writers attested to seeing ghostly restorations of Stuart figures and behaviors everywhere on the political one, the upheavals from the French Revolution to the 1832 Reform Bill having brought them into focus. A generation of postrevolutionary writers echoed Victor Frankenstein's conviction that the seventeenth-century Stuart past was "the most animating epoch of English history."[11] Edmund Burke's *Reflections on the Revolution in France* (1790) and Thomas Babington Macaulay's *History of England from the Accession of James the Second* (1848) placed the Stuarts' constitutional crises at the center of British history, drawing parallels between such events and their own age of revolution and reform. Other purveyors of history followed suit, assembling an array of analogies to fit every possible ideological outlook: the execution of Louis XVI was a repeat of Charles I's fate; parliamentarian reformers in the 1640s and Whig martyrs such as John Hampden and Algernon Sidney served as behavioral models for radicals looking to cast the Bourbons and the Hanoverians as reincarnations of the tyrannous Stuarts; conservatives pilloried their Jacobin and Napoleonic opponents as dangerous Cromwellian upstarts.[12] Nineteenth-century playwrights did not fail to capitalize—ideologically, if not always financially—on this trend. In the 1820s, both Percy Shelley and Mary Russell Mitford wrote tragedies starring Charles I and Cromwell; Lamb's unproduced *John Woodvil* (1802) and William Godwin's *Faulkener* (1807) unfolded their dramas of family discord and partisan strife in the days of the Restoration, while plays such as Francis Lee's *The Glorious Revolution* (1821),

Robert Taylor's *Swing* (1831), and John Robert Haines's *The Rye-House Plot* (1838) detailed the revolutionary conspiracies of the 1680s.

Such drama has been recognized for its staging of "politics by indirection." Part of the British government's reactionary measures in the wake of the French Revolution, the censorship of all topical political representations in the theater only intensified in the age of reform; using the tumultuous but safely distant past of the seventeenth century was a tactic of displacement that allowed dramatists to broach potentially subversive questions under the veil of analogy.[13] To understand representations of the Stuart past solely in this way, however, fails to account for the fact that the crises of autocratic monarchy, corrupt aristocracy, and popular radicalism that defined the period from the civil wars to 1688 were, for many British citizens, more than apt historical parallels to present turmoil: they were performances that remained unresolved in British social and political life. "The very same vice assumes a new body," Burke claimed in his *Reflections*, chastising readers for their myopia regarding the repetition of revolutionary events, "The spirit transmigrates; and, far from losing its principle of life by the change of its appearance, it is renovated in its new organs."[14] Same spirit, new body: well known for reading politics as theater, Burke proffers here a vision of history-as-performance that anticipates Marvin Carlson's theory of "ghosting," in which the "spirit" or trace of past theatrical events inevitably inheres in each subsequent revival, "renovated"—restored and revised—in their repetition by different corporeal actors. Such a view of historical event as performance event implies a conception of the past not as discrete and distanced, but as ongoing.[15]

Many Romantic writers felt they were still somehow in Stuart time, recognizing that past's ongoingness in the restoration of its political behaviors. In a review of Walter Scott's Popish Plot novel *Peveril of the Peak* (1823)—a tale featuring cameos by Charles II and his courtiers—Hazlitt remarked, "at a time . . . when we bid fair to revive the principles of the Stuarts, it is interesting to bring us acquainted with their persons."[16] The word "revive" occurs frequently in Hazlitt's dramatic criticism; reminiscent of Burke's language, it underscores a serious supposition that the Stuart past lives on, reenacted in present-day political "principles" that undercut the progressive, triumphalist narrative of Whig history that writers such as Macaulay drew on. The unfinished Stuart past troubled Hazlitt particularly in the period following the 1815 Bourbon Restoration and the subsequent bolstering of royal power in Britain against popular sovereignty. One such principle is "legitimacy"—a claim of hereditary royal right to rule that "haunts" the Hanoverian present "like a frightful spectre" from the Stuart past: "Such is the old doctrine of Divine Right, new-vamped up under the style and title of Legitimacy. . . .

We wonder where our English politicians picked it up. Is it an echo from the tomb of the martyred monarch, Charles the First? Or was it the last word which his son, James the Second, left behind him in his flight[?]"[17] Monarchical right contains a spectral echo of the Stuart past. For Hazlitt, this is more than polemical historical analogy; like the rhythms of the repertory theaters, such politics are performances worryingly subject to perpetual returns.

The unresolved crisis of Stuart tyranny was often correlated with the revival of Stuart libertine behavior, both of which put public liberty at risk. While Lamb and Hazlitt separate their nostalgia for the supposedly disappeared form of Restoration libertine comedy from their distaste for revived Stuart politics, in reality this divide is not always clear. The rake's performances of autonomy and absolutism repeatedly factor in polemical critiques of restored Stuart behavior. Hazlitt's portrayal of Charles II in his collected essays as "amiable," "witty," but largely ornamental condemns the king for the very predilections that often make his comic stage avatars appealing: "Instead of regulating his conduct by public opinion and abstract reason, [Charles] did every thing from a feeling of personal convenience. Charles would have been more annoyed with the rejection of a licentious overture than with the rebellion of a province; and poured out the blood of his subjects with the same gaiety and indifference as he did a glass of wine. He had no idea of his obligations to the State, and only laid aside the private gentleman, to become the tyrant of his people."[18] Turning Charles's wine into the blood of British subjects, Hazlitt correlates libertine behavior with dangerous political outcomes. What, under the auspices of stage comedy, he or Lamb might read as Restoration libertine pranks—Charles's sexual promiscuity, his drinking, his blasé self-centeredness—are here merged with and raised as motivating causes for the king's tyrannous politics, his disregard for the public good. Hazlitt's description of Charles registers some of the fundamental tensions that animated the liberal reform movement in post-Waterloo Britain: Charles's contempt for public opinion and his exploitation of the bodies of his subjects correspond with the view that many reformers had of the nation's current governors as corrupt, self-serving, and indifferent to the people.[19]

Nor was the Stuart libertine a purely liberal bugbear. Samuel Taylor Coleridge, in his famous attack on "modern jacobinical drama" in his *Biographia Literaria* (1817), was alternately to criticize political radicalism by affiliating it with the anarchic will of Thomas Shadwell's antihero in *The Libertine* (1675).[20] In privileging autonomous selfhood against all social bonds and traditional authorities, as Jeffrey Cox has noted, the hero-villains of Gothic tragedy were dramatic descendants of the Restoration libertine.[21] The same notion occurs to Coleridge; he compares Gothic plays such as Charles Robert Maturin's *Bertram* (1816) with

Shadwell's work for the way they present a "subversion of the natural order of things . . . by representing the qualities of liberality, refined feeling, and a nice sense of honour" in "those criminals whom law, reason, and religion have excommunicated from our esteem." The difference is that *Bertram* revives the élan of Shadwell's libertine and the seductive promise of the "individual's self-will" but strips them of the morally ordered universe by which they may ultimately be contained.[22] As Coleridge sees it, the subversiveness of "modern" Jacobinism lies not solely in the novelty of its political doctrine, but in the way it conjures the dangerous spirit of the Stuart rake's excessive liberties, reviving in the new embodiment of the everyday individual the lawlessness of the absolute king.

An index of Romantic historical and political self-understanding, the Restoration Stuart past was no less crucial to Romantic theatrical history and its own questions of reform. In recent years, scholars of Romantic theater have unanimously attested that the issue of parliamentary reform was virtually inseparable from the issue of the reform of London's patent stages, Drury Lane and Covent Garden. From the Old Price Riots of 1809 to the parliamentary debates surrounding reform in the early 1830s, the degeneracy of the patents was perhaps the defining obsession of Romantic-era writing for and about the stage.[23] Due to a commercial monopoly system derived from Charles II's original grant of theatrical patents to William Davenant and Thomas Killigrew in 1662—and in perpetuity to their heirs—holders of the patents possessed the sole right to perform five-act tragedy and comedy in London and assumed responsibility as trustees of the nation's dramatic heritage. For all other "minor" venues of performance—spaces such as the Haymarket and Sadler's Wells in the eighteenth century and the Adelphi, Olympic, Surrey, and Coburg theaters in the nineteenth century—drama with spoken dialogue was off-limits, their licenses granting them the power to produce only spectacular entertainments. As Jane Moody has revealed, by the Regency era, "Drury Lane and Covent Garden theatres had come to be identified as the cultural synecdoche of a corrupt political state," their practices accused by liberal critics of promoting entrenched aristocratic privilege against the rights of expanding, multiclassed audiences, debasing Britain's dramatic traditions for their own monetary gain, and arbitrarily suppressing all attempts by alternative theatrical venues to break their monopolistic sway.[24] The minor theaters emerged as oppositional sites of popular resistance and plebeian counterculture, at first surreptitiously staging "legitimate" drama under the guise of musical or physical forms such as burletta and pantomime and, increasingly, becoming public rallying centers for the movement to abolish the patent monopolies altogether and establish dramatic free trade.[25]

As advocacy for parliamentary and theatrical reform intensified, London's theater monopoly system was not just labeled by its detractors as corrupt, but also imagined specifically as an institution in which the illiberal Stuart past still held sway. In part, such a rendering was made feasible by the chaotic history of theatrical licensing. The 1737 Stage Licensing Act effectively authorized the Lord Chamberlain's office to license additional minor theaters within London and ensured that Drury Lane and Covent Garden would remain the only theaters operating under the protection of a royal patent. But the legislation opened the door for confusion between the powers of the Lord Chamberlain and the powers of the crown regarding theatrical matters; the former had been asserted by parliamentary law, the latter by royal fiat. Throughout the long eighteenth century, Drury Lane and Covent Garden were officially referred to as the "Theatres Royal" and their personnel as "His Majesty's Servants," nomenclature that, as Dewey Ganzel indicates, denotes the technical legal fact that, from the Restoration until the abolition of theatrical monopoly in 1843, these theaters were granted license to operate not by Parliament but by the "royal prerogative" of Charles II.[26] In other words, when it came to laws governing theatrical rights, Drury Lane and Covent Garden were temporally out of sync with the rest of London; the very material conditions by which they functioned secured a space in which the Restoration was not over. In spite of all the political measures passed from 1688 forward to limit royal prerogative and to debar James II's heirs from the throne, the patent theaters remained a space over which the Stuarts could be said to still reign.

Such associations between the performances of illiberal monopoly and those of Stuart privilege grew popular among reformers by the 1830s. On May 31, 1832, liberal Member of Parliament and novelist Edward Bulwer spoke before the House of Commons, urging Parliament to approve the establishment of a Select Committee to investigate the nation's need for dramatic reform. His argument hangs on a carefully wrought history of dramatic decay, rooted "in the licentious period in which the first patents were granted, viz. the time of Charles 2nd": "It happened, curiously enough, that no sooner were the two great theatres in possession of this patent, than the national drama began to deteriorate, and a love for scenic effect to supersede it. It was reproached to Sir Wm. Davenant, it was reproached to all the stage managers under the new patents. . . . This reproach, with more or less justice, had constantly existed—this reproach, with peculiar justice, existed at the present time."[27] Reversing the standard historical narrative in which Charles recovers the drama from the antitheatrical prejudices of puritan Interregnum rule, Bulwer isolates the Restoration as the origin of dramatic decline, productive of a lineage of corrupt patent managers that continues to plague London's theatrical scene.

Bulwer's polemic relies on a vision of theater history concocted by his radical colleagues during the preceding months. Prompted by recent attempts of the patent managers to prosecute their minor opponents for staging plays, Benjamin

Rayner, Thomas Serle, and George Davidge convened a series of public meetings with the intent of developing a petition to Parliament for the liberalization of theatrical trade. Attended by managers, actors, playwrights, and politicians, their discussions were reported regularly in *The Morning Chronicle*, and their efforts eventually led to the formation of Bulwer's 1832 Select Committee on Dramatic Literature.[28] In the early meetings, their rhetoric recycled the standard indictment of the patent managers as an unreformed aristocracy. For Serle, they were akin to an oligarchy, "determined to use their prescriptive rights and their privileges to shut out their fellow-citizens from the exercise of their rights."[29] Eugene Macarthy, an associate of the Dublin theater, suggested that their "pecuniary embarrassments" made their case "similar to that of a profligate libertine, who has wasted his fortune, and plunged himself into debt by a riotous course of unprincipled extravagance."[30] Their financial situation tottering since the days of the Old Price Riots, the patents were perceived as squandering their funds in the hope of big returns on elaborate spectacles rather than producing the national drama.[31] For Macarthy and Serle, they embodied the wastefulness of an upper-class rake bent on self-involved pleasure rather than invested in the national community.

While such language was not novel in Romantic-era discussions of the monopoly, the 1832 reformers were unique in tying these allegations to a specifically Stuart heritage that resonated in contemporary performance. As the meetings progressed, speakers began to locate a historical precedent in Charles II's court for the patents' illiberal behavior. Serle, for example, cast current theatrical culture as behind the times: "At the very time when all other arts are gaining new life under the influence of perfect freedom," the theaters were "languishing under the bondage of monopoly." Untouched by the promise of progressive reform, according to Serle, theater's temporal lag was the fault of "tyrannical" patent practices derived from their Stuart origins: "What, then, was the case of the patent theaters? They were created in the first instance by tyranny, and now the over-exertion of tyranny . . . would destroy them."[32] Imagined genealogically, the patents are the archaic offspring of an absolutist dynasty that Britain had ousted for its violations of liberty and property over a hundred years ago.

The "tyranny" here describes the use of royal prerogative to grant exclusive rights of theatrical ownership. Though the patent managers claimed that they were simply safeguarding their property rights, Serle argues that the means by which they obtained those rights were unconstitutional:

> In the time of Shakespeare . . . there were seventeen theatres, each possessing equal rights—equal authority, to perform whatever plays they chose to accept and exhibit for the best interests of themselves and the

> public. . . . Upon the restoration of Charles it was thought necessary to raise the drama from its ashes, to collect its scattered materials, which had been thrown all over England. To do that it was considered necessary to establish something like a monopoly in order that there might be an exclusive enjoyment on behalf of some; this was rather a difficult task, but, from the exercise of a most arbitrary power, patents were created for services which I need not name. Thus those monopolies have commenced, and they have proceeded in a manner worthy of their origin; they began in infamy and ended in treachery.[33]

Rehearsing a narrative familiar from the theater histories of Hazlitt and Walter Scott, in which the liberal values of popular sovereignty anachronistically associated with the Renaissance stage devolve into a post-1660 absolutist system, Serle describes the modern patent theaters as having the "arbitrary power" of the Stuarts in their blood.[34] Paid in dramatic property for their suspect "services" to Charles, the managers' right to the national theaters is based in court corruption. Such actions might be "infamy" in the Stuart era, but under Britain's modern parliamentary rule they are treason. In protecting their rights, Serle suggests, the managers are propagating a heritage of absolutist self-interest that infringes on the competing rights of their compatriots.

Charles II served as a particularly apt scapegoat; his cultural memory as arbitrary king, founder of the modern monopoly system, and chief among libertines was a liberal anathema. Agreeing with Serle that the monopoly had "originated in arbitrary power," a radical lawyer, Mr. Mahon, enlarged on this theme:

> The law that gave a monopoly to the patent Theatres . . . was the product of an age when public liberty was ill understood, and public morals were grossly relaxed [hear, hear!]. A sensual despot was then upon the Throne, who thought of nothing but his pleasures. The actors and actresses were then, as the cant goes now, his Majesty's Servants, dependent upon his high pleasure, which pleasure lay more among the female, than the male performers. . . . We no longer wear the flowing wigs, rolled stockings, and high shoes of the days of the Stuarts, and why should we be fettered by their monopoly [loud applause]?[35]

With the comparison to sartorial fashion, Mahon implies that theatrical monopoly is a fad that unfortunately has refused to fade. The patent managers continue to perform in the style of the Stuarts, their commercial abuse of the public an extension of the sexual abuses of the original "sensual despot," Charles himself. Manifested in his predatory sexuality, the king's performance of tyranny is linked to that of the patent managers: they are both imagined to violate the rights of their subjects by pursuing their own pleasures at the expense of "public liberty."

Unlike Serle or Bulwer, however, Mahon does not ascribe to Charles's excesses the immediate decline of theatrical culture, but instead characterizes the Restoration and early eighteenth century as "those better days" in which "legitimate tragedy and comedy prevailed": "Congreve, Wycherley, Cibber, and their compeers in comedy held the full mirror up to nature—and though license too often marked their pens, wit and moral pointed and closed their lines. . . . Every hit of Gay at the profligate courtiers of the day was caught at and approved."[36] Not exactly approving of ribald libertine comedy, Mahon nonetheless reads in its performance a critique of the abuse of power by a king and court whose public irresponsibility conditioned the politics of theater management thereafter. His historical vision extends the hope of reform in the shape of "legitimate" dramatists willing to take a similar stand against public corruption. For Mahon, the restoration of something like Restoration comedy is imagined to be a potential resolution to the crisis of the Stuarts' persistence in the patent monopoly system.

Locating, in Serle's words, the "origin" of current theatrical disorder in Charles II's monopoly rather than in any number of other causes—actors' cartels, the economics of the repertory, the effects of the 1737 Licensing Act—the stage reformers of the early 1830s revived a powerful scenario of Stuart tyranny versus public liberty, one that had shaped British political thought since the seventeenth century and, as Melinda Zook notes, was deployed by Whig historians looking to "frame [their] history as a story of continuing liberal progress."[37] Against older accounts that read in this era the triumph of a free stage, revisionist historians such as Jacky Bratton argue Bulwer's movement instead to have instituted a set of hierarchical oppositions—literature/theater, author/performer, high/low—that policed theatrical culture to conservative, elitist ends and, eventually, paved the way for its domination by a middle-class commercial hegemony.[38] That this brand of theatrical reform was so successful, I suggest, is in part due to the way its cause was mobilized by a paradigmatic pattern of liberal historical thought. Insisting that the theatrical scene was still under Stuart rule, the reform movement cast its adherents as participants in a long-running historical drama, representing their local cause as part of a venerable, supposedly universal defense of British rights, liberty, and property and as a repeat of 1688 in which the specter of the Stuarts may once again be deposed. Normalized through the scenario of Stuart tyranny and liberty, the minor theaters' cause was accorded center stage in the national debate over the reform of Old Corruption. As one skeptic, the conservative Member of Parliament Charles Wetherall, put it, "to hear what was said on the subject [of theater reform], it might be supposed that the liberty of the people was invaded—that the Habeas Corpus Act was suspended, so much was made of dramatic liberty being infringed and violated."[39] Seeing the practices of Stuart absolutism persist in patent monopoly was a powerful tactic for making just such (in Wetherall's opinion) hyperbolic statements ring true.

Though derisive of the association, Wetherall links the discourses of state and stage reform through the question of bodily freedom versus corrupt centers of power. In the rest of this chapter, I turn to a set of comedies—written by pro-reform dramatists between Waterloo and the early 1830s—that animate this question in the theatrical setup and action of actual bodies on London's stages. In allusions to Charles II's exploitation of his subjects, reform advocates such as Hazlitt, Bulwer, and Mahon depict how Stuart absolutism inheres in public institutions specifically in the form of private, libertine, and often threateningly sexualized bodily behavior. The playwrights Jerrold, Addison, and Payne share a similar outlook with regard to the incompleteness of the Stuart past; in their comedies, however, Stuart libertine conduct becomes the staging ground on which the reform of the nation's political and cultural systems of governance is produced. In schematic plotlines involving the sexual misadventures and eventual disciplining of royal or aristocratic Stuart bodies, their plays imagine national reform to occur through the regulation of manners. Taken collectively, they render the scenario of tyranny and liberty comically as a scenario of libertine seduction and reform, using the theatrical reenactment of the Stuart past rather than its juridical repression to pose alternative interpretations of how that past's persistence affects the present and future of a reformed Britain.

SCENARIO II: SOVEREIGN SEDUCTION AND BARE BODIES

Douglas Jerrold's two-act comic afterpiece *The Bride of Ludgate* opened at Drury Lane on December 8, 1831. The author's debut on the patent stages and his first foray in high comedy, it details the "licentious frolics" of Charles II, in which the king and his courtiers, disguised as commoners, pursue amorous dalliances with the wives and daughters of London's citizens.[40] Though the play was well received, almost all of the reviewers remarked on it as a latecomer in a series of Restoration-era period pieces that flooded the theaters from the Regency forward. For Leigh Hunt, *The Bride of Ludgate* "too closely reminded us of some of its predecessors"; making specific reference to John Howard Payne's *Charles the Second*, which had premiered seven years earlier, another writer declared that it "might with great propriety have been called 'Charles the Second *the Second*.'"[41] Such criticism did neither Jerrold nor the phenomenon itself any harm; Jerrold went on successfully to produce *Nell Gwynne* (1833) at Covent Garden, and this was followed by Addison's *The King's Word* (1835), James Robinson Planché's *The Court Beauties* (1835), and Moncrieff's *The "Tobit's Dog!"* (1838). By the 1830s, as a third review claimed, Charles II period pieces had become a very popular "staple commodity of the stage."[42]

Such mass appeal, as I have noted earlier, may be partially explained by Romantic theatergoers' increasing fascination with scenic realism. Described by Planché as a "little attempt to illustrate the manners and costume of the time of 'Sauntering Charles,'" for instance, *The Court Beauties* eschewed originality of plot in favor of spectacular historical verisimilitude, with a set that produced a full-scale version of London's Mall, "scrupulously correct" period costuming, and even a pack of King Charles spaniels.[43] In its epilogue, the manager and leading actress of the Olympic theater, Eliza Vestris, announced,

> We have attempted here to-night, to shew
> Of Charles's Court, the Beauty and the Beau,
> Each in their habit as they lived and walked
> The mall, and flirted, frolicked, sung, and talked. (32)

Associating scenic authenticity—Restoration personalities "as they lived and walked"—with the finery of fancy dress, flirtation, and courtly frolic, Vestris presents such drama as a vehicle for pleasurable escape, as Lamb had put it, from "the all devouring drama of common life."[44]

Recent critical reaction similarly reads these plays as formulaic and escapist, their comic focus on Charles's extra-marital amours devoid of any political significance.[45] Such approaches, however, are problematic on two fronts: they rehearse the antitheatrical equation of repetition with debased, empty copy, and they presume the sexual to be a sign of the apolitical rather than a site through which bodies and national populations may be regulated to political ends. Regarded as scenarios—"culturally specific imaginaries" that mobilize "ways of conceiving conflict, crisis, and resolution"—the repetitive, stock situations of libertine frolic in these plays, I would argue, ritualistically register and attempt to allay the anxieties surrounding the performance of cultural and political governance in the 1820s and 1830s.[46] Staged at the height of parliamentary and theatrical reform, these plays offer scenarios of rakish seduction and reform that reveal the underlying fantasies animating those movements: the overhauling of ruling-class privilege and corruption without courting the dangers of revolution and the advance of a liberal future through a return to the (middle-class Whiggish) values ensconced in Britain's past.[47] Representative of the misappropriation of legitimate power for lawless ends that reformers saw in Parliament and the patent theaters, Charles's sexual misbehavior in these comedies becomes the grounds on which the conflict over who counts as part of the political community is played out. In their reanimation of Stuart misrule, the plays articulate a problem of the permeation of governmental forms of power by a "spectral" or "resurgent" sovereignty that, for theorists such as Giorgio Agamben and Judith Butler, is the mark of political modernity.[48]

That the plays' claims to comic escapism mask deeper political import is apparent in the reviews of *The Bride of Ludgate*. "King Charles the Second, of profligate memory," Hunt writes, "is a great favourite with playwrights, novelists, and actors. . . . *The Bride of Ludgate* follows the usual course, and represents the King as a wild, good-humoured, and generous rambler; constantly seeking libertine adventures, but as often abandoning his intended prey, when he finds that another has superior claims to it."[49] What makes Charles a "great favourite" is precisely the derivativeness of the action, "the usual course" of libertine seduction and reform. The stock scenario that Jerrold's play rehearses underscores a thematic of reform—the "profligate" king is brought from sexually preying on his subjects to recognizing their rights; Stuart libertinism at once threatens a social order that guarantees the liberty, property, and rights of the British subject and is dispelled in comic resolution. Other reviews testify to a similar social unease regarding the play's light-heartedness; they describe Jerrold's Charles as "frolic[king]" among "petticoated commoners" and "merry at his subjects' expence," quietly underscoring the inextricability of the discourse of frivolity from the sexual and socioeconomic disparities that liberals such as Hazlitt, Bulwer, and Mahon denounced in the Stuart past.[50]

As such reviews suggest, these scenarios of comic libertinism bear political ramifications, particularly in rendering the pervasive sexualization and exploitation of a disenfranchised laboring populace by an illegal sovereign prerogative. *The Bride of Ludgate*, *The King's Word*, and *Charles the Second* all take place in working-class urban and rural settings where Stuart royalty abuses its power in quest of sexual pleasure. *The King's Word* follows Charles into the English countryside, where he makes unwanted advances on Kate, a newly married milliner's daughter. Charles's libertine frolics are here underwritten with a dark air of class exploitation; he is described by various characters as selecting his female victims from "amidst the more beautiful classes—such as milliners, and farmer's wives"—and as loving to "take advantage of his rank" in his amours.[51] Kate too assesses her predicament of being subject to the king's will in political terms as "persecuted by a sovereign prince" (13). Similarly, *The Bride of Ludgate* opens on a scene of authority run amok in which London's ruling elite have swarmed the vintner Must's house in pursuit of his new young wife. "Half the court are there," reports the servant Doeskin, "you might, any hour in the day, pick a new ministry from his back parlour" (12). As courtly privilege migrates from Whitehall and the Mall to middling-class locales, such scenarios unearth some of the social tensions driving contemporary reform.

As Doeskin's remark implies, with the merriment of Restoration comic escapism comes a failure of ministerial duty. The reneging of national responsibility among England's ruling and propertied classes was a hallmark of out-of-doors reformist discourse, an accusation that Jerrold and other radicals wove into their work.[52] *The Bride of Ludgate* portrays London's state ministers as corrupt public servants, having abandoned their governmental duties in favor of their own self-serving desires. Foremost among them are the king and the libertine wit Sir Charles Sedley. As this pair loiter incognito at the vintner's establishment, their conversation reveals the extent to which Charles's right to rule has been displaced by his libertine will. Responding to Sedley's accidental slip in calling him "your majesty," Charles chastises him: "Sedley, I this morning left my majesty with my star and garter at Whitehall. I pray you, do not disturb it" (18). The slip is repeated by another of the king's associates shortly later, and Charles exclaims, "There again! Do for once let my head come out of my coinage, and appear without '*Carolus, Dei Gratia Rex*.' . . . Can't you bring me an account of another man's wife, without letting me know that I am King of England, and—" (19). Sedley sardonically finishes his sentence with "Defender of the Faith!" (19). This exchange renders Charles culpable of splitting asunder the king's two bodies, separating the vestments of his legally sanctioned sovereignty from his extra-legal pursuit of personal pleasure. Libertine frolic is made tantamount to renouncing royal responsibility while also retaining royal privilege over subjects' bodies. As Sedley's quip makes clear, Charles is not defending his subjects' faith (religious, sexual, and otherwise) but actively violating it in rehearsing the scenario of Restoration comic seduction.

The King's Word, as well, shows Charles's libertinism to result in a fracturing of lawful kingly behavior into illegitimate personal sovereignty. Alone with Kate toward the middle of the play, the king offers her "riches," "power," and "rank" in exchange for sex, manipulating his privilege and legitimacy toward extra-legal ends (14). Kate rebuts these advances with a political argument that hangs on the theory of the king's two bodies: "Sire, you are the father of a mighty nation. To you a people look for succour and protection. To you, then, as the defender of the rights even of your meanest subject, I appeal, to save the wife of an honest man from the base lures of a great and too fascinating prince" (14). Challenging Charles with a double vision of himself, Kate redefines his frivolous sexuality as loss of patriarchal accountability for his nation. She represents subjects' "rights" as, ideally, coextensive with the sovereign will and as the purview of patrician custodial activity—a stance that, as Linda Colley argues, was adopted by the Whigs under Lord Grey and that served as their rationale for the reform of the nation's wayward public servants in the early 1830s.[53] In good Lockean fashion, Kate's argument suggests that a king retains his power and privilege only so long as he acts as a servant to his people, whereas Charles here makes a tactic of his legitimate sovereign prerogative in pursuit of self-centric ends, wielding, in his sexualization of his subjects' bodies, a lawless power.

Faced with corrupt state ministers, it is the common people who emerge as the bulwark of British order in these plays. Against the confusions of Charles's identity, *The King's Word* presents Kate as consistently loyal to her king despite his recognizable abuses of power. As Charles offers sexual and economic temptations, she holds fast to her marriage vow and to her values; as she tells him, she desires to remain "your most devoted, but your virtuous subject" (15). Her denial of libertine sexuality is formulated in terms at once patriotic and moderate, her chastity affiliated with her devotion to the standing political order that Charles both represents and perverts. The juxtaposition of patriotism and aristocratic sexual misrule structures the main plot of *Charles the Second* as well. Rendering the scenario of Stuart seduction with a twist of nautical drama, Payne's play presents Charles and Rochester, disguised as common sailors, haunting a tavern in the maritime borough of Wapping and harassing Mary, the niece of tavern keeper and former sailor Captain Copp. Adapting a common trend of Romantic nautical drama, in which sailors are stereotyped as either degenerate and mutinous or humanitarian and loyal, Payne casts the upper-class rakes as sexually piratical, "rovers" and "desperate rogue[s] among the petticoats."[54] Their lawless exploitation of the public is countered by Copp, who, despite his disapproval of their misbehavior, remains an enduringly loyal subject. In portraying common citizens as the seat of both patriotic duty and a liberal defense of rights, plays such as *The King's Word* and *Charles the Second* illustrate the seemingly paradoxical position to which Romantic middle-class reform adhered: a relentless critique of the sociopolitical inequalities harbored within Britain's traditional system of government and a fundamental fidelity to the terms of the system itself.[55]

In depicting Charles's thoroughgoing sexual objectification of the public, these comedies stage a principal feature of reformist discourse, positing the state's directors as petty absolutists whose privilege works exploitatively and outside the rule of law to displace an entire subset of the national community from its political rights. But, as we have seen earlier, for liberal writers, Charles II's libertine performances served likewise as convenient shorthand for representing the corrupt legacy of London's patent theaters. The same playwrights who made the Charles II comedies a "staple commodity" of the era were all actively invested in the theater reform movement: Jerrold attended Serle's and Bulwer's radical meetings, spoke out against monopoly in front of the Select Committee, and wrote extensively in defense of the rights of dramatists; Planché promoted the rights of the minor theaters; Addison was a member of the pro-reform Dramatic Author's Society, founded by Jerrold, Serle, and Planché in 1833; Payne and Planché campaigned for the reform of dramatic copyright law.[56] Appearing during this concentrated push, many of their Stuart libertine scenarios thematically embody the particular anxieties that animated theatrical reform.

One recurrent argument of theater reform rhetoric was that the monopolistic tyranny authorized under the current constitution of the stage had sunk Britain's "national drama" into a state of degeneracy. The despotism and greed that reigned at Drury Lane and Covent Garden, pro-reform writers claimed, coupled with the minor theaters' legal proscription from producing spoken drama, had caused lowbrow theater to run rampant on the Romantic stages.[57] Accusations of lowness spanned all political stripes. In a letter to the patent managers in the conservative *Blackwood's Edinburgh Magazine*, for instance, "Philo-Dramaticus" complained that "all [writers] of a higher class have abandoned you, and the public have flown with them."[58] But liberals especially were critical of the patent managers for selfishly inducing a decline in taste. Standard fare for Bulwer and his associates, this argument was also widespread throughout the decades surrounding reform, from early liberal tracts such as *The Modern Stage* (1819), a petition to the radical Member of Parliament George Lamb to curb "the Decay and Degradation of English Dramatic Literature" caused by the monopoly, to such works as Jerrold's "The Rights of Dramatists" (1832) and *Bajazet Gag* (1841–1842), which depicted theater managers as petty absolutists, debasing the quality of the nation's dramatic entertainment and taking advantage of authors and audiences for their own private profit.[59]

The Charles II comedies share this thematic interest in tracing the "low" performances of national managers, marking the king's corrupt nature by his use of theatrical disguises that debase his royalty and call into question his legitimacy. Across the series of plays, Charles's various costumes run the gamut of the unkingly: from sailors and country peasants to Dutch wine merchants and lawyers. His theatricality is described by one character in *Charles the Second* in terms of degrading "nocturnal rambles" from which he needs to be brought "back to reason" (8). More explicitly, *The King's Word* forces Charles to confront the effects of his theatricality as he tries to end his seduction plot when challenged with Kate's husband, Martin:

> CHARLES: I must put a stop to this disgraceful scene. I am the King!
>
> MARTIN: Ha—ha! the King—you the King! it is useless thus to endeavour to deceive me by an accidental likeness you yourself explained. Ha—ha!

> caught in your own trap. No, no; I am not to be imposed upon; the King, though he is a Stuart, is an upright Prince—a man of honour, . . . not a vile intriguing base seducer. You are not the King. (17)

Collectively, such scenarios depict Charles literally lowering himself to a point beyond recognition as rightful sovereign. Just as the patent managers were conceived as deceiving audiences with degraded forms of drama, here the king's theatrical antics reveal only a "base seducer" and a "disgraceful scene." The sovereign's double body on which plays such as *The King's Word* remark is—like the patent monopoly derived from Charles's reign—both licit and illicit, product of national law but one that has been arbitrarily distorted for personal advantage.

Beyond thematic resonances, some of the plays adapt the seduction scenario in ways that accentuate the parallel between the problematic sovereignty of state and stage. Jerrold's *Nell Gwynne* develops the usual conflict between the rapacious propertied classes and the disenfranchised subject; the play's eponymous heroine is an honest, generous, working-class girl trying to forge an entry into London's theatrical world while dodging the sexual advances of the men who would turn her to a life of prostitution: the miserly lawyer Crowsfoot and the king. Despite Jerrold's predilection for historical authenticity, he knowingly rearranges the facts of Nell's life, having her introduction to Charles II occur simultaneously with her commencement as actress at the King's Company and prior to her notorious liaisons with Charles Hart and Lord Buckhurst. In part, Jerrold does this to replace her cultural memory as "the Protestant whore" with a sympathetic portrayal of a victim of social inequality whose "error," as he declares in the preface, "had been forced upon her by circumstances, rather than indulged from choice."[60]

But this chronological change also foregrounds an analogy between the "illegitimate" behavior of the nation's cultural and political directors.[61] Alongside Charles and Nell, Jerrold revives the historical actor-managers Thomas Betterton, Charles Hart, and Michael Mohun, whose floundering fortunes at the two patent theaters drive much of the play's comedy and cultural politics. While the king dons lower-class disguises (the country cousin of one of his courtiers, a mercer) to seduce Nell, the managers are mocked for their encouragement of lowbrow sensationalism at the patent theaters: everything from "speaking doll[s] from France" and "new treble[s] from Italy" to "unicorn[s]" (*Nell Gwynne*, 5). Yielding to commercial pressures, the managers have even "improved Shakespeare," cutting his tragedies and putting them to music, an action that one skeptical character compares to the "mutilation" of his subjects by "the grand Turk" (5). The crisis of *Nell Gwynne*, then, is as much about the state of British dramatic culture, and its implications for the liberties of the subject, as it is about the protagonist. As in Bulwer's condemnation of Davenant for allowing the national drama to "deteriorate" into "scenic effect," Betterton, Hart, and Mohun are here rendered "grand Turks[s]," cultural absolutists, lawless in their disregard for public opinion and for the national heritage they are tasked to preserve. Their management results in a decline in theatrical quality, a desecration of dramatic tradition, and an influx of foreign spectacle. In the comparison between mutilated subjects and Shakespeare's mutilated plays, Jerrold updates a prominent strand of theater reform discourse that correlates the nation's theatrical corpus to the health of its body politic. The managerial defacing of the national poet is made akin to a loss of rights, under the terms of resurgent absolutism, for Britain's free theatergoing public. Jerrold's humanitarian sympathy for Nell thus extends to sympathy for a nation and a national heritage abused by the powers instituted to safeguard it.

The fate of Britain's dramatic corpus at the hands of unscrupulous managers, in Jerrold's play, is also similar to that of ordinary citizens like Nell: both are subject to a loss of identity, to a reduction to their most bodily elements, at the hands of a lawless sovereign power. In the main plot, Charles competes with the lawyer Crowsfoot to make Nell his mistress, treating her as a sexual prize to be bought and sold with the perquisites of his royalty. At the same time, in the subplot, the theater managers, in order to raise their fortunes, compete among themselves for the chance to exploit Nell's bodily labor economically on the stage.[62] At the end of the first act, Betterton and Hart quarrel over who has the "first claim" to her (24). "This girl must be ours," Hart declares (25), and Betterton makes a similar bid for possession: "The king seems dazzled with this wench—I must secure her for the Duke's" (22). The object of the king's sexual desires and his public servants' commercial desires, Nell is stripped of social and political identity—responsible citizen, Lockean self-owner, liberal humanitarian. She is reduced to the utilitarian value of her body in a metric determined solely by the pleasure and self-interest of a devolved absolutism and made representative of the political inconsequentiality of the citizen under a system of Stuart governance: excluded from full subjecthood yet included in the matrix of politics as a body to be manipulated. On top of forsaking patrician responsibility for libertine frivolity, *Nell Gwynne* reveals the nation's political and cultural authorities to have the constitutionally suspect effect of reducing the body politic to property, actual bare bodies.

In line with the liberal rhetoric of Hazlitt, Bulwer, or Mahon—in which Stuart libertine pleasure equates with the sexual objectification of laboring British subjects, the turning of their blood into wine—these Charles II plays dramatize the ways that Stuart tyranny lurks at the heart of Stuart libertine frolic, the ways that both haunt the mechanisms of governance in Britain's political and theatrical present. Their imaginary Restoration world reflects liberal reform's polemical nightmare image of the real-life Romantic one: a world whose lawful ministers have gone astray, no longer the guardians of the public but self-centric sovereign despoilers who reduce the body politic to purely visceral, manipulatable bodies. In staging this effect of legally sanctioned yet illicit Stuart rule reanimated, the plays gesture toward a critique not just of the inequalities ensconced in Britain's governing institutions, but also of what Giorgio Agamben defines as the modus operandi of sovereign power itself: the creation of "bare life," life that is subject to political calculation but that is itself stripped of political or social significance.[63] Concerned less with sovereignty as political theory and more with sovereignty as pose, however, these seduction scenarios literalize this effect, depicting the libertine king's sexual desire for the "bare" (naked) bodies of the British people as analogous to the suspension of their rights—a stripping of all identity beyond the physical—by the spectral performances of Stuart absolutism in the nineteenth-century political and theatrical world.

THE LIBERTINE REFORMED

Ultimately, however, while Addison's, Jerrold's, and Payne's work embodies the pro-reform motif of libertine exploitation, their distinct political edge arises from the terms of their preferred genre. Unlike the damning rhetoric of Hazlitt or Bulwer or the tragic outlook of earlier period-piece drama such as *Faulkener* or *John Woodvil,* these plays treat the Stuart past in a comic mode. Their opening scenarios of Restoration cavalier corruption resolve not in the disintegration of the polity but in the rake's reform, a rerighting of the sociopolitical order that had been upended by the cross-class seduction plot. Invariably in these plays, Charles II is led to see the error of his ways and, as Hunt's gloss of *The Bride of Ludgate*'s plot suggests, good-naturedly relinquishes his libertine desires in favor of establishing social cohesion and respecting the rights of his citizens.

This portrayal of an essentially benevolent Charles II has been read as a necessity in the increasingly moral climate of the theaters. To comply, like Gay's Beggar, with the "taste of the town," even liberal playwrights deeply critical of the Stuarts' political and sexual offenses had to suppress the explicit theatrical representation of such matters.[64] The plays' recourse to a comic resolution of the rake's socialization is motivated by a drive to brand political reform as non-radical, non-revolutionary, in accordance with traditional, moderate middle-class British values. Reacting to older accounts of 1832 as a moment of unified democratic triumph, recent historians have illustrated the extent to which entrenched partisan and class interests competed for control over the terms of what social and parliamentary reform would actually entail. Above all, reform never escaped its affiliation with the dangers of French radicalism: its conservative opponents insisted that the proposed sociopolitical changes would precipitate an all-out revolution, while many advocates, including those in Lord Grey's pro-reform ministry, viewed reform not as a means of opening up the floodgates of democracy but as the only solution for shoring up ruling-class power against recent social unrest.[65] Despite the radical leanings of some of their authors, these Charles II plays dramatize reform so as to foreclose on its subversive potential, fashioning it as the comic rerighting of liberal relations between the people and public authority rather than as the new modeling of the social order.

Broadly in late Enlightenment culture, the idea of reform turned on an imbrication of the institutional and the individual; campaigns to reform the personal behavior of citizens were part and parcel of calls for more sweeping societal changes.[66] The plays rely on a similar association, imagining the possibility of institutional reform in the disciplining of the physical manifestation of state and cultural power: Charles's body. In part, they describe Charles's transformation as an effect of his exposure to the liberal ideals of the British citizens with whom he mingles. In *Nell Gwynne*, for instance, the king's rejection of libertinism begins as he is subjected to Nell's social values. Responding to Charles's sexual advances, she relates to him a dream in which she pities a "poor old soldier without any arms or legs," and the king, swayed by her sympathy, establishes an asylum for aged and disabled veterans to which flock "heaps of old soldiers . . . all with their rough faces looking so happy and contented" (27, 28–29). Here Nell identifies with the humanitarian causes, such as poor relief, that Jerrold regularly championed in his social melodramas.[67] The narration of her dream educates Charles in responsible kingship, showing him a future in which his libertine conduct—"baring" the bodies of his subjects—is transformed into liberal conduct, literally, the protection of downtrodden public bodies. In Jerrold's representation, liberal reform develops not from parliamentary edict but from the sympathetic will of the British people and its ability to rechannel the power of the privileged to socially productive ends.

The plays often represent Charles's concession to liberal ideals in markedly visceral fashion. The comic device of mistaken identity that allows the king to stage-manage his seduction plots ultimately strips him of control over his circumstances and forces him to identify with the public he exploits. As Jerrold acknowledges in his preface, *Nell Gwynne* stages the reversal of Charles's libertine fortunes by borrowing an apocryphal tale, "variously related in the Chroniques Scandaleuses of his 'merry' and selfish days," in which "the king sup[s] at a tavern with Nell, and find[s] himself without money to defray the bill" (vii).[68] Toward the middle of the final act, the tavern keeper Stockfish "make[s] prisoners" of Charles and his courtier associates, locking them in his back room for their inability to pay for the lavish meal they use to entice Nell (33). Payne adapts the same anecdotal source material in *Charles the Second.* In his rendering, Charles's lack of funds is part of a deliberate scheme orchestrated by Rochester—at the behest of the queen—to "trick [the king] into some ridiculous dilemma" and teach him a "lesson," thereby curing his libertinism (8, 13). Caught out at Captain Copp's with no money, Charles is accused of being "a barefaced, impudent swindler" and made "a prisoner" in the tavern (29–30). *The King's Word* and John Walker's *Nell Gwynne* (1830) also lead an incognito Charles to be variously robbed, incarcerated, and humiliated. In Walker's version, Charles describes these un-kingly circumstances in terms that comically allude to the fear of the democratizing effects of liberal reform: "Here's a situation for royalty—the levelling system with a vengeance."[69]

As I suggested in the previous section, the plays attend anxiously to the Stuart libertine's body—legal yet illicit—as a site of sovereign power that makes "bare" bodies out of the rights-bearing populace. In these scenes of "levelling" and imprisonment, the initial scenario of "baring" is reversed as Charles is stripped of his sovereign identity and privileges and made into a commoner and a body subject to forms of disciplinary power. Ironically, the production of Charles as a "bare" body is the effect of the comedy of mistaken identity that the king himself initiates as a tactic of his exploitative will. His revival of libertine performances—disguise, theatricality, seduction—grants him the appearance of sovereign autonomy but ends in the comic collapse of his absolutist pose into subjected body.

Containing Charles's sovereign corruption, such acts of visceral discipline catalyze his transformation to liberal subjecthood and the plays' overall production of their vision of reform. The end result of the "baring" of the king's vulnerable body is the resignation of his absolutist will. In *Nell Gwynne* and *The King's Word,* his farcical predicament leads him to a new respect for his citizens' rights of self-possession; in *Charles the Second,* it causes him to resolve to "change [his] course of life" (32). Such resolutions set the stage for the comic denouement in which the social order that was threatened by corrupt authority is restored. In *The Bride of Ludgate* and *Charles the Second,* the king facilitates the marriage of the young lovers, removing the plays' other blocking agents; in *The King's Word,* he reaffirms Kate's marriage and grants her husband a dukedom; in *Nell Gwynne,* he endorses Nell's career on the stage; in all the scenario's variants, he accepts the role of public servant, promoting the good of the nation.

The social order produced through Charles's rehabilitation conforms to the ideals of moderate middle-class—rather than revolutionary—reform. As in so many Restoration comedies and their eighteenth-century successors, the marriages that result from the taming of the rake's disruptive sexual energies consolidate a patrilinear elite power bloc by keeping property all in the family.[70] By and large, the lower classes do not stay low. Mary, in *Charles the Second*, is melodramatically ennobled at the last minute, revealed to be a relation of Rochester's, and she marries one of Charles's courtiers. Melissa and Mapleton, the protagonists of *The Bride of Ludgate*, have only been made lower class because their fortunes and estates were forfeited due to their familial connections to the parliamentarians in the English civil wars; in fostering their marriage, Charles also returns their property. The same kind of upward mobility happens for Martin, the dispossessed republican husband of Kate in *The King's Word*. As Charles reconciles partisan strife, reform bequeaths peace on the nation, but it also solidifies—in its emphasis on marriage and the resumption of inheritances—the bourgeois Whiggish value for property. Thus, while the plays pay lip service to the ordinary citizen's right to resist absolutist authority, the reforms in no way radically broaden the terms of enfranchisement. Whereas radical reformers called to abolish the propertied establishment as the hinge on which sociopolitical injustice turns, these scenarios depict reform as "safe" for the nation's propertied middle classes, an extension of representative politics that is nonetheless a non-revolutionary return to British values traditionally associated with 1688.[71]

Such scenarios treat theatrical reform as well in terms of the concerns and values of its elite middle-class proponents. This is especially apparent in Jerrold's *Nell Gwynne*. The play's final scenes are set in the "interior of the King's Theatre," where Nell has been hired by the managers Hart and Mohun to speak the prologue on the opening night of Dryden's *The Conquest of Granada* (47). The king is in attendance, having exchanged his pursuit of Nell's sexual body for the sponsorship of the "success" of her theatrical body, her career as actress (45). Whereas earlier in the play, Charles's desires are aligned with those of the commercially rapacious managers, the concluding scenes do not emphasize Nell's exploitation. Rather, his reform enables her accession to the stage, which in turn promises the return of legitimate, literary drama to the patent theaters. Prior to meeting Nell, the managers sought to replace Dryden's prologue with one designed for a fashionable highwayman: "Advertize that he will appear with the identical pistols with which he robbed the money-broker at Finchley.—Depend on't, the pistols would do more than the heroic verse" (18). Nell, however, ends the play by reciting "Dryden's syllables," forgoing the sensational spectacle that the managers had planned in favor of giving center stage to the dramatist's words (48). In the ordinary citizen's wresting of the final performance from the hands of the managers, Jerrold dramatizes the triumph of the interests of Bulwer's reform movement: the victory of public liberty over absolutist monopoly, the encouragement of dramatic authorship over theatrical spectacle.

As *Nell Gwynne* closes, however, Dryden's words are upstaged by Nell's own; she improvises the prologue's conclusion, advising her audience:

> Of good and ill all character is made;
> The good accept—the rest cast into shade. (48)

This plea refers to Jerrold's goal of rehabilitating Nell's image, but applies equally to how the plays handle the cultural memory of Restoration comedy itself. Under the influence of dramatists who "cast into shade" the radical provocations of the genre's legacy and stress its scenarios of rakish reform, the revival of something like Restoration comedy—as Mahon similarly posited—may be imagined as a "good" in the cause of liberal reform. These plays not only reflect an anxiety over the persistence of absolutist performances in modern, supposedly representative institutions but also negotiate the scenarios of Restoration comedy to reshape absolutist into liberal behavior. Thus, the social effect of these plays depends not on the disappearance of the Stuarts' political and theatrical past, but on the logic of reenactment that, as Rebecca Schneider argues, offers the hope of difference in time's recurrence. Their repetitive theatricalization of the Stuart past suggests both that that past is not over and that its reenactment may yield alternative outcomes.[72] Reenacting Charles's libertine rule not as it was but as it might have been—socialized into public responsibility as a final stage in the rake's progress—these scenarios reframe Stuart history as comedy as a way of posing possibilities for Britain's liberal future.

These playwrights, then, share with their liberal colleagues in the 1820s and early 1830s a vision of the Stuart past as a historical blot on Britain's liberal progress, one that continues to haunt the present. But whereas Bulwer worked through the official channels of legal power to resolve the incompleteness of this past, they circulate a reformist discourse whose efficacy relies on acting bodies rather than acts of Parliament. "The Stage," Nell tells Charles in Walker's play, "has more effect than public laws" in matters of reform.[73] Sounding very much like Steele in *The Spectator*, Nell's maxim recognizes the nonjuridical regulatory power of the theater, a power that these Restoration scenarios of the rake's reform harness to reproduce the ideals of non-radical reform and, importantly, to naturalize and universalize them. Rendering reform not a matter of law, but as the customary, even timeless resolution of the comic genre, these scenarios naturalize the normative values of the middle-class parliamentary and theatrical reformers as universal and desirable for all British subjects, occluding their local contingency and establishing their dominance in such a way as to discount alternative possibilities of what reform might entail. Popular repertory staples, they exemplify how dramatic performance established a middle-class hegemony that permeated both national politics and theatrical culture in the wake of 1832.[74]

While "pass[ing] as universally valid," however, according to Taylor, the real power of the scenario lies in the vagaries of its local embodiment, the flexibility of its "cultural agency" produced by a critical distance between set roles and the different social actors who may inhabit them.[75] The plays we have examined so far were all produced at the patent theaters, their authors largely sympathetic to the terms of Bulwer's reform program. In the final section of the chapter, I turn to a reading of William Thomas Moncrieff's *Rochester* (1818), a play that stages familiar Stuart libertine scenarios but to very different effect. Read as dramatic text, the play resembles the imaginative work of Jerrold, Addison, and Payne, especially in its interest in leveling a critique of the absolutist Regency state. But read as performance—its self-aware production at a minor theater with anti-authoritarian proclivities in particular—*Rochester* recuperates the libertine transgressions of its Stuart court wits to reveal how the universalist platform of liberal Reform itself is composed of a set of arbitrary and exclusionist tactics that restrict both the liberty of the political subject and the free trade of the de-monopolized theaters.

THE LIBERTINE RECLAIMED

Billed as a three-act burletta, *Rochester* was first produced on November 16, 1818, at the Olympic, a minor theater in close proximity to Drury Lane and run, at the time, by the actor-manager Robert William Elliston. Elliston starred as Rochester, his well-known status as a rakish role-icon suited to a play that the author averred to be a genealogical descendant of George Farquhar's *The Beaux' Stratagem* (1707).[76] The play met with unparalleled success; it ran for approximately eighty nights before the Olympic closed for the season in April 1819 and was revived frequently thereafter.[77] Its plot borrows from an apocryphal anecdote, included in Saint-Évremond's early "life" of Rochester, that details the sexual exploits of Rochester and Buckingham, who, banished to the countryside, set up as innkeepers and don a variety of disguises in order to seduce local women.[78] In Moncrieff's rendering, Rochester and Buckingham have been exiled from Charles II's court for refusing to marry at the king's command; they set up an inn at Newport—appropriately named "The Horns"—where they play the alternating roles of master and servant, holding nightly revels and staging a series of theatrical plots to seduce the wives and daughters of the boorish townsfolk. Their main target is the young country heiress Silvia Golden, who is simultaneously attempting to escape from her puritan guardian, Starvemouse, and to elope with her lover, Romeo

Dunstable, a provincial actor. At each turn, the libertines' plots are foiled by the Countess of Lovelaugh and Lady Gay, their would-be wives. In the end, Rochester extorts a pardon from Charles II, and all the characters return to the court.

Rochester establishes a scenario of libertine frivolity that at first conceals its political implications. As Planché and Vestris would do with *The Court Beauties* years later, Moncrieff concludes his play with a song that affiliates the Stuart past with comic escapism:

> Let some praise Norman William's days,
> The warlike and the older ones;
> While some more fond of peace may praise,
> Our old Queen Bessy's golden ones:
> We hope you'll for the laugh's sake praise,
> King Charles the Second's merry days.[79]

As David Worrall, Julia Swindells, and Katherine Newey have recognized, however, Moncrieff over the course of his long theatrical career consistently attuned his comedy to radical political ends.[80] *Rochester* is no different, its representation of Charles's "merry days" reflecting to satirical ends the not-so merry ones of Moncrieff's own. After Waterloo, postwar economic distress and renewed campaigns for parliamentary reform had generated agitation among the working and middle classes. Lord Liverpool's ministry responded with reactionary measures—the "Gagging Acts"—intended to stifle oppositional ferment, including a ban on seditious meetings and a suspension of habeas corpus that led to a number of unwarranted arrests. The suspension was lifted in early 1818, but reform proponents kept alive the memory of the state's violations of British civil rights. By the time *Rochester* debuted, the nation was beginning to witness a second wave of radical activity.[81]

The very moments produced seemingly for "the laugh's sake" are when *Rochester* levels its critique of the Regency state's oppressions. The play contains frequent scenes of illegal imprisonment that allude to Liverpool's persecutions, most of which arise from the mistaken identities generated by the libertines' theatrical antics. After Rochester is discovered impersonating the parish beadle Squeak as part of an attempt to kidnap Silvia, he convinces Buckingham to switch roles with him. Newport's perpetually befuddled mayor Muddle and his constables promptly arrive at the inn and arrest the duke in his place. Buckingham's attempts to convince the officials of their error—"Confusion! I tell you I am not the man"—are ignored; the mayor determines his fate without evidence or trial: "Away with him [Buckingham]; gag him, bind him, harden him" (32–33). As the duke is stripped arbitrarily of his verbal and bodily liberty, he represents the stereotypical victim of the Gagging Acts. The mayor defends his action as a "decisive extermination of justice," warning Buckingham that "the law knows no extinction of personages" (31). His mistake of "execution" for "extermination" insinuates that justice itself has been countermanded in this wrongful arrest. Moreover, presumably substituting "extinction" for "distinction" of personages, Muddle exposes the sweeping indifference of the Regency state's reactionary policies. Questions of evidence and identity, guilt and innocence, are laid aside as one person is as good as the next in the state's push to imprison agitators. Reviving a Restoration scenario of comic intrigue in which indistinguishability is the driving force, the play uses this form as political satire: allowing for indiscriminate arrests, the Gagging Acts have made an intrigue comedy of real life, in which mistakes of identity perpetuate unconstitutional policies.

Muddle's assertion that identity is extinguishable comments further on the consequences of the ministry's alarmism. Though the majority of English radicals pressed peacefully for constitutional change, many Members of Parliament exaggerated the country's unrest and were quick to label the reformers as insurrectionists looking to demolish the monarchy in a French-style revolution. In a speech before the House of Lords, Lord Sidmouth argued that "a traitorous conspiracy has been formed in the metropolis for the purpose of overthrowing, by means of a general insurrection, the established Government, laws, and Constitution of this kingdom."[82] Moncrieff portrays Muddle as taking similar liberties in arbitrarily redefining the identities of the other characters. In act 3, he arrests Dunstable and Silvia as they abscond from Starvemouse's house:

> MUDDLE: Sieze them, the traitorous benefactors!—emancipate them!—bring them along!
>
> DUNSTABLE: Zounds, rascals, what are you at? Unhand me slaves; or by the bright heavens— . . .
>
> MUDDLE: Here's an incendiary—oh, that we had some of the malicious officers of the next town at hand; but I'll make a pattern of him—Barnacle him with the handcuffs there—I'll make an abominable restitution of him—away there—barnacle him, I say.
>
> SILVIA: Mercy! mercy! your worship—indeed we have done no mischief.
>
> MUDDLE: Not yet, but you may. (51)

The mayor's language parodies the public responses of conservative ministers such as Sidmouth, branding the innocent Dunstable and Silvia traitorous incendiaries. His dismissive acknowledgment that the lovers have committed no crime but might do so in the future is a satirical jab at the ministry's paranoia in 1817, its eagerness to see conspiracies everywhere and to preemptively strike out at the radical reform movement.

In the end, *Rochester* makes all of this laughable. If Muddle is the play's agent of state authority, he is a bumbling one at best. As he orders his constabulary to arrest Dunstable and Silvia, he invokes habeas corpus: "Whoever falls on their habeas corpusses, may appropriate them at their own penalty in the watch-house, under peril and authority of the King's Majesty, like a loyal and most deficient subject" (51). As before, Muddle's malapropisms touch on some truth, as he collapses any distinction between the "loyal" and the "deficient" public servant. In his loyalty to "the King's Majesty" and to law and order in Newport, he is a "deficient subject" as he unjustly infringes on the liberties of his fellow citizens. It is not clear whether Muddle actually understands what habeas corpus signifies, but allusions to such hot-button topics usually incurred the ire of the Lord Chamberlain's censors. The fact that the reference was not excised indicates *Rochester*'s facility in masking its political overtones under comedic guise. Libertine laughter is protective and subversive. As Muddle gets so much wrong, the play reveals the ridiculous fallibility of the state, mocking the ministry's hunt for revolutionaries as simply the blundering of incompetent authority while simultaneously raising audience awareness of the dangers to civil liberties that such incompetence promotes.

Reversing the scenarios of the other plays we have examined, *Rochester* appropriates rather than rejects the libertine theatricality of the Stuart court, revealing its participation in a genealogy of performances in which, as James Turner notes, "sexually charged carnival (masquerading as innocent merriment) was used to protest abuses in power in all the theatres of authority."[83] Undoubtedly, Rochester and Buckingham's sexual adventuring is coded as illicit. In the first act, after Rochester has exempted his male patrons from paying for their drinks, he asks his manservant to produce his "bill of fare for the day," that is, the "bill of the fair of Newport," a list of potential sexual targets (4). His generosity is a lure by which to dupe the townsmen into forgetting to look after their wives and daughters. As the name of the inn the libertines run ("The Horns") suggests, it is an establishment that allows them to pillage their clientele sexually, linking them to characters such as Muddle who abuse their role as public servants. But overall, the play's interest lies more in using the libertines' theatrical pursuit of seduction to expose abuses of the subject's rights rather than to stand in for such abuses.

This interest is emphasized in Moncrieff's singular commitment to keeping his Rochester unreformed and unrepentant at the end of the play. Moncrieff's rationale for avoiding the reform plot of his liberal playwright colleagues emerges in the preface to the 1825 edition of *Rochester*, a largely flippant rebuttal to the censures of James Plumptre, an Anglican clergyman and moralistic stage reformer. Answering Plumptre's complaints that "the Earl and his profligacy are held up as a subject of good humour and complacency" and to his suggestion that "he who shall dramatise his *Death*, shall do him and the world a kindness," Moncrieff argues that "playing a *reformed* Rochester" would fail in the London theaters.[84] Moreover, he proceeds to imply, scenarios of reform are yet another tactic by which the ministry imposes its absolutist will on the populace. As an example, Moncrieff cites the case of the once "irreverend" George Colman the Younger, "the erewhile sinful George" who had, in 1824, succeeded John Larpent as Examiner of Plays. Colman, he claims, has forsaken his early career as a bawdy playwright and turned religious "convert": "The new light . . . has broken in upon him; since he has obtained a place, he is of the elect, and tacked to the tail of the Court."[85] A "rake reformed" scenario, Colman's career illustrates that scenario to mask a merely self-interested capitulation to a state power that will continue to censor or "gag" its subjects (political and theatrical) indiscriminately.

In Moncrieff's embrace of the unreformed libertine, he presents himself as the reverse of the hypocritical "Saint George the Younger": "the free author of this same 'Rochester'—the naughty deviser of 'Don Giovanni'—the desperate perpetrator of 'Tom and Jerry.'"[86] The catalogue playfully juxtaposes *Rochester* with two of Moncrieff's other works—the burletta afterpiece *Giovanni in London; or, The Libertine Reclaimed* (1817) and *Tom and Jerry; or, Life in London* (1821)—both of which proved to be incredibly popular but were also vilified for their licentiousness.[87] For Moncrieff, however, it is exactly these sorts of productions that make for a "free author." Whereas Colman appears a slave to the court, Moncrieff equates liberty with libertinism and with his authorial ability to resist the moral and theatrical impositions of the state's censors. During much of its opening run, *Rochester* was played with *Giovanni in London*, a burlesque continuation of the Don Juan legend in which the libertine hero returns from hell to cause havoc in nineteenth-century London and, notably, is not punished for his new offenses. As David Worrall observes, *Giovanni in London* bears affinities with the Cockney School and its "mixture of libertinism and radical politics," inverting Shadwell's "libertine destroyed" scenario and reclaiming the figure instead for a radical agenda.[88] The double billing is significant as it promotes two versions of rakish reclamation. Whereas *Giovanni in London* quite literally revives the corpse of the libertine, *Rochester* does so metaphorically, recuperating Stuart rakishness in making it emblematic of the liberty of the subject opposed to the repressive hand of the state.

Moncrieff's suspicion of reform's ultimate betrayal of the principles of freedom that it was supposed to protect extends to the liberal reform movement of the London stages to which he at least nominally belonged. In 1832, he testified in front of Bulwer's Select Committee on Dramatic Literature in favor of reforming the stage. Over the course of his long career working for the minor playhouses—over two hundred plays, by his own count—his was a notable voice in the argument for dramatic free trade against the exclusionary practices that the patent monopolies had instituted.[89] But if Moncrieff agreed in theory with the movement's desire to overhaul the theatrical institution, he differs from his colleagues in seeing the practical consequences of liberal reform as detrimental to the creation of a genuine theatrical commons that might envelop all forms and classes of dramatic production. Moncrieff's most innovative contribution to theatrical reform comes in his persistent radicalism, his misgivings about how the liberals subtly revive the Stuart-esque authoritarianism they purport to resist.

Moncrieff's stance first becomes clear in his involvement in the 1832 meetings that would eventually lead to the formation of the Select Committee. During a meeting on February 25, the "cause of the Minor Theatres," *The Morning Chronicle* reports, was quickly superseded by the "cause of dramatic literature"; the reformers' recurrent argument became that the state of the drama was "mutilated and crippled" by the degradations of the patents and the consequent lowness of the minors, that "the genius of English [dramatic] authors [was] in this age degenerate," and that what was required was for the minor theaters to wrest back the rights to older legitimate drama in order not only to reform the monopoly but also to revitalize the production of literary works of original genius such as those of Shakespeare.[90] Present, Moncrieff recognized in this turn a devaluation of writers for the minor stages such as himself who had built careers on such successful, if technically illegitimate, productions as *Giovanni in London* and *Rochester*. "The proper course for the minor Theatres would be, to assert their rights," he argued in rebuttal, "to give the best support they could to the production of new pieces. . . . There was no dearth of dramatic talent. The Olympic and the Adelphi were remarkable instances of the success of what might be expected from the Theatres confining themselves to the class of performance suited to their peculiar circumstances."[91] Refusing to concede to the narrative of dramatic decline and suggesting that "dramatic talent" does not conform to the literary elitism of Bulwer and his compatriots, he suggests the minor theaters to be capable of high dramatic standards without having to fall back on Shakespeare. His objections were quickly dismissed by Serle, who persisted in demanding that the minor theaters needed access to the national drama of Britain's past if they were to recover dramatic literature from degeneration.

Moncrieff recycled this argument when he testified in front of the Select Committee. Many of his statements repeat familiar reformist demands: dramatic free trade and protection of authors' rights from unscrupulous managers and publishers. But on the question of abolishing monopoly, he again veers significantly from the liberal script: "Let the great houses have the privilege of representing Shakespeare and Massinger. . . . I think it is for the benefit of the drama that the theatres royal should have the exclusive privilege of playing pieces that have descended down to this period. . . . But at the same time I give them the exclusive privilege of playing those pieces, I would restrict them from performing those monstrosities they have been playing."[92] Abolishing the patents' "privilege" to older spoken drama is not the issue. Moncrieff insists rather on a theatrical balance in which the patent stages would give up the "monstrosities" of illegitimate spectacle, a kind of restoration to their original purpose as protectors of the national dramatic heritage. At the same time, the minor theaters need not cling to older literary drama to thrive, but they should be legally allowed the freedom to compete for any new drama they might desire, legitimate or otherwise: "If the minor theatres can get the legitimate drama written, and they find it worth their while, I should say it would be better to allow them to perform it. . . . Let the minor theatres play any piece they can get written for them; if they can start a Shakespeare, in Heaven's name let them do it."[93] For Moncrieff, access to old Shakespeares is not obligatory for the minors' success; new ones may crop up if constraints on spoken drama were to be lifted. Citing the Olympic as a pattern of success, he argues that "those theatres which confined themselves to the peculiar class of pieces which seemed to be natural to their house, have always made money."[94] Theatrical prosperity does not necessarily correspond to the standards of literary achievement espoused by his pro-reform colleagues.

Emerging collectively from Moncrieff's contributions to the 1830s debates is an implicit opposition to the liberal reformers who would use the rhetoric of the death of drama in the promotion of their cause. As in the preface to *Rochester*, reform is suspect as it obscures self-interested ideologies that the elite literary bourgeois would impose on the theatrical field. Moncrieff critiques the liberal agenda of Bulwer as erecting a set of restrictive borders between the high and the low, the elite and the popular, in essence acting the part of sovereign absolutist that they would foist onto the patent managers as they seek to rule London's theatrical scene solely on the basis of their self-constructed definition of literary drama. In contrast, in his preface to his comedy *Reform* (1831), Moncrieff imagines a theatrical field of impressive openness, one that even borders on chaotic freedom: "The drama should be one free and equal arena, in which genius of every grade and class might strive for the mastery."[95] Dramatic genius is here not confined to a certain "class" of production. Refusing the liberal elitism that grants sovereign privileges only to certain forms of theater, Moncrieff rehearses a vision of dramatic liberty that defends the national drama and takes up a more inclusive view of what such a term may describe.

Fourteen years earlier, *Rochester* reclaims its Restoration libertine heroes in a similar ideological defense of a radical version of free trade for the minor theaters. It engages in these debates with meta-theatrical play, rendering in its ontic register the commitment to the dramatic openness of Elliston's Olympic theater. A "main nice house" that offers a "good bill of fare, and rational entertainment," the inn represents the Olympic, its libertine landlord (played by Elliston) a stand-in for the manager (1–2). Over the summer of 1818, Elliston had renovated the theater, pouring significant funds into improving the space and the company, with the aim of "attracting the *beau monde*" to "a theatre previously considered 'low.'"[96] *Rochester* was the "bill of fare" on the night of the theater's reopening in November, and Elliston's real-life duty as manager was purposely blurred with his mimetic role. As Moncrieff's prologue suggests, the play's self-proclaimed status as "rational entertainment" is a competitive dig at the patent theaters, whose recently expanded spaces began to house extravagant and foreign entertainments at the expense of British drama:

> However vast, magnificent, and grand,
> Uprise the scenic structures of our land;
> What do their pomp and space avail, if there
> The Drama's followers in vain repair;
> If there, those arts which all our cares have charmed,
> Be most subverted, or be unperformed;
> If English sentiment must quit the field,
> And to the Melo trash of Gallia yield;
> While all the Drama's laws unnoticed go,
> And *Sense* is sacrificed to sound and show.[97]

Opposed to the "huge space," "gaudy show," and "empty noise" of Drury Lane and Covent Garden, Elliston's tastefully renovated minor theater was marketed as a haven for "infant merit" and "veteran talent" in dramatic production, a "little" space where theatrical traditions may be preserved and the "rights" of audiences and authors protected.[98]

Critics recognized that, with *Rochester*, the Olympic audaciously proclaimed itself a venue for traditional drama with a genealogical link to legitimate Restoration comedy, an assault on the very heart of monopoly. George Daniel went so far as to suggest that the play was "remarkable for being the first regular drama produced at a minor theatre, without an accompanying tinkle on the piano."[99] Moncrieff further informs us in his 1825 preface that "all the fashion, and nearly all the population of London, were attracted by *Rochester* to a Theatre previously almost wholly unknown and unattended."[100] If in *Giovanni in London*'s urban libertine antics, Moncrieff announced his radical politics, the choice for an accompanying mainpiece of a genteel historical comedy set in the Restoration signals the Olympic's ambitions to compete with the patents for a more fashionable audience and literary repertoire.[101] But it is the fact that the Olympic would pair *Giovanni in London* and *Rochester* that suggests its establishment as a site of the open, non-hierarchical mingling of dramatic classes and audiences that Moncrieff would come to champion later. This is again registered in *Rochester*'s play between ontic and mimetic registers as the libertine-managers' "house" becomes a site of liberality for theatergoers. At the close of act 2, the cast gathers for a banquet at the inn, and in unison they sing a metatheatrical welcome to the audience to the refurbished Olympic:

> Come haste to our house warming,
> Lads gay, and lasses charming,
> And do whate'er you will;
> For if you gold could eat here,
> You'd freely with it meet here,
> And eat and drink your fill,
> But still between each blythe carouse,
> We'll drink success to our new house. (45)

The libertines' festive "house" is a place of liberty where guests may do "whate'er [they] will," where the individual's will is not coerced as it is in the play's scenes of suspended habeas corpus or under the rule of censorship.

That *Rochester*'s performance in 1818 extends a self-referential comment on the Olympic specifically and on the intellectual scene of theater reform broadly is indicated not only in the analogy of inn/house and rake/manager, but also in the play's reliance on the scenarios of the Restoration libertine. Rochester and Buckingham's penchant for disguising their true identities is similar to the situation of the Olympic. Staging an anecdotal account of upper-class Restoration rakes slumming it incognito as publicans in the provinces suggests that the Olympic's appropriation of a traditional dramatic heritage needed to be surreptitious, hidden under the "low" reputation historically attached to the minor theaters. Restoration rakishness—its play of bodies engaging in disguise and its behavioral blurring of high and low, refined and abject—is here repurposed as an act of radical brinksmanship, symbolic of the Olympic's defiance of the legal constraints brought on by the patents' monopoly on "regular" drama. The play solicits identification with the minor theater's libertine self-willed theatricality, presenting in its protagonists' behavior a saturnalian response to the censoring tactics of the state, a celebratory disorder that is not violently transgressive but that is nonetheless freeing in positing an inclusive theatrical field.

If the anti-authoritarian activities of the exiled Rochester and Buckingham signal the possibilities for the license of illegitimate theater (similarly cut off from the beneficence of Charles II in operating outside of, but still defined by the terms of, his monopoly), it is fitting that the rakes' rival for the affections of Silvia is the "strolling player" Dunstable (*Rochester*, 5). An impoverished but professional working-class actor who makes his livelihood in the provincial vicinity of the minor theaters, Dunstable possesses no courtly connections, suggesting his symbolic dissociation from the patents. But his frequent quotations from Shakespeare and his first name (Romeo) render him an heir to legitimate British drama. Dunstable spends most of the play trying to free Silvia from Starvemouse, but the only disguise he wears in doing so is that of a "beggar," a role that more reveals his true self than hides it (14). He is thus linked to the fallen state of the national drama, as reformers saw it: beggared and banished from the patent theaters.

In drawing these meta-theatrical analogies, *Rochester* not only registers the cultural concerns over theatrical liberty that would intensify in the two decades following the play's premiere, but also mobilizes an imaginative solution to the state of the nation's stages, forgoing the reform of the Restoration aristocratic libertine in favor of a radically inclusive reordering of the theatrical establishment indebted to the Restoration rake's revived tactics. At the end of the play, as Rochester and Buckingham's plots fail to come to fruition, they grow weary of Newport and seek a way back into Charles II's good graces. Catching the king on one of his "incognito" rambles through the village, Rochester dons a mountebank disguise and slips him an opiate in order to get him to the inn (53). Once there, Rochester and Buckingham—dressed again as the landlords—try to extort a pardon. When Charles refuses, they accuse him of being an "imposter" with "a plan to rob the house" (58). Declaring that Charles is in on a "plot against [their] lives," Rochester simulates Muddle's earlier paranoid tactics, ordering the servants to bind and gag the king as a dangerous radical: "Away with him to the cellar, lock him up; away with him—don't hear a word" (58). Though wary of being accomplices to "high treason," the servants obey, and as Charles is led out, he calls Rochester and Buckingham "traitors" and threatens, "scoundrels, I'll hang you" (59). In this climactic scene, Moncrieff revisits the play's earlier suspensions of habeas corpus but with the roles reversed, in that the figure of the state is exposed to the arbitrary will of his subjects. In effect, Rochester and Buckingham are, like Muddle, "loyal" yet "most deficient" servants to the king. They bear no actual treasonous designs, yet they are "deficient" in enacting the desire of the subject in terms of the will of the monarch, parodying the sovereign state's tactics of coercion as a form of radical resistance to Charles's edicts.

Having set up the analogy of the libertines to the minor theaters, however, *Rochester* does not push their resistance to established authority beyond bounds, producing instead a nonviolent resolution that is yet radical in its refusal to harmonize with the normative middle-class values reflected in the later period pieces. Immediately deflating any real political threat, Rochester laughs off their treatment of Charles, playing on the cultural memory of the king's clemency: "Ha! ha! ha! I know my Royal master's disposition well. Shall I fear his resentment? Charles is the essence of wit and good humor combined. . . . We shall gain our pardons, and though he may be angry at first, he'll laugh at the joke bye and bye" (59). The play supports his prediction; once the mistaken identities are clarified, Charles indeed pardons his courtiers under the condition that their ladies serve as "pledges of [their] future conduct" (62). Rochester's agreeing to these terms constitutes not so much his reform as it does his surrender to expediency. The libertines' sovereign privileges and theatrical licentiousness do not ultimately threaten the liberty of the subject as they do in the 1830s comedies but rather allow the subject, in imitating the will of the sovereign, to have his desires fulfilled: their return to status in Charles's court. Moncrieff, true to his word in the preface, keeps Rochester unrepentant. In refusing to admonish its hero's theatrical tricks in the guises of the lower classes (indeed, it is that "low" theatricality that procures him his return to status), *Rochester* suggests that illegitimate theater is only illegitimate when used for illicit purposes. Opposed to the liberal reformers' distrust of "low" theatricality and disorder in the patents and the minors, Moncrieff's play extends the possibility that popular forms of performance—like the farces and pantomimes that Rochester and Buckingham enact in their exile and that the minor theaters such as the Olympic meld with the spoken drama—possess the same capacities as "higher" forms of drama to benefit the British public and its traditions, thus disentangling the reformist cause from any necessary correlation to the elevation of dramatic literature.

In the end, then, *Rochester* does not call for the reform of Restoration libertine comedy but uses a revived version of it in which Charles II may act as rightful theatrical governor, providing an order to the stage that at once restores old traditions of Britain's dramatic heritage yet expands that heritage's sociocultural constitution. Charles's last act in the play is a restructuring of the theatrical system in favor of not only Rochester and Buckingham's accession to the court, but also that of Dunstable. "Be it so," Charles declares with reference to Silvia and Dunstable, "I take them into my favour—he shall belong to my establishment—it shall be so!" (62). Advanced to legitimacy, Dunstable's fate represents the imagined hopeful return of the national drama from its state of beggary to a state of respectability at the center of Britain's culture.

But, importantly, the restoration performed here is not an act of conservative nostalgia that reestablishes a rearguard order but an act of making a new future through an imaginative revival of the past. As Moncrieff would later advocate with regard to the British stage, Charles's authority embraces all "classes" of theater in a cohesive whole, accepting "lower" and "higher" theatrical entertainments as part of the same order without necessarily signaling a hierarchical relationship between them: Rochester, Buckingham, and Dunstable (and the varieties of theater they represent) are all part of Charles's "establishment." Reclaiming the Restoration libertine's theatrical scenarios in this way allows *Rochester* to emphasize the regenerative and forward-looking possibilities of reenacting a past that, for other reformers, only haunts the present as a demon of political corruption. Charles's inclusion of all of Newport's "actors" into his "establishment" institutes a theatrical order that refuses to subjugate the radical freedom of different values and ideologies. Moncrieff's success at Elliston's Olympic in 1818—his ability to attract the fashionably genteel and the Cockney lower classes with his mix of "low" theater such as *Giovanni in London* and "regular" drama such as *Rochester*—indicates a kind of radical stage reform that at once resists the shoring up of theatrical hierarchy endemic to the authoritarians of patent monopoly and to their liberal opponents alike, while furthermore disclosing this indistinction between them. As Charles's nondiscriminatory "establishment" is promised within the play's mimetic register, the Olympic is transformed into a site of theatrical free trade that is at once liberal in its openness to difference yet still chaotic in its mixing of classes, tastes, and personalities. As it fluctuates between a space of gentility, lowness, literary drama, performative entertainment, the Restoration past, and the Romantic present, the Olympic serves, for Moncrieff, as a memorial to what reformed theater might look like, a space that cultivates a legitimate theatrical culture not by purging the old but by appropriating and adapting old scenarios to new ends.

CONCLUSION

ULTIMATELY FAILING TO PASS in the House of Lords in 1833, the Select Committee's bill for the deregulation of the national theaters would have to wait another decade before coming to fruition. It was not until the Theatre Regulation Act of 1843 that the patent monopoly was legally broken. This legislation, however, produced neither Bulwer's elite aspirations for drama as a literary and intellectual enterprise nor the emergence of Moncrieff's vision of a hybrid commons of theatrical production, but an overwhelming commercialization of the stage in the spread of bourgeois mass culture.[1] Post-Reform Britain, then, marks one possible resting place within, if not a definitive conclusion to, the long-running Restoration. In the 1843 collapse of monopoly, Charles II's sovereign prerogative over the theater—a prominent site, as we have seen, in which Stuart rule haunts its Hanoverian successors—ends. Restoration period pieces continued to be written and staged in the later nineteenth century—witness George Alexander McFarren's operatic *King Charles II* (1849) and Gilbert Arthur à Beckett's *Charles II, or Something like History* (1872)—but they possess little of the political edge manifested collectively in the spate of post-Waterloo Charles II comedies. Moreover, with the dominance of bourgeois propriety in the spaces of theatrical entertainment, it is as if the radical draw of the libertine—traditional puncturer of middle-class values—was also curtailed. Though, as Oscar Wilde's 1890s reinvention of the comedy of manners (with its elitist posturing, verbal wit, sexual transgressions, and impatience with bourgeois-capitalist pretensions) suggests, such endings are never final.

"The power of seeing through performance," Diana Taylor writes, "is the recognition that we've seen it all before—the fantasies that shape our sense of self, of community, that organize our scenarios of interaction, conflict, and resolution."[2] Restoration libertine drama offered writers and performers after 1688 with an abundance of such fantasies. In its particular definition of the long-running Restoration, this book has specifically traced one of them: the role of the sovereign Stuart dramatic rake in the development and contestation of the liberal, often Whiggish discourse of the liberty of the British subject. Restoration libertine drama was not monolithic in form at the time of its origin, and it similarly did not persist in the eighteenth-century imaginary in one guise only. Rather than define the rake solely as tyrannical absolutist, elitist aristocrat wit, or radical libertarian, I have argued that his performances more often than not collapse such competing subject positions together, offering a tool or a mode in a series of cultural and political debates over the nature of liberty and its basis in the sovereign desire of the individual. As my examples have suggested throughout, in the spaces of sovereign desire marked by the reappearance of Restoration dramatic poses and scenarios—on the stage, in literature, and in political argumentation—emerge a set of debates in which postrevolutionary claims about the powers and limits of the freeborn subject, liberal institutions, and forms of social governance were played out. Moreover, as the poses and scenarios of Restoration libertine drama, with its complex representations of liberty and absolutism, persist in the moments of its supposed cultural obsolescence—Collier's and Rowe's suspicion of the rake as leveler, Steele's attack on Dorimant, Garrick's midcentury moralizing of the stage, the disappearance of the rake's drama from the repertory in the nineteenth century—they reveal a history of the liberal subject predicated on the perpetual if sporadic revival of, not the chronological or ideological distancing from, the sovereign self's will to power.

Furthermore, my readings of the eighteenth-century adoption and adaptation of the figures, poses, and scenarios of the Restoration stage libertine offer a theoretical understanding of corpsing as a driving force in the historical process. In the specific stage bloopers that afflicted early productions of *The Fair Penitent* (which I discuss in the introduction and chapter 1), corpsing signifies the ontic unruliness of Lothario's body, its potential to betray its mimetically dead status and challenge the authority of the script. The scriptedness of standard post-1688 literary and theatrical histories of Restoration libertine drama, I suggest, comes similarly under threat when faced with evidence of how the bodily behavior of the Stuart rake materializes in the period. Onstage corpsing generates unease and a breakdown of theatrical illusion (and of the order predicated on that illusion) in the failure of a copy (actor) to conform to an ideal original (script). To think of history as inclusive of moments of corpsing is to take seriously how the messiness of time—the unavoidable reappearances of actions and actors thought to be "over" and thus to fail to fit within historical meaning—affords the opportunity to see around and beyond the order imposed by the illusion of historical straightforwardness. Abstracted in this way, from an individual action to a historiographical idea, corpsing reflects the fundamental power of history grounded in performance. The literal and metaphorical moments of corpsing that I have charted (often attached to figures, such as Dennis or Boswell, considered behind the times) unsettle the borders that our usual histories draw using the obsolescence of Restoration libertine drama and all that it signifies. The long-running Restoration—as a period organized around reappearance, revival, and reenactment rather than linearity, progress, and disappearance—asks us not only to reflect on a major facet of eighteenth-century theater history but also to embrace self-reflexivity in how we perform the work of literary and theatrical history ourselves.

I conclude here with one last, very short anecdote about the Restoration's libertine king himself. Allegedly, Charles II's last words on his deathbed are supposed to have been an apology to his court for having taken such an unconscionable time in dying. It has been the aim of *Lothario's Corpse* to show that, figuratively, the death of the sovereign Restoration libertine took a very long time indeed and is, perhaps, still ongoing.

ACKNOWLEDGMENTS

The first half of chapter 2 appeared, in slightly altered form, in *Modern Philology* 112, no. 2 (2014): 358–380 as "The Rake's Revival: Steele, Dennis, and the Early Eighteenth-Century Repertory." Parts of the introduction appeared in *Restoration* 40, no. 2 (2016): 83–89 as "On Getting over the Restoration." I am thankful to the editors of these journals for their permission to reprint this material.

My efforts on this book have been long-running, but so too—I am happy to say—have been the care and support of the many people I wish to thank here. Joseph Roach, Misty Anderson, and Elliott Visconsi, who were and still are energizing mentors, belong at the very top of this list. The intellectual inspiration they continue to provide me is matched only by their unflagging dedication in promoting all my academic pursuits. As model teachers and scholars, they are incomparable.

I have been fortunate in the institutional support I have received for this project. A series of grants from the Research Foundation of CUNY supplied me with both time and funding in the early stages. An enjoyable two-month joint fellowship at the Lewis Walpole Library and the Beinecke Rare Book and Manuscript Library was crucial in moving the book from draft to final product. In particular, I would like to thank Nicole Bouché, Cindy Roman, Sue Walker, and the entire staff at the Lewis Walpole Library for their generosity and expert advice. Thanks also to the editorial staff and my anonymous readers at Bucknell University Press for their aid in bringing this project to publication.

It is no exaggeration to say that I would not be where I am today without the Yale Boswell Editions. As a junior Warnock Fellow and ever since, I have been happily indebted to Nadine Honigberg for her warm friendship and to James Caudle for teaching me how to think and research like a historian. I am forever grateful to Gordon Turnbull for his guidance and his faith in my work.

I have also been fortunate to benefit from the expertise and encouragement of an amazing set of colleagues and friends in the field, especially Ala Alryyes, Emily Anderson, Thomas Bonnell, Jill Campbell, James Carson, Al Coppola, Jenny Davidson, Molly Farrell, Julia Fawcett, Evan Gottlieb, Andrew Heisel, Elizabeth Kraft, Katie Mannheimer, Jean Marsden, Hilary Menges, Melina Moe, Daniel

O'Quinn, David Quint, Claude Rawson, Stuart Sherman, Kristina Straub, Alan Vardy, and Brett Wilson. For carefully reading parts of this book in draft, I am especially grateful to Lisa Freeman, Michael Gavin, James Horowitz, Kathy Lubey, Laura Rosenthal, and Jason Shaffer.

My colleagues, former and current, in the English Department at The City College of New York have constituted a stimulating community for intellectual exchange and sociability. I owe much to Lindsay Goss, Robert Higney, Kristina Huang, Yana Joseph, Václav Paris, Michelle Valladares, Harold Veeser, and Fuson Wang. Very special thanks go to Mikhal Dekel, András Kiséry, and Elizabeth Mazzola, without whom, quite literally, this book would never have been completed.

My thanks to the following two people belong in a category all their own. Matthew Vernon has read every word of this book, probably twice. A friend and intellectual companion I cannot do without, he has always believed in the importance of my work, even in the moments when I could not. Deborah Laycock, of course, has been reading my writing for as long as I can remember. She inspired my initial fascination with Restoration drama, taught me what it means to be a good teacher, and, as a friend and mentor, continues to offer me more than I can put into words. All that I have accomplished here is due to her.

I want to thank my parents, Linda and Waino Gustafson, for a lifetime of support and patience, especially in moments when the road has gotten difficult. Finally, this book is dedicated to Serena Klempin, who has made the journey to its completion not only possible, but also worthwhile, and whose love sustains me every day.

NOTES

NOTES TO INTRODUCTION

1. *New Monthly Magazine and Literary Journal*, vol. 20 (London, 1827), 480.
2. *The Times*, February 25, 1813. For similar reviews, see *The Morning Post*, December 10, 1811, January 12 and 29, 1813, and February 25, 1813. For a narrative account of Coates's death scene performances, see John Robinson and Hunter Robinson, *The Life of Robert Coates* (London, 1891).
3. The theater as a site and a mode of both enacting and contesting the governance of the body public has been a preoccupation of eighteenth-century scholarship for some time; see Paula Backscheider, *Spectacular Politics: Theatrical Power and Mass Culture in Early Modern England* (Baltimore, Md.: Johns Hopkins University Press, 1993); Daniel O'Quinn, *Staging Governance: Theatrical Imperialism in London, 1770–1800* (Baltimore, Md.: Johns Hopkins University Press, 2005); Elizabeth Maddock Dillon, *New World Drama: The Performative Commons in the Atlantic World, 1649–1849* (Durham, N.C.: Duke University Press, 2014); and Lisa Freeman, *Antitheatricality and the Body Public* (Philadelphia: University of Pennsylvania Press, 2017). I return more fully in chapter 1 to Lothario's death in relation to social regulation.
4. Samuel Johnson, *The Lives of the Most Eminent English Poets; with Critical Observations on Their Works*, ed. Roger Lonsdale, 4 vols. (Oxford: Clarendon Press, 2006), 2:200. Richardson himself emphasizes the similarity of Lovelace to Lothario in the novel; see *Clarissa; or, The History of a Young Lady*, ed. Angus Ross (New York: Penguin, 2004), 1205.
5. "Libertine offensive" is Maximillian Novak's term in "Margery Pinchwife's 'London Disease': Restoration Comedy and the Libertine Offensive of the 1670s," *Studies in the Literary Imagination* 10 (1977): 1–23. Further scholarship that analyzes libertine drama across these periods includes Thomas H. Fujimura, *The Restoration Comedy of Wit* (Princeton, N.J.: Princeton University Press, 1952); John Traugott, "The Rake's Progress from Court to Comedy," *Studies in English Literature* 6 (1966): 381–407; Virginia Ogden Birdsall, *Wild Civility: The English Comic Spirit on the Restoration Stage* (Bloomington: Indiana University Press, 1970); Robert Jordan, "The Extravagant Rake in Restoration Comedy," in *Restoration Literature: Critical Approaches*, ed. Harold Love (London: Methuen, 1972), 69–90; Laura Brown, *English Dramatic Form, 1660–1760: An Essay in Generic History* (New Haven, Conn.: Yale University Press, 1981); Robert D. Hume, *The Rakish Stage: Studies in English Drama, 1660–1800* (Carbondale: Southern Illinois University Press, 1983); Michael Neill, "Heroic Heads and Humble Tails: Sex, Politics, and the Restoration Comic Rake," *The Eighteenth Century: Theory and Interpretation* 24 (1983): 115–139; Harold Weber, *The Restoration Rake-Hero: Transformations in Sexual Understanding in Seventeenth-Century England* (Madison: University of Wisconsin Press, 1986); Robert Markley, *Two-Edg'd Weapons: Style and Ideology in the Comedies of Etherege, Wycherley, and Congreve* (Oxford: Clarendon Press, 1988); Richard Braverman, *Plots and Counterplots: Sexual Politics and the Body Politic in English Literature, 1660–1730* (Cambridge: Cambridge University Press, 1993); Susan J. Owen, *Restoration Theatre and Crisis*

(Oxford: Clarendon Press, 1996); Derek Hughes, *English Drama, 1660–1700* (Oxford: Clarendon Press, 1996); J. Douglas Canfield, *Tricksters and Estates: On the Ideology of Restoration Comedy* (Lexington: University Press of Kentucky, 1997); Jeremy Webster, *Performing Libertinism in Charles II's Court: Politics, Drama, Sexuality* (New York: Palgrave, 2005); and Laura Rosenthal, "'All Injury's Forgot': Restoration Sex Comedy and National Amnesia," *Comparative Drama* 42 (2008): 7–28.

6. B. A. Kachur, *Etherege and Wycherley* (New York: Palgrave, 2004), 12.
7. Thomas Shadwell, *The Libertine*, in *Four Restoration Libertine Plays*, ed. Deborah Payne Fisk (Oxford: Oxford University Press, 2005), 55.
8. On the "long" Restoration, see Corrinne Harol, "1688: Literature, Politics, and the Long Restoration," *Restoration* 39 (2015): 5–16, and the essays in Blair Hoxby and Ann Baynes Coiro, eds., *Milton in the Long Restoration* (Oxford: Oxford University Press, 2016). Joseph Roach and Elizabeth Kraft have stretched the length of the Restoration even further in their studies of the period's impact in twentieth-century mass culture; see Roach, *It* (Ann Arbor: University of Michigan Press, 2007), and Kraft, *Restoration Stage Comedies and Hollywood Remarriage Films: In Conversation with Stanley Cavell* (New York: Routledge, 2017). I am deeply indebted to Joseph Roach for the concept of the "long-running."
9. Charles Lamb, "On the Artificial Comedy of the Last Century," in *The Works of Charles and Mary Lamb*, ed. E. V. Lucas, 7 vols. (New York: AMS Press, 1968), 2:141.
10. Samuel Johnson, *A Dictionary of the English Language*, 2nd ed., 2 vols. (London, 1756).
11. The documentary methods of the period's theater history have been driven by the invaluable information in *The London Stage, 1660–1800: A Calendar of Plays, Entertainments, and Afterpieces*, ed. William Van Lennep, Emmett L. Avery, Arthur H. Scouten, George Winchester Stone Jr., and Charles Beecher Hogan, 5 parts in 11 vols. (Carbondale: Southern Illinois University Press, 1960–1968). As repertory theaters, London's eighteenth-century playhouses relied economically on revivals from a reserve of older plays, and over time theatrical offerings from the Restoration tradition made up significantly less of this stock. By the 1760s, the libertine plays of Behn, Etherege, Crowne, D'Urfey, Ravenscroft, Southerne, and Shadwell were purged from the repertory almost entirely; those of Dryden, Wycherley, Vanbrugh, and Congreve were revived, but much more rarely than the works of Shakespeare or their post-1700 descendants. Plays that were retained often existed in redacted or adapted form, and expurgation was a facet of print culture's treatment of Restoration drama as well. See James J. Lynch, *Box, Pit, and Gallery: Stage and Society in Johnson's London* (Berkeley: University of California Press, 1953); George Winchester Stone Jr., "The Making of the Repertory," in *The London Theatre World, 1660–1800*, ed. Robert D. Hume (Carbondale: Southern Illinois University Press, 1980), 181–209; Robert D. Hume "Theatres and Repertory," in *The Cambridge History of British Theatre*, vol. 2, ed. Joseph Donohue (Cambridge: Cambridge University Press, 2004), 53–70; Robert Markley, "The Canon and Its Critics," in *The Cambridge Companion to English Restoration Theatre*, ed. Deborah Payne Fisk (Cambridge: Cambridge University Press, 2000), 226–242; and Brian Corman, "Restoration Drama after the Restoration: The Critics, the Repertory and the Canon," in *A Companion to Restoration Drama*, ed. Susan J. Owen (Oxford: Blackwell, 2001), 177–192.
12. Lamb, "Artificial Comedy," 2:141–143.
13. Jeremy Collier's *Short View of the Immorality and Profaneness of the English Stage* (London, 1698) has long been assigned the blame for the death of Restoration drama, but moral reactions to Stuart culture and theater were widespread by the late seventeenth century. See Tony Claydon, *William III and the Godly Revolution* (Cambridge: Cambridge University Press, 1996), and Aparna Gollapudi, *Moral Reform in Comedy and Culture, 1696–1747* (Burlington, Vt.: Ashgate, 2011). For a history of Restoration drama's rela-

tionship to moralizing culture, see John Harwood, *Critics, Values, and Restoration Comedy* (Carbondale: Southern Illinois University Press, 1982).

14. Richard Bevis, *The Laughing Tradition: Stage Comedy in Garrick's Day* (Athens: University of Georgia Press, 1980), 85.
15. See assessments by Robert D. Hume, *The Development of English Drama in the Late Seventeenth Century* (Oxford: Clarendon Press, 1976), 376; Brown, *English Dramatic Form*, 142; John Loftis, *Comedy and Society from Congreve to Fielding* (Stanford, Calif.: Stanford University Press, 1959), 101; and Hughes, *English Drama*, 454.
16. In particular, see Lisa Freeman, *Character's Theater: Genre and Identity on the Eighteenth-Century English Stage* (Philadelphia: University of Pennsylvania Press, 2002); O'Quinn, *Staging Governance*; Daniel O'Quinn, *Entertaining Crisis in the Atlantic Imperium, 1770–1790* (Baltimore, Md.: Johns Hopkins University Press, 2011); and the scholarship in *The Oxford Handbook of the Georgian Theatre, 1737–1832*, ed. Julia Swindells and David Francis Taylor (Oxford: Oxford University Press, 2014).
17. Freeman, *Character's Theater*, 5. Freeman elaborates further along in the book, positioning the difference as one of concerns with sovereignty and aristocratic power versus concerns with liberal forms of governance in a broader sociopolitical realm: "In short, as was the case with eighteenth-century tragedy, comedy too left behind the preoccupations with Stuart authority and aristocratic privilege that had so consumed the Restoration stage and turned instead toward the work of socializing the newly mobile middling classes for their role in an emerging public order" (146–147).
18. Respectively, the following writers associate the eclipse of Stuart sovereignty with the rise of nationalist communities and the decline of the court, the popularization of republican political theory, and the development of a public sphere, civil society, and bourgeois political economy: Benedict Anderson, *Imagined Communities: Reflections on the Origins and Spread of Nationalism* (London: Verso, 1983); J.G.A. Pocock, *Virtue, Commerce, and History: Essays in Political Thought and History, Chiefly in the Eighteenth Century* (Cambridge: Cambridge University Press, 1985); Jürgen Habermas, *The Structural Transformation of the Public Sphere: An Inquiry into a Category of Bourgeois Society*, trans. Thomas Burger with the assistance of Frederick Lawrence (Cambridge, Mass.: MIT Press, 1989); and Steve Pincus, *1688: The First Modern Revolution* (New Haven, Conn.: Yale University Press, 2009).
19. Michael McKeon, *The Secret History of Domesticity: Public, Private, and the Division of Knowledge* (Baltimore, Md.: Johns Hopkins University Press, 2005), xxii, 6.
20. See, for example, Carol Kay, *Political Constructions: Defoe, Richardson, and Sterne in Relation to Hobbes, Hume, and Burke* (Ithaca, N.Y.: Cornell University Press, 1988); Erin Mackie, *Market à la Mode: Fashion, Commodity, and Gender in "The Tatler" and "The Spectator"* (Baltimore, Md.: Johns Hopkins University Press, 1997); and Erik Bond, *Reading London: Urban Speculation and Imaginative Government in Eighteenth-Century Literature* (Columbus: Ohio State University Press, 2007). The term "governmentality," which I adopt throughout, is Michel Foucault's coinage; see *Security, Territory, Population: Lectures at the Collège de France, 1977–1978*, ed. Michael Senellart, trans. Graham Burchell (New York: Picador, 2004), 87–114.
21. Erin Mackie, *Rakes, Highwaymen, and Pirates: The Making of the Modern Gentleman in the Eighteenth Century* (Baltimore, Md.: Johns Hopkins University Press, 2009), 12. For the rake's connection to Stuart politics, see Neill, "Heroic Heads"; Braverman, *Plots and Counterplots*; and James G. Turner, *Libertines and Radicals in Early Modern London: Sexuality, Politics, and Literary Culture, 1630–1685* (Cambridge: Cambridge University Press, 2002).
22. Neill, "Heroic Heads," 132; Warren Chernaik, *Sexual Freedom in Restoration Literature* (Cambridge: Cambridge University Press, 1995), 4–5.

23. Elaine McGirr, *Eighteenth-Century Characters: A Guide to the Literature of the Age* (New York: Palgrave, 2007), 27. See also Mackie: "After his heyday in the 1660s and 70s, the rake came under increasing, and to a significant extent effective, assault through the rest of the seventeenth and eighteenth centuries" (*Rakes*, 39).
24. See Elaine McGirr, "Why Lovelace Must Die," *NOVEL: A Forum on Fiction* 37 (2003–2004): 5–23.
25. See Raymond Williams, *Marxism and Literature* (Oxford: Oxford University Press, 1977).
26. In *Take Up the Bodies: Theater at the Vanishing Point* (Urbana: University of Illinois Press, 1982), Herbert Blau claims that performance exists on the cusp of its disappearance. So too in Peggy Phelan's *Unmarked: The Politics of Performance* (New York: Routledge, 1993): "performance . . . becomes itself through disappearance" (146). Alternatively, more attuned to performance history, Rebecca Schneider repeats Phelan's influential definition with a difference: "Performance becomes itself through messy and irruptive reappearance"; see her *Performing Remains: Art and War in Times of Historical Reenactment* (New York: Routledge, 2011), 102. On other theories of performance that stress its reappearance or displacement in time and space, see Joseph Roach, *Cities of the Dead: Circum-Atlantic Performance* (New York: Columbia University Press, 1996); and Elin Diamond's introduction to *Performance and Cultural Politics*, ed. Elin Diamond (New York: Routledge, 1996), 1–13.
27. Schneider, *Performing Remains*, 33.
28. Reinhart Koselleck, *The Practice of Conceptual History: Timing History, Spacing Concepts*, trans. Todd Samuel Presner (Stanford, Calif.: Stanford University Press, 2002), 168.
29. See Richard Schechner, *Between Theater and Anthropology* (Philadelphia: University of Pennsylvania Press, 1985), and Marvin Carlson, *The Haunted Stage: The Theatre as Memory Machine* (Ann Arbor: University of Michigan Press, 2001).
30. Schneider, *Performing Remains*, 29.
31. Roach, *It*, 44.
32. On the seventeenth-century perception of the political past repeating itself, see Phillip Harth, *Pen for a Party: Dryden's Tory Propaganda in Its Contexts* (Princeton, N.J.: Princeton University Press, 1993), and Jonathan Scott, *England's Troubles: Seventeenth-Century English Political Instability in European Context* (Cambridge: Cambridge University Press, 2000).
33. J. Scott, *England's Troubles*, 26.
34. Schneider, *Performing Remains*, 55.
35. See Michel de Certeau, *The Practice of Everyday Life*, trans. Steven Rendall (Berkeley: University of California Press, 1984).
36. Charles Lamb, "Modern Gallantry," in *Works*, 2:79.
37. Schneider, *Performing Remains*, 90.
38. Diana Taylor, *The Archive and the Repertoire: Performing Cultural Memory in the Americas* (Durham, N.C.: Duke University Press, 2003), 28.
39. Taylor, *The Archive and the Repertoire*, 28.
40. Taylor, *The Archive and the Repertoire*, 31.
41. John Zomchick, "Force, Contract, and Power in *The Woman-Captain*," *Restoration* 20 (1996): 181.
42. *The London Magazine; or, Gentleman's Monthly Intelligencer*, vol. 40 (London, 1771), 483. I return to a fuller reading of Brute and *The Provoked Wife*'s performance history in chapter 3.
43. *The London Chronicle*, March 3–5, 1757.
44. *The London Chronicle*, October 14, 1758.

45. John Vanbrugh, *The Provoked Wife*, in *John Vanbrugh: Four Comedies*, ed. Michael Cordner (New York: Penguin, 1989), 197–199.
46. Mackie, *Rakes, Highwaymen, and Pirates*, 43, 120. In that Mackie offers a compelling exploration of the libertine's persistence in eighteenth-century literature, I am indebted to her insights. But, as I suggest later in this introduction, I part ways from her significantly in my conclusions about the stage rake's attraction in post-Restoration culture and about how this attraction frames liberal modernity.
47. Catherine Gallagher, "Embracing the Absolute: The Politics of the Female Subject in Seventeenth-Century England," *Genders* 1 (1988): 26. See also McKeon, *Secret History*, 3–48.
48. On the temporality of nostalgia, see Susan Stewart, *On Longing: Narratives of the Miniature, the Gigantic, the Souvenir, the Collection* (Durham, N.C.: Duke University Press, 1993), and Svetlana Boym, *The Future of Nostalgia* (New York: Basic Books, 2001).
49. If, as James Turner notes, recent critics "challenge the liberationist claims of libertinism, since its doctrine of sexual freedom is always complicated by the politics of class and gender," earlier scholars read the rake's behaviors of sovereign license as coding for progressive sexual liberation and rebellion against moral and social authoritarianism (*Libertines and Radicals*, ix–x). For such earlier readings, see Birdsall, *Wild Civility*, and Bonamy Dobrée, *Restoration Comedy, 1600–1720* (Oxford: Oxford University Press, 1924). My point is that at different stages in the history of its interpretations, the rake's sovereignty has signified different things; this diversity of signification holds as well in the character's eighteenth-century performance history.
50. Algernon Sidney, *Discourses Concerning Government*, ed. Thomas G. West (Indianapolis, Ind.: Liberty Fund, 1996), 24. On Sidney's defense of individual liberty, see Alan Houston, *Algernon Sidney and the Republican Heritage in England and America* (Princeton, N.J.: Princeton University Press, 1991), 114–122.
51. My account expands on James Turner's claim that seventeenth-century libertinism may best be described as a set of theatrical "props" rather than a coherent philosophy; see his "The Properties of Libertinism," *Eighteenth-Century Life* 9 (1985): 75–87.
52. Neill, "Heroic Heads," 116. Following the work of Neill, Markley, Turner, and others, my account understands that libertine drama's skeptical assessment of its world often includes the absolutist poses and ethos of its own rakish heroes.
53. Michel Foucault, *"Society Must Be Defended": Lectures at the Collège de France, 1975–1976*, ed. Mauro Bertani and Alessandro Fontana, trans. David Macey (New York: Picador, 2003), 36–38. Reversing Foucault's terms somewhat, Giorgio Agamben argues that sovereignty is always already invested in circumscribing a "threshold beyond which life ceases to be politically relevant," or what he calls "bare life," and its effects only intensify under totalitarian regimes; see *Homo Sacer: Sovereign Power and Bare Life*, trans. Daniel Heller-Roazen (Stanford, Calif.: Stanford University Press, 1998), 139. For Judith Butler, alternatively, the modern mechanisms of Foucauldian governmentality themselves, in "mak[ing] concrete the understanding of power as irreducible to law," allow for sovereignty's self-grounded extralegal power to be "resurrected"; see *Precarious Life: The Powers of Mourning and Violence* (New York: Verso, 2004), 94, 56.
54. See Christopher Loar, *Political Magic: British Fictions of Savagery and Sovereignty, 1650–1750* (New York: Fordham University Press, 2014); Peter DeGabriele, *Sovereign Power and the Enlightenment: Eighteenth-Century Literature and the Problem of the Political* (Lewisburg, Pa.: Bucknell University Press, 2015); and Dillon, *New World Drama*.
55. Judith Butler, *Excitable Speech: A Politics of the Performative* (New York: Routledge, 1997), 78.

56. Michel Foucault, *Power/Knowledge: Selected Interviews and Other Writings, 1972–1977*, ed. Colin Gordon (New York: Pantheon, 1980), 121.
57. Foucault, *"Society Must Be Defended,"* 36.
58. Foucault, *"Society Must Be Defended,"* 39.
59. See Emmett Avery, "The Reputation of Wycherley's Comedies as Stage Plays in the Eighteenth Century," *Research Studies of the State College of Washington* 12 (1944): 131–154; Avery, *Congreve's Plays on the Eighteenth-Century Stage* (New York: Modern Language Association, 1951); Barry Olshen, "The Original and 'Improved' Comedies of Sir John Vanbrugh: Their Nineteenth-Century London Stage History," *Restoration and Eighteenth-Century Theatre Research* 13 (1974): 27–52; and Jane Spencer, "*The Rover* and the Eighteenth Century," in *Aphra Behn Studies*, ed. Janet Todd (Cambridge: Cambridge University Press, 1996), 84–107.
60. See Hume, *The Rakish Stage*. On the variations of types of Restoration libertine drama and on the fact that those sex comedies often considered the canonical heart of Restoration drama were not always so, see Canfield, *Tricksters and Estates*, and Rosenthal, "'All Injury's Forgot.'"

NOTES TO CHAPTER 1

1. Nicholas Rowe, *The Tragedy of Jane Shore*, ed. Harry William Perdicord (Lincoln: University of Nebraska Press, 1974), 74.
2. For the "china scene" and the metatheatrical discussion of it, see act 4, scene 3, of *The Country Wife* and act 2 of *The Plain Dealer* in William Wycherley, *The Country Wife and Other Plays*, ed. Peter Dixon (Oxford: Oxford University Press, 1996).
3. Rowe, *The Tragedy of Jane Shore*, 74–75.
4. Charles Beckingham, "A Poem to the Memory of Nicholas Rowe, Esq," in *Musarum Lachrymae: or, Poems to the Memory of Nicholas Rowe, Esq.; By Several Hands* (London, 1719), 14, 17, 19.
5. Nicholas Rowe, *The Fair Penitent*, ed. Malcolm Goldstein (Lincoln: University of Nebraska Press, 1969), 23. Further citations refer to this edition and appear parenthetically in the text.
6. Out of the many histories of this period and the emergence of Whig doctrine within it, I am particularly indebted to J. P. Kenyon, *Revolution Principles: The Politics of Party, 1689–1720* (Cambridge: Cambridge University Press, 1977); H. T. Dickinson, *Liberty and Property: Political Ideology in Eighteenth-Century Britain* (New York: Holmes and Meier, 1977); Tim Harris, *Politics under the Later Stuarts: Party Conflict in a Divided Society, 1660–1715* (London: Longman, 1993); and Julian Hoppit, *A Land of Liberty? England, 1689–1727* (Oxford: Oxford University Press, 2000).
7. Brett Wilson, *A Race of Female Patriots: Women and Public Spirit on the British Stage, 1688–1745* (Lewisburg, Pa.: Bucknell University Press, 2012), 13.
8. On the "godly revolution" and the state ideology of Williamite moral reform, see Tony Claydon, *William III and the Godly Revolution* (Cambridge: Cambridge University Press, 1996). On moral reform under Williamite culture more broadly, see Dudley Bahlmann, *The Moral Revolution of 1688* (New Haven, Conn.: Yale University Press, 1957); and Rachel Weil, *Political Passions: Gender, the Family, and Political Argument in England, 1680–1714* (Manchester: Manchester University Press, 1999), 86–160. Tim Harris discusses pre-1688 moral reactions to the Stuarts in "'There Is None that Loves Him but Drunk Whores and Whoremongers': Popular Criticism of the Restoration Court," in *Politics, Transgression, and Representation at the Court of Charles II*, ed. Julia Marciari Alexander and Catharine MacLeod (New Haven, Conn.: Yale University Press, 2007), 35–60.

9. For these trends in comedy, see Joseph Wood Krutch, *Comedy and Conscience after the Restoration*, rev. ed. (New York: Columbia University Press, 1949); Laura Brown, *English Dramatic Form, 1660–1760: An Essay in Generic History* (New Haven, Conn.: Yale University Press, 1981); Derek Hughes, *English Drama, 1660–1700* (Oxford: Clarendon Press, 1996), 331–357; J. Douglas Canfield, "Shifting Tropes of Ideology in English Serious Drama, Late Stuart to Early Georgian," in *Cultural Readings of Restoration and Eighteenth-Century English Theater*, ed. J. Douglas Canfield and Deborah Payne (Athens: University of Georgia Press, 1995), 195–227; Matthew J. Kinservik, *Disciplining Satire: The Censorship of Satiric Comedy on the Eighteenth-Century London Stage* (Lewisburg, Pa.: Bucknell University Press, 2002); and Aparna Gollapudi, *Moral Reform in Comedy and Culture, 1696–1747* (Burlington, Vt.: Ashgate, 2011).
10. *Proposals for a National Reformation of Manners* (London, 1694), 14; *An Account of the Societies for the Reformation of Manners* (London, 1699), 131.
11. Daniel Defoe, *Reformation of Manners, a Satyr* (London, 1702), 58. Though Defoe satirizes the ineffectuality and class biases of moral reform in this tract, he nevertheless also laments the deleterious social effect of libertine theater.
12. George Ridpath, *The Stage Condemn'd* (London, 1698), 36; Jeremy Collier, *A Short View of the Immorality and Profaneness of the English Stage* (London, 1698), 164. See Lisa Freeman, "Jeremy Collier and the Politics of Theatrical Representation," in *Players, Playwrights, Playhouses: Investigating Performance, 1660–1800*, ed. Michael Cordner and Peter Holland (New York: Palgrave, 2007), 135–151.
13. Collier, *A Short View*, 2, 176.
14. Richard Blackmore, *Prince Arthur: An Heroick Poem in Ten Books* (London, 1695), iv.
15. Steve Pincus, *1688: The First Modern Revolution* (New Haven, Conn.: Yale University Press, 2009), 483. Other revisionist accounts of 1688 and William's reign include Kenyon, *Revolution Principles*; Claydon, *William III and the Godly Revolution*; Craig Rose, *England in the 1690s: Revolution, Religion, and War* (Malden, Mass.: Blackwell, 1999); Tim Harris, *Revolution: The Great Crisis of the British Monarchy, 1685–1720* (New York: Penguin, 2006); and the essays in Esther Mijers and David Onnekink, eds., *Redefining William III: The Impact of the King-Stadholder in International Context* (Burlington, Vt.: Ashgate, 2007).
16. Michael Hardt and Antonio Negri, *Commonwealth* (Cambridge, Mass.: Harvard University Press, 2009), 9.
17. L. Brown, *English Dramatic Form*, 42. For the rake's ideological similarities to seventeenth-century radicalism, see also Michael Neill, "Heroic Heads and Humble Tails: Sex, Politics, and the Restoration Comic Rake," *The Eighteenth Century: Theory and Interpretation* 24 (1983): 115–139; and Laura Rosenthal, "'All Injury's Forgot': Restoration Sex Comedy and National Amnesia," *Comparative Drama* 42 (2008): 7–28.
18. Anita Pacheco, "Reading Toryism in Aphra Behn's Cit-Cuckolding Comedies," *Review of English Studies* 55 (2004): 690. See also J. Douglas Canfield, *Tricksters and Estates: On the Ideology of Restoration Comedy* (Lexington: University Press of Kentucky, 1997).
19. Hughes, *English Drama, 1660–1700*, 388.
20. Richard Braverman, *Plots and Counterplots: Sexual Politics and the Body Politic in English Literature, 1660–1730* (Cambridge: Cambridge University Press, 1993), 210–237.
21. John Vanbrugh, *The Provoked Wife*, in *John Vanbrugh: Four Comedies*, ed. Michael Cordner (New York: Penguin, 1989), 194.
22. Catharine Trotter, *Love at a Loss; or, Most Votes Carry It*, in *The Broadview Anthology of Restoration and Early Eighteenth-Century Drama*, ed. J. Douglas Canfield and Maja-Lisa von Sneidern (Peterborough, Ont.: Broadview, 2001), 901.
23. Richard Blackmore, *A Satyr against Wit* (London, 1700), 5.

24. For the details of this controversy, I have relied on Richard C. Boys, *Sir Richard Blackmore and the Wits* (Ann Arbor: University of Michigan Press, 1949); Robert C. Krapp, "Class Analysis of a Literary Controversy: Wit and Sense in Seventeenth-Century English Literature," *Science and Society* 10 (1946): 80–92; Abigail Williams, *Poetry and the Creation of a Whig Literary Culture, 1681–1714* (Oxford: Oxford University Press, 2005); and Michael Gavin, *The Invention of English Criticism, 1650–1760* (Cambridge: Cambridge University Press, 2015), 50–73.
25. See A. Williams, *Whig Literary Culture*, 32–37.
26. *Commendatory Verses, on the Author of the Two Arthurs, and the Satyr against Wit* (London, 1700), 5, 25.
27. *Commendatory Verses*, ii.
28. Tom Brown, *The Works of Mr. Thomas Brown, in Prose and Verse; Serious, Moral, and Comical*, 2 vols. (London, 1707), 1:32.
29. *Commendatory Verses*, i.
30. *Commendatory Verses*, 23. For wit's genealogical connections with Stuart cavalier gentility and its politics of style, ease, and pleasure, see Krapp, "Class Analysis"; Robert Markley, *Two-Edg'd Weapons: Style and Ideology in the Comedies of Etherege, Wycherley, and Congreve* (Oxford: Clarendon Press, 1988); Anna Bryson, *From Courtesy to Civility: Changing Codes of Conduct in Early Modern England* (Oxford: Oxford University Press, 1998); and A. Williams, *Whig Literary Culture*.
31. For the example of Tom Brown, see Benjamin Boyce, *Tom Brown of Facetious Memory: Grub Street in the Age of Dryden* (New York: Johnson Reprint, 1968). Boyce characterizes Brown as a libertine if professional and non-aristocratic man of letters, an admirer of the Stuart court wits and the dramatists who emulated their convivial lifestyle. See also Richard Steele's eulogy of Brown as a "careless fellow" pursuing "Merriment" in *Tatler* no. 101, December 1, 1709, in Richard Steele, *The Tatler*, ed. Donald F. Bond, 3 vols. (Oxford: Clarendon Press, 1987), 2:121.
32. Abel Boyer, *Letters of Wit, Politicks and Morality* (London, 1701), 216. See also Gavin, *The Invention of English Criticism*, 67–70.
33. Boys labels the *Commendatory Verses* as "Tory-tinged" (*Sir Richard Blackmore*, 143), but his list of contributors includes Whig writers such as Steele and John Dennis. Abigail Williams declares that "the controversy did not develop along exclusively Whig/Tory lines" (*Whig Literary Culture*, 32).
34. Blackmore, *A Satyr against Wit*, 3–4, 7.
35. Blackmore, *A Satyr against Wit*, 9 10, 13.
36. Blackmore, *A Satyr against Wit*, 8.
37. *Commendatory Verses*, 10.
38. Richard Steele, *The Christian Hero: An Argument Proving that no Principles but those of Religion are Sufficient to make a Great Man*, in *Tracts and Pamphlets by Richard Steele*, ed. Rae Blanchard (New York: Octagon Books, 1967), 7.
39. John Wilmot, Lord Rochester, *Against Reason and Mankind*, in *The Works of John Wilmot, Earl of Rochester*, ed. Harold Love (Oxford: Oxford University Press, 1999), 58.
40. See Joseph Roach, *It* (Ann Arbor: University of Michigan Press, 2007).
41. Rowe is mentioned as affiliated with the wits at Will's in Boyer's *Letters of Wit, Politicks and Morality*, 216.
42. *The Fair Penitent*'s popularity is deduced from its high rate of performance. For statistics and performance records, see Malcolm Goldstein's introduction to *The Fair Penitent*, xiv; and George Winchester Stone Jr., "The Making of the Repertory," in *The London Theatre World, 1660–1800*, ed. Robert D. Hume (Carbondale: Southern Illinois University Press, 1980), 201–203. Goldstein here lists the numerous eighteenth-century celebrities who, in

portraying Calista, Lothario, and Horatio, ensured the play's appeal. Works that discuss these celebrity portrayals in more detail include Shaun Strohmer, "'My Eyes Take Pleasure to Behold Thee': Spectatorship and the Mastery of Passion in *The Fair Penitent*," *Restoration and Eighteenth-Century Theatre Research* 14 (1999): 55–65; and Felicity Nussbaum, *Rival Queens: Actresses, Performance, and the Eighteenth-Century British Theater* (Philadelphia: University of Pennsylvania Press, 2010).

43. See Laura Brown, "The Defenseless Woman and the Development of English Tragedy," *Studies in English Literature* 22 (1982): 429–443; Vaska Tumir, "She-Tragedy and Its Men: Conflict and Form in *The Orphan* and *The Fair Penitent*," *Studies in English Literature* 30 (1990): 411–428; Strohmer, "Spectatorship and Mastery"; Lisa Freeman, *Character's Theater: Genre and Identity on the Eighteenth-Century English Stage* (Philadelphia: University of Pennsylvania Press, 2002), 125–134; Jean Marsden, *Fatal Desire: Women, Sexuality, and the English Stage, 1660–1720* (Ithaca, N.Y.: Cornell University Press, 2006), 149–159; Kathleen Wilson, "Rowe's *Fair Penitent* as Global History; or, A Diversionary Voyage to New South Wales," *Eighteenth-Century Studies* 41 (2008): 231–251; and B. Wilson, *A Race of Female Patriots*, 33–68.
44. Brett Wilson advances this argument in the greatest detail; see *A Race of Female Patriots*, 33–68.
45. Scholars have noted Lothario's Stuart heritage but persist in reading him as archetypal in his libertinism; see Elaine McGirr, *Eighteenth-Century Characters: A Guide to the Literature of the Age* (New York: Palgrave, 2007), 32–22; and B. Wilson, *A Race of Female Patriots*, 54–55. Even works such as Tumir's "She-Tragedy and Its Men," which purport to examine the play's masculine figures, have very little to say about Lothario in detail.
46. See Rochester, *Against Reason and Mankind*, 57–63. This doctrine is voiced to greater or lesser degree in most libertine plays of the Restoration but is perhaps the most clearly articulated by Don John and his cronies in Thomas Shadwell's *The Libertine* (1675).
47. On the post-1688 shift in the stage rake's fortunes, see Robert D. Hume, *The Rakish Stage: Studies in English Drama, 1660–1800* (Carbondale: Southern Illinois University Press, 1983), 165, and Braverman, *Plots and Counterplots*, 211–213. This development is in accordance with the demonization of Stuart excesses found more broadly in Williamite culture.
48. Braverman, *Plots and Counterplots*, 66.
49. The valuation of present pleasure is central to the anti-puritan politics of earlier seventeenth-century cavalier poetry and is adapted to new libertine purposes in poems such as Rochester's "Love and Life" and, as we saw earlier, in the 1690s wits' resistance to bourgeois industry.
50. Thomas Shadwell, *The Libertine*, in *Four Restoration Libertine Plays*, ed. Deborah Payne Fisk (Oxford: Oxford University Press, 2005), 11. This creed is also attributed by Sir Jaspar Fidget to Horner in Wycherley's *The Country Wife*: "Go, go, to your business, I say—pleasure, whilst I go to my pleasure—business" (220).
51. B. Wilson, *A Race of Female Patriots*, 231.
52. *A Prologue sent to Mr. Row, to his new Play, call'd The Fair Penitent* (London, 1706), 2.
53. Rosenthal, "'All Injury's Forgot,'" 26.
54. The image of the fifth-act corpse is included in most editions of *The Fair Penitent* from 1714 until the 1750s, as well as in the *Dramatick Works of Nicholas Rowe* (London, 1720, 1725, 1728, 1733), the *Works of Nicholas Rowe* (London, 1728), and *Plays Written by Nicholas Rowe* (London, 1736). Variants of the image of the fourth-act corpse are included in the 1759, 1763, 1770, 1775, and 1795 editions of *The Fair Penitent*.
55. Calista's conflicted characterization, evoked in this scene particularly, has been a critical crux for centuries. For some critics, her persistent desire for Lothario makes her a "Fair

Wanton," hardly deserving of the title "penitent"; see Charles Gildon, *A New Rehearsal; or, Bays the Younger* (London, 1714), 57–63, and Theophilus Cibber, *The Lives of the Poets of Great Britain and Ireland* (London, 1753), 276. For others, this scene evokes Calista's solemnity; see Francis Gentleman, *The Dramatic Censor; or, Critical Companion* (London, 1770), 267. Scholarly discussions of this issue include Lindley Wyman, "The Tradition of Formal Meditation in Rowe's *The Fair Penitent*," *Philological Quarterly* 42 (1963): 412–416; Tumir, "She-Tragedy and Its Men"; Freeman, *Character's Theater*; and Marsden, *Fatal Desire*.

56. John Milton, *Paradise Lost*, in *Complete Poems and Major Prose*, ed. Merritt Y. Hughes (Indianapolis, Ind.: Hackett, 2003), 224. On the "sons of Belial" as referring to the Restoration court, see James G. Turner, *Libertines and Radicals in Early Modern London: Sexuality, Politics and Literary Culture, 1630–1685* (Cambridge: Cambridge University Press, 2002), 164–166.
57. Milton, *Paradise Lost*, 297.
58. Aphra Behn, *The Rover; or, The Banished Cavaliers*, in *The Rover and Other Works*, ed. Jane Spencer (Oxford: Oxford University Press, 1995), 78.
59. Thomas Hobbes, *Leviathan*, ed. C. B. Macpherson (New York: Penguin, 1985), 190.
60. Milton, *Paradise Lost*, 300.
61. The biblical reading of temptation in *The Fair Penitent* is pursued in greatest detail by J. Douglas Canfield, *Nicholas Rowe and Christian Tragedy* (Gainesville: University Press of Florida, 1977), 111–145. For Satan as a corrupter of liberty, see Elliott Visconsi, *Lines of Equity: Literature and the Origins of Law in Later Stuart England* (Ithaca, N.Y.: Cornell University Press, 2008), 75–112.
62. Quoted in Kenyon, *Revolution Principles*, 46.
63. On the split in the Whig party between the Williamite "junto" Whigs, who tenuously became the party of the court and throne, and opposition Whigs, who continued to espouse older radical strands of republicanism such as resistance theory, see Kenyon, *Revolution Principles*, 35–60; T. Harris, *Politics under the Later Stuarts*, 147–176; and Claydon, *William III and the Godly Revolution*, 148–226.
64. Charles Gildon, *The Patriot; or, The Italian Conspiracy* (London, 1703), 55.
65. J. Douglas Canfield, "Nicholas Rowe," in *Restoration and Eighteenth-Century Dramatists*, second series, ed. Paula Backscheider (Detroit, Mich.: Gale Research, 1989), 280.
66. My reading of Calista over the next few pages is similar to that of Brett Wilson, who sees her as representative of an amalgamation of republican and Tory feminist thought that must be expelled from Rowe's affective civic order (*A Race of Female Patriots*, 35). While I agree with Wilson's reading here, I come to different conclusions regarding Rowe's relation to earlier Whig republicanism and to the tragedy's representation of postrevolutionary values and sovereign desire.
67. Nicholas Rowe, *The Ambitious Step-mother* (London, 1701), 7.
68. See Lawrence Klein, *Shaftesbury and the Culture of Politeness: Moral Discourse and Cultural Politics in Early Eighteenth-Century England* (Cambridge: Cambridge University Press, 1994).
69. Weil, *Political Passions*, 6.
70. Elizabeth Maddock Dillon, *New World Drama: The Performative Commons in the Atlantic World, 1649–1849* (Durham, N.C.: Duke University Press, 2014), 50.
71. Yael Shapira has shown that the staged spectacle of corpses, while violating the neoclassical rules of propriety dominant in early eighteenth-century tragedy, could also serve hegemonic purposes in governing audiences; see "Shakespeare, *The Castle of Otranto*, and the Problem of the Corpse on the Eighteenth-Century Stage," *Eighteenth-Century Life* 36 (2012): 8–10.

72. On this function of *Tamerlane*, see John Loftis, *The Politics of Drama in Augustan England* (Oxford: Clarendon Press, 1963), 33–34.
73. See Susan Cannon Harris, "Outside the Box: The Female Spectator, *The Fair Penitent*, and the Kelly Riots of 1747," *Theatre Journal* 57 (2005): 33–56; K. Wilson, "Rowe's *Fair Penitent* as Global History"; and Dillon, *New World Drama*, 206–208.
74. Andrew Sofer, *The Stage Life of Props* (Ann Arbor: University of Michigan Press, 2003), 2.
75. William Rufus Chetwood, *A General History of the Stage* (London, 1749), 253–254.
76. The anecdote is recycled in John Genest, *Some Account of the English Stage from the Restoration in 1660 to 1830*, 10 vols. (Bath, U.K., 1832), 2:281–282; and, most recently, in Judith Milhous and Robert D. Hume, eds., *The London Stage, 1660–1800: A New Version of Part 2, 1700–1729*, http://personal.psu.edu/faculty/h/b//hbl/London%20Stage%20 2001/. In describing a failure late in the production, the anecdote accords with the rendering of *The Fair Penitent*'s premiere in John Downes's *Roscius Anglicanus*, ed. Judith Milhous and Robert D. Hume (London: Society for Theatre Research, 1987): it was, Downes claims, "a very good Play for three Acts; but failing in the two last, answer'd not [the company's] Expectation" (95). *The Fair Penitent* opened in the spring of 1703 for one night only; it was not revived again until after the successes of Rowe's other she-tragedies in the wake of 1714, after which it went on to be one of the century's most revived tragedies.
77. Nicholas Ridout, *Stage Fright, Animals, and Other Theatrical Problems* (Cambridge: Cambridge University Press, 2006), 135.
78. On theatrical failure, see Ridout, *Stage Fright*; and Sara Jane Bailes, *Performance Theatre and the Poetics of Failure: Forced Entertainment, Goat Island, Elevator Repair Service* (New York: Routledge, 2011). For theories of failure, performance, and subjectivity more broadly, see Judith Butler, *Gender Trouble: Feminism and the Subversion of Identity* (New York: Routledge, 1990); Judith Halberstam, *The Queer Art of Failure* (Durham, N.C.: Duke University Press, 2001); and Rebecca Schneider, *Performing Remains: Art and War in Times of Theatrical Reenactment* (New York: Routledge, 2011).
79. Bailes, *Performance Theatre*, 3.
80. See the entry for George Powell in Philip H. Highfill Jr., Kalman A. Burnim, and Edward A. Langhans, eds., *A Biographical Dictionary of Actors, Actresses, Musicians, Dancers, Managers, and Other Stage Personnel in London, 1660–1800*, 16 vols. (Carbondale: Southern Illinois University Press, 1973–1993), 12:107–114.
81. Colley Cibber, *An Apology for the Life of Colley Cibber*, ed. B.R.S. Fone (New York: Dover, 2000), 134. See also Vanbrugh's preface to *The Relapse* (1696), in Cordner, *John Vanbrugh*, 44, and Daniel Defoe, *More Reformation. A Satyr upon Himself* (London, 1703), 44–45.
82. On Rochester's fame for yelling at his servants, see John Dennis, *A Defence of Sir Fopling Flutter* (1722), in *The Critical Works of John Dennis*, ed. Edward Niles Hooker, 2 vols. (Baltimore, Md.: Johns Hopkins University Press, 1943), 2:248.
83. Ridout, *Stage Fright*, 142, 34.
84. See Dillon, *New World Drama*, 1–30.

NOTES TO CHAPTER 2

1. Joseph Addison and Richard Steele, *The Spectator*, ed. Donald F. Bond, 5 vols. (Oxford: Clarendon Press, 1965), 1:278–280.
2. John Dennis, *A Defence of Sir Fopling Flutter*, in *The Critical Works of John Dennis*, ed. Edward Niles Hooker, 2 vols. (Baltimore, Md.: Johns Hopkins University Press, 1943), 2:243.

3. See Richard Braverman, "The Rake's Progress Revisited: Politics and Comedy in the Restoration," in *Cultural Readings of Restoration and Eighteenth-Century English Theater*, ed. J. Douglas Canfield and Deborah Payne (Athens: University of Georgia Press, 1995), 141–168. For broader accounts of the decline of the stage and shifting political and social ideologies, see J. Douglas Canfield, "Shifting Tropes of Ideology in English Serious Drama, Late Stuart to Early Georgian," in Canfield and Payne, *Cultural Readings*, 195–227; Laura Brown, *English Dramatic Form, 1660–1760: An Essay in Generic History* (New Haven, Conn.: Yale University Press, 1981); and Susan Staves, *Players' Scepters: Fictions of Authority in the Restoration* (Lincoln: University of Nebraska Press, 1979).
4. See Horace Walpole, "Thoughts on Comedy," in *The Works of Horatio Walpole, Earl of Orford*, 5 vols. (London, 1798), 2:315–322, and Charles Lamb, "Modern Gallantry," in *The Works of Charles and Mary Lamb*, ed. E. V. Lucas, 7 vols. (New York: AMS Press, 1968), 2:79–82.
5. Robert D. Hume, "Theatres and Repertory," in *The Cambridge History of British Theatre*, ed. Joseph Donohue, vol. 2 (Cambridge: Cambridge University Press, 2004), 60.
6. Diana Taylor, *The Archive and the Repertoire: Performing Cultural Memory in the Americas* (Durham, N.C.: Duke University Press, 2003). For "restored behavior," see Richard Schechner, *Between Theater and Anthropology* (Philadelphia: University of Pennsylvania Press, 1985).
7. Thomas King, *The Gendering of Men, 1600–1750*, vol. 2: *Queer Articulations* (Madison: University of Wisconsin Press, 2008), 22. See also Joseph Roach, "Power's Body: The Inscription of Morality as Style," in *Interpreting the Theatrical Past: Essays in the Historiography of Performance*, ed. Bruce McConachie and Thomas Postlewait (Iowa City: University of Iowa Press, 1989), 99–118.
8. See Erin Mackie, *Rakes, Highwaymen, and Pirates: The Making of the Modern Gentleman in the Eighteenth Century* (Baltimore, Md.: Johns Hopkins University Press, 2009).
9. See Shirley Strum Kenny, "Humane Comedy," *Modern Philology* 75 (1977): 29–43; Hume, "Theatres and Repertory," 59–70; and Harold Weber, *The Restoration Rake-Hero: Transformations in Sexual Understanding in Seventeenth-Century England* (Madison: University of Wisconsin Press, 1986), 179–221.
10. Some of Steele's many attacks on the Restoration stage can be found in *The Spectator* and *The Tatler*, particularly in the following essays: *Spectator* nos. 14, 51, 65, 158, 208, 270, 352, 370, 446; *Tatler* nos. 3, 8, 42. The modern edition of the latter is Richard Steele, *The Tatler*, ed. Donald F. Bond, 3 vols. (Oxford: Clarendon Press, 1987).
11. Hannah Smith has shown that despite George I's boorish reputation, he was actively interested in theatrical entertainments; see *Georgian Monarchy: Politics and Culture, 1714–1760* (Cambridge: Cambridge University Press, 2006), 68–69; and John Loftis, *The Politics of Drama in Augustan England* (Oxford: Clarendon Press, 1963), 63–69.
12. Detailed information on Steele's accession as Drury Lane manager and on the role of the actor-managers can be found in John Loftis, *Steele at Drury Lane* (Berkeley: University of California Press, 1952), 11–54, and in Charles Knight, *A Political Biography of Richard Steele* (London: Pickering and Chatto, 2009), 171–204. For Steele's appropriation of the nickname "Censor of Great Britain," see *Tatler* no. 144.
13. For readings that understand the Dorimant debate in terms of satiric versus sentimental comedy, see Lisa Freeman, *Character's Theater: Genre and Identity on the Eighteenth-Century English Stage* (Philadelphia: University of Pennsylvania Press, 2002), 206; Loftis, *Steele at Drury Lane*, 195–213; and Robert D. Hume, "Theory of Comedy in the Restoration," *Modern Philology* 70 (1973): 302–318. The most thoughtful consideration of the Dorimant debate remains Brian Corman's "Interpreting and Misinterpreting *The Man of Mode*," *Papers on Language and Literature* 13 (1977): 35–53.

14. Lawrence Klein, "Property and Politeness in the Early Eighteenth-Century Whig Moralists: The Case of *The Spectator*," in *Early Modern Conceptions of Property*, ed. John Brewer and Susan Staves (New York: Routledge, 1995), 228.
15. Anthony Ashley Cooper, 3rd Earl of Shaftesbury, *Characteristics of Men, Manners, Opinions, Times*, ed. Lawrence E. Klein (Cambridge: Cambridge University Press, 1999), 31.
16. I rely on a number of studies of politeness and the public sphere; see Jürgen Habermas, *The Structural Transformation of the Public Sphere: An Inquiry into a Category of Bourgeois Society*, trans. Thomas Burger with the assistance of Frederick Lawrence (Cambridge, Mass.: MIT Press, 1989); J.G.A. Pocock, *Virtue, Commerce, and History: Essays in Political Thought and History, Chiefly in the Eighteenth Century* (Cambridge: Cambridge University Press, 1985); Klein, "Property and Politeness"; Lawrence Klein, "Liberty, Manners, and Politeness in Early Eighteenth-Century England," *The Historical Journal* 32 (1989): 583–605; Erin Mackie, *Market à la Mode: Fashion, Commodity, and Gender in "The Tatler" and "The Spectator"* (Baltimore, Md.: Johns Hopkins University Press, 1997); Brian Cowan, "Mr. Spectator and the Coffeehouse Public Sphere," *Eighteenth-Century Studies* 37 (2004): 345–366; Terence Bowers, "Universalizing Sociability: *The Spectator*, Civic Enfranchisement, and the Rule(s) of the Public Sphere," in *The Spectator: Emerging Discourses*, ed. Donald J. Newman (Newark: University of Delaware Press, 2005), 150–174; Anna Bryson, *From Courtesy to Civility: Changing Codes of Conduct in Early Modern England* (Oxford: Oxford University Press, 1998); and Phillip Carter, *Men and the Emergence of Polite Society, Britain 1660–1800* (New York: Pearson, 2000).
17. For a more detailed analysis of Shaftesbury and his effect on Addison and Steele, see Klein, "Property and Politeness," and Bowers, "Universalizing Sociability."
18. *Spectator* no. 370, in Addison and Steele, *The Spectator*, 3:393.
19. Richard Steele, *The Conscious Lovers*, in *The Plays of Richard Steele*, ed. Shirley Strum Kenny (Oxford: Clarendon Press, 1971), 299. For Steele's language of "Goths," see also *Spectator* no. 367, in Addison and Steele, *The Spectator*, 3:382.
20. *Spectator* no. 65, in Addison and Steele, *The Spectator*, 1:278.
21. *Spectator* no. 65, in Addison and Steele, *The Spectator*, 1:278.
22. *Spectator* no. 65, in Addison and Steele, *The Spectator*, 1:278–279.
23. *Guardian* no. 34, in Richard Steele, *The Guardian*, ed. John Calhoun Stephens (Lexington: University Press of Kentucky, 1982), 143.
24. Leonard Welsted, *A Prologue occasioned by the Revival of a Play of Shakespear*, in *The Works, in Verse and Prose, of Leonard Welsted*, ed. John Nichols (London, 1787), 77.
25. Welsted, *A Prologue*, 79.
26. Welsted, *A Prologue*, 80.
27. On the worry of the libertine and national decline, see Laura Rosenthal, "'All Injury's Forgot': Restoration Sex Comedy and National Amnesia," *Comparative Drama* 42 (2008): 7–28.
28. Mackie, *Market à la Mode*, 21, 26.
29. See George Winchester Stone Jr., "The Making of the Repertory," in *The London Theatre World, 1660–1800*, ed. Robert D. Hume (Carbondale: Southern Illinois University Press, 1980), 181–209.
30. The inclusion of Shadwell's *The Libertine* (1675) in the figure and the table may seem odd, given that it is not a straightforward comedy like the plays of Etherege. As Deborah Payne Fisk argues in her introduction to *Four Restoration Libertine Plays* (New York: Oxford University Press, 2005), *The Libertine*'s popularity on the eighteenth-century stage may be accounted for by its moral stance against libertinism (xxviii). Shadwell's disapproval of libertinism is not in question; however, as we shall see later in this chapter, Steele's critics ranked *The Libertine* together with *The Man of Mode* as morally dangerous, suggesting

either that the play's didacticism was not always apparent in performance or that audiences may have appreciated it just as much for Don John's extravagant villainies as for its moral message. I include it here because of both its popularity and its classification as pernicious by Steele's contemporaries.

31. For other such explanations, see Loftis, *Steele at Drury Lane*, 57–61; Hume, "Theatres and Repertory," 60–65; and Knight, *A Political Biography*, 180–181.
32. Daniel Defoe, *The Fears of the Pretender turn'd into the Fears of Debauchery* (London, 1715), 8, 16.
33. Samuel Butler, *Satires and Miscellaneous Poetry and Prose*, ed. René Lamar (Cambridge: Cambridge University Press, 1928), 42.
34. Defoe, *The Fears of the Pretender*, 32.
35. Defoe, *The Fears of the Pretender*, 36.
36. For Defoe's antitheatricalism and puritanism, see J. A. Downie, "Defoe's *Review*, the Theatre, and Anti-High-Church Propaganda," *Restoration and Eighteenth-Century Theatre Research* 15 (1976): 24–32.
37. Daniel Defoe, *The Great Law of Subordination Consider'd*, in *Religious and Didactic Writings of Daniel Defoe*, ed. J. A. Downie, vol. 6 (London: Pickering and Chatto, 2007), 81.
38. Defoe, *The Fears of the Pretender*, 24–25.
39. Defoe, *The Fears of the Pretender*, 20.
40. Defoe, *The Fears of the Pretender*, 20–21.
41. See Mackie, *Market à la Mode*, 154–156.
42. *The State of the Case, between the Lord Chamberlain of his Majesty's Household, and Sir Richard Steele, as Represented by that Knight. Restated in Vindication of King George, and the Most Noble the Duke of Newcastle* (London, 1720), 14. Steele's own pamphlet was also entitled *The State of the Case* and had been initially published earlier in March 1720. For details on the quarrel with Newcastle over theatrical licensing at Drury Lane, see Loftis, *Steele at Drury Lane*, 121–180.
43. *The State of the Case . . . Restated*, 14.
44. *The State of the Case . . . Restated*, 16.
45. Richard Steele, *The State of the Case between the Lord Chamberlain of His Majesty's Household, and the Governor of the Royal Company of Comedians*, in *Tracts and Pamphlets by Richard Steele*, ed. Rae Blanchard (New York: Octagon Books, 1967), 598.
46. Steele, *The State of the Case*, 595, 604. For similar language, see also Richard Steele, *The Correspondence of Richard Steele*, ed. Rae Blanchard (Oxford: Oxford University Press, 1941), specifically the letter from Steele to the Duke of Newcastle, December 19, 1719 (146–147), and Steele's journal entry for April 9, 1721 (541).
47. *The State of the Case . . . Restated*, 27.
48. See Michael McKeon, *The Secret History of Domesticity: Public, Private, and the Division of Knowledge* (Baltimore, Md.: Johns Hopkins University Press, 2005), 3–48.
49. John Dennis, *The Characters and Conduct of Sir John Edgar, call'd by Himself Sole Monarch of the Stage in Drury-Lane* (1720), in *Critical Works*, 2:214. Further citations of Dennis's works refer to this edition and are cited parenthetically in the text. Sir John Edgar was Steele's pseudonym in his 1720 periodical *The Theatre.*
50. Corman, "Interpreting and Misinterpreting," 39.
51. No doubt due to Dennis's reputation as "the Critick" and parodies of him as such by Pope, Gay, and others, he has received far more scholarly attention for his aesthetics than he has for the way his work fits into the political, religious, and cultural contexts of his moment. But see John Morillo, "John Dennis: Enthusiastic Passions, Cultural Memory, and Literary Theory," *Eighteenth-Century Studies* 34 (2000): 21–41.

52. For Dennis and literary professionalization, see Paul D. Cannan, *The Emergence of Dramatic Criticism in England: From Jonson to Pope* (New York: Palgrave, 2006), 116–124.
53. Most scholars read 1711 as the major turning point in Dennis's career; see Cannan, *The Emergence of Dramatic Criticism*, 116–117, 124; and Brean Hammond, *Professional Imaginative Writing in England, 1670–1740: "Hackney for Bread"* (Oxford: Clarendon Press, 1997), 177.
54. Cannan, *The Emergence of Dramatic Criticism*, 116–124.
55. Cannan, *The Emergence of Dramatic Criticism*, 123.
56. See Hammond, *Professional Imaginative Writing*, 49–69.
57. For the associations between the rise of manners and sociability in the early eighteenth century and the culture's turn to commerce, see Pocock, *Virtue, Commerce, and History*, and Klein, "Property and Politeness."
58. See Cannan, *The Emergence of Dramatic Criticism*, 121, and Matthew J. Kinservik, "Reconsidering Theatrical Regulation in the Long Eighteenth Century," in *Players, Playwrights, Playhouses: Investigating Performance, 1660–1800*, ed. Michael Cordner and Peter Holland (New York: Palgrave, 2007), 160–161.
59. See Kinservik, "Reconsidering Theatrical Regulation," 160–161.
60. For a political reading of *The Rehearsal*, see Margarita Stocker, "Political Allusion in *The Rehearsal*," *Philological Quarterly* 67 (1988): 11–35.
61. See James G. Turner, *Libertines and Radicals in Early Modern London: Sexuality, Politics and Literary Culture, 1630–1685* (Cambridge: Cambridge University Press, 2002).
62. See Joseph Roach, *It* (Ann Arbor: University of Michigan Press, 2007), 98–101, 116, and Robert D. Hume and Harold Love, "General Introduction," in George Villiers, *Plays, Poems, and Miscellaneous Writings associated with George Villiers, Second Duke of Buckingham*, vol. 1 (Oxford: Oxford University Press, 2007), xlii–xliv.
63. In *Spectator* no. 65, however, Steele reads libertine wit as capable of breaking down the barriers of social class it purports to uphold. For a similar reading, see Robert Markley, *Two-Edg'd Weapons: Style and Ideology in the Comedies of Etherege, Wycherley, and Congreve* (Oxford: Clarendon Press, 1988), 100–137.
64. See Bryson, *From Courtesy to Civility*, 250–252, 262–264, and Mackie, *Market à la Mode*, 20–21.
65. Mackie, *Rakes, Highwaymen, and Pirates*, 45; Turner, *Libertines and Radicals*.
66. John Gay, *John Gay: Dramatic Works*, ed. John Fuller, 2 vols. (Oxford: Clarendon Press, 1983), 1:222–223.
67. See Habermas, *The Structural Transformation of the Public Sphere*, 52–53. For similar articulations, see Mackie, *Market à la Mode*, 21, and Peter Uwe Hohendahl, *The Institution of Criticism* (Ithaca, N.Y.: Cornell University Press, 1982), 52.
68. See Loftis, *The Politics of Drama*, 87, and Charles Harold Gray, *Theatrical Criticism in London to 1795* (New York: Columbia University Press, 1931), 57. Loftis provides an extensive account of the immediate responses to *The Conscious Lovers* in *Steele at Drury Lane*, 204–213.
69. Benjamin Victor, *An Epistle to Sir Richard Steele* (London, 1722), 4, 26.
70. *The Freeholder's Journal*, December 5 and 12, 1722.
71. Steele, *The Conscious Lovers*, 304.
72. See John Locke, *Second Treatise of Government*, in *Two Treatises of Government*, ed. Peter Laslett (Cambridge: Cambridge University Press, 1988), 380–384, 398–405.
73. *The Freeholder's Journal*, December 5, 1722. For a related reading of the politics of sentimentality, see Brett Wilson, "Bevil's Eyes; or, How Crying at *The Conscious Lovers* Could Save Britain," *Eighteenth-Century Studies* 45 (2012): 497–518.

74. *The St. James's Journal,* November 22, 1722. For the prior letter to which this writer refers, see *The St. James's Journal,* November 15, 1722.
75. *The St. James's Journal,* November 22, 1722.
76. On this irony, see also Loftis, *Steele at Drury Lane,* 207.
77. The scenes are as follows: 3.2, 4.1, 5.2. For Dorimant as spectator, see also Thomas King, *The Gendering of Men, 1600–1750,* vol. 1: *The English Phallus* (Madison: University of Wisconsin Press, 2004), 228–240.
78. Robert D. Hume, *The Rakish Stage: Studies in English Drama, 1660–1800* (Carbondale: Southern Illinois University Press, 1983), 155. See also Weber, *The Restoration Rake-Hero,* 78–79; Derek Hughes, *English Drama, 1660–1700* (Oxford: Clarendon Press, 1996), 154; and Virginia Ogden Birdsall, *Wild Civility: The English Comic Spirit on the Restoration Stage* (Bloomington: Indiana University Press, 1970), 89.
79. George Etherege, *The Man of Mode; or, Sir Fopling Flutter,* in *Restoration and Eighteenth-Century Comedy,* 2nd ed., ed. Scott McMillin (New York: W. W. Norton, 1997), 127.
80. Habermas, *The Structural Transformation of the Public Sphere,* 32–33, 40–43.
81. The phrase "little Senate" is Pope's; see his letter to James Craggs, July 15, 1715, in *The Correspondence of Alexander Pope,* ed. George Sherburn, 5 vols. (Oxford: Clarendon Press, 1956), 1:306–307. For Button's, see Loftis, *The Politics of Drama,* 86, 90, and Bryant Lillywhite, *London Coffee Houses: A Reference Book of Coffee Houses of the Seventeenth, Eighteenth, and Nineteenth Centuries* (London: G. Allen and Unwin, 1963), 143–144.
82. *The St. James's Journal,* December 15, 1722.
83. *The St. James's Journal,* December 15, 1722. For Pope's later variants, see *Miscellanies. The last volume* (London, 1727), 132–133; and *Epistle to Arbuthnot,* in *The Poems of Alexander Pope,* ed. John Butt (New Haven, Conn.: Yale University Press, 1963), 604–605. Modern scholarship rejects the theory that "Dorimant" was actually Pope. That the lines are here printed without permission is suggested by Pope himself in the "Testimonies of Authors" section of the *Dunciad Variorum* (1729), where Pope accuses the public journals of pirating the Addison lines (*Poems,* 332). For the history of the lines and Pope's relations with Addison, see Arthur Case, "Pope, Addison, and the 'Atticus' Lines," *Modern Philology* 33 (1935): 187–193, and Norman Ault, "Pope and Addison," *Review of English Studies* 17 (1941): 428–451.
84. Pope, letter to James Craggs, July 15, 1715, in *The Correspondence of Alexander Pope,* 1:306–307; *Applebee's Original Weekly Journal,* March 20, 1720; *The Freeholder's Journal,* December 5 and 12, 1722.
85. Bertrand Goldgar, *Walpole and the Wits: The Relation of Politics to Literature, 1722–1742* (Lincoln: University of Nebraska Press, 1976), 51.
86. *Weekly Journal, or the British Gazetteer,* March 25, 1727; *Weekly Journal, or the British Gazetteer,* June 22, 1728.
87. For "Dorimant's" attacks on the oppositional press, see *Weekly Journal, or the British Gazetteer,* January 14, 1727, and October 28, 1727. For his defense of Drury Lane, see *Weekly Journal, or the British Gazetteer,* March 25, 1727, and March 30, 1728. The literary tactics of pro-ministry and oppositional writing at this time are discussed in Matthew J. Kinservik, *Disciplining Satire: The Censorship of Satiric Comedy on the Eighteenth-Century London Stage* (Lewisburg, Pa.: Bucknell University Press, 2002), 60–65; Loftis, *The Politics of Drama,* 94–98; and Goldgar, *Walpole and the Wits,* 28–63.
88. Goldgar, *Walpole and the Wits,* 72.
89. *The London Journal,* March 23, 1728; *An Essay upon the Taste and Writings of the Present Times* (London, 1728), 15–16. Similar ministry attacks can be found in *The Senator* (London, 1728); *The London Journal* for March 30 and April 20, 1728; and *The Twickenham*

Hotch-Potch (London, 1728). See also Goldgar, *Walpole and the Wits*, 70–74, and William Eben Schultz, *Gay's Beggar's Opera: Its Content, History, and Influence* (New York: Russell and Russell, 1967), 226–269.

90. See *Twickenham Hotch-Potch*, i–vii, and *A View of the Town; or, Memoirs of London* (London, 1731), vii. The comment by Dennis is from his *Remarks upon Mr. Pope's Translation of Homer* (1717).
91. Modern scholarship is at odds about the political thrust of *The Beggar's Opera*. Political in itself or not, however, it is certain that the opposition politicized the play quickly after its premiere. See Kinservik, *Disciplining Satire*, 60–65; Goldgar, *Walpole and the Wits*, 69–70; Calhoun Winton, *John Gay and the London Theatre* (Lexington: University Press of Kentucky, 1993), 103–107; David Nokes, *John Gay: A Profession of Friendship* (Oxford: Oxford University Press, 1995), 433–436; and Schultz, *Gay's Beggar's Opera*, 178–203.
92. *Weekly Journal, or the British Gazetteer*, March 30, 1728.
93. For Oldfield, see James Peck, "Anne Oldfield's Lady Townly: Consumption, Credit, and the Whig Hegemony of the 1720s," *Theatre Journal* 49 (1997): 397–416.
94. *Weekly Journal, or the British Gazetteer*, March 30, 1728.
95. See Jonathan Kramnick, *Making the English Canon: Print-Capitalism and the Cultural Past, 1700–1770* (Cambridge: Cambridge University Press, 1998), 15–53.
96. For a review of the scholarly debate over *The Spectator*'s relation to coercive and consensual forms of sociocultural power, see King, *The Gendering of Men, 1600–1750*, 1:201–202.
97. *Spectator* no. 10, in Addison and Steele, *The Spectator*, 1:44; *Weekly Journal, or the British Gazetteer*, March 30, 1728.
98. See Isaac Kramnick, *Bolingbroke and His Circle: The Politics of Nostalgia in the Age of Walpole* (Cambridge, Mass.: Harvard University Press, 1968), 223–230; William Empson, *Some Versions of Pastoral* (London: Chatto and Windus, 1950), 195–252; J. Douglas Canfield, "The Critique of Capitalism and the Retreat into Art in Gay's *Beggar's Opera* and Fielding's *Author's Farce*," in *Cutting Edges: Postmodern Critical Essays on Eighteenth-Century Satire*, ed. James E. Gill (Knoxville: University of Tennessee Press, 1995), 320–334; Michael Denning, "Beggars and Thieves," *Literature and History* 8 (1982): 41–55; and Sven Armens, *John Gay: Social Critic* (New York: Octagon, 1966), 51–71.
99. John Gay, *The Beggar's Opera*, ed. Bryan Loughrey and T. O. Treadwell (New York: Penguin, 1986), 49, 107. Further citations refer to this edition and appear parenthetically in the text.
100. "Newgate pastoral" is originally Swift's term; see Swift's letter to Pope, August 30, 1716, in *The Correspondence of Alexander Pope*, 1:360.
101. See Weber, *The Restoration Rake-Hero*, 207–211; Canfield, "The Critique of Capitalism," 322; Mackie, *Rakes, Highwaymen, and Pirates*, 71–96; Peter Tasch, "*The Beggar's Opera* and *The Libertine*," *Notes and Queries* 36 (1989): 52; and Dianne Dugaw, *Deep Play: John Gay and the Invention of Modernity* (Newark: University of Delaware Press, 2001), 162–192.
102. *Memoirs Concerning the Life and Manners of Captain Mackheath* (London, 1728), 7. Further citations refer to this edition and appear parenthetically in the text. For other readings of this text, see Roach, *It*, 217–218, and Cheryl Wanko, *Roles of Authority: Thespian Biography and Celebrity in Eighteenth-Century Britain* (Lubbock: Texas Tech University Press, 2003), 62–65.
103. Goldgar, *Walpole and the Wits*, 71–72.
104. Examples of "moral" writings on *The Beggar's Opera* that thinly disguise opposition politics include *An Epistle from Matt of the Mint, lately deceased, to Captain Macheath* (London, 1729); *Mist's Weekly Journal*, July 6, 1728; and *The Craftsman*, March 2, 1728, and April 20, 1728.

105. *The Craftsman*, May 18, 1728.
106. See Henry Fielding, *Shamela*, in *Joseph Andrews and Shamela*, ed. Judith Hawley (New York: Penguin, 1999), 21.
107. On this point, see Winton, *John Gay*, 92–93, 99.
108. Weber, *The Restoration Rake-Hero*, 209.
109. Denning, "Beggars and Thieves," 48, 53; Canfield, "The Critique of Capitalism."
110. Canfield, "The Critique of Capitalism," 326.
111. See I. Kramnick, *Bolingbroke*, 223–230; Canfield, "The Critique of Capitalism"; Mackie, *Rakes, Highwaymen, and Pirates*; Weber, *The Restoration Rake-Hero*, 203–211; and Armens, *John Gay*, 51–71.
112. Roach, *It*, 205–231.

NOTES TO CHAPTER 3

1. Hester Thrale's annotations in *The Spectator*, 8 vols. (London: Payne, Rivington, et al., 1789), 1:384, GEN MSS Vol. 527, Beinecke Rare Book and Manuscript Library, Yale University, New Haven, Conn. *The Man of Mode*'s final eighteenth-century performance was at Covent Garden on March 15, 1766.
2. See James J. Lynch, *Box, Pit, and Gallery: Stage and Society in Johnson's London* (Berkeley: University of California Press, 1953), 40–44, 270–271.
3. Charles Churchill, *The Poetical Works of Charles Churchill*, ed. Douglas Grant (Oxford: Clarendon Press, 1956), 198.
4. See Lynch, *Box, Pit, and Gallery*, 252–253; Thomas Kaiser, "The Drama of Charles Edward Stuart, Jacobite Propaganda, and French Political Protest, 1745–1750," *Eighteenth-Century Studies* 30 (1997): 365–381; and Elaine McGirr, *Heroic Mode and Political Crisis, 1660–1745* (Newark: University of Delaware Press, 2009), 167–204.
5. Readings that address *Clarissa*'s engagement with the 1745 Jacobite threat most directly include Tom Keymer, *Richardson's "Clarissa" and the Eighteenth-Century Reader* (Cambridge: Cambridge University Press, 1992), 142–198, and Elaine McGirr, "Why Lovelace Must Die," *NOVEL: A Forum on Fiction* 37 (2003–2004): 5–23. Richardson's dependence on Restoration libertines and Restoration drama for the characterization of Lovelace is also traced admirably in Mark Kinkead-Weekes, *Samuel Richardson: Dramatic Novelist* (Ithaca, N.Y.: Cornell, University Press, 1973), 395–461; Margaret Anne Doody, *A Natural Passion: A Study of the Novels of Samuel Richardson* (Oxford: Clarendon Press, 1974), 107–128; James G. Turner, "Lovelace and the Paradoxes of Libertinism," in *Samuel Richardson: Tercentenary Essays*, ed. Margaret Anne Doody and Peter Sabor (Cambridge: Cambridge University Press, 1989), 70–88; and Jocelyn Harris, "Protean Lovelace," in *Passion and Virtue: Essays on the Novels of Samuel Richardson*, ed. David Blewett (Toronto: University of Toronto Press, 2001), 92–113.
6. McGirr, "Why Lovelace Must Die," 8.
7. Denis Diderot, letter to Sophie Volland, September 28, 1761, quoted in *Clarissa: The Eighteenth-Century Response, 1747–1804*, 2 vols., ed. Lois Bueler (New York: AMS Press, 2010), 1:390.
8. Thomas Wilkes, *A General View of the Stage* (London, 1759), 25.
9. *The Whitehall Evening Post*, October 16, 1766; Francis Gentleman, *The Dramatic Censor; or, Critical Companion*, 2 vols. (London, 1770), 1:273; Elizabeth Inchbald, *Remarks for the British Theatre*, ed. Cecilia Macheski (Delmar, N.Y.: Scholars' Facsimiles and Reprints, 1990), n.p.
10. Henry Fielding, *The Champion*, January 3, 1740, in *Contributions to The Champion and Related Writings*, ed. W. B. Coley (Oxford: Oxford University Press, 2003), 104.

11. Francis Gentleman, for instance, describes how different actors portrayed their various roles; see *The Dramatic Censor*, 1:269–274.
12. For discussions of Garrick's "natural" style and its revolutionary qualities, see Alan Downer, "Nature to Advantage Dressed: Eighteenth-Century Acting," *PMLA* 58 (1943): 1002–1037; Michael Wilson, "Garrick, Iconic Acting, and the Ideologies of Theatrical Portraiture," *Word and Image* 6 (1990): 368–394; Joseph Roach, *The Player's Passion: Studies in the Science of Acting* (Ann Arbor: University of Michigan Press, 1993); and Lisa Freeman, *Character's Theater: Genre and Identity on the Eighteenth-Century English Stage* (Philadelphia: University of Pennsylvania Press, 2002), 32–39.
13. Peter Thomson, "Acting and Actors from Garrick to Kean," in *The Cambridge Companion to British Theatre, 1730–1830*, ed. Jane Moody and Daniel O'Quinn (Cambridge: Cambridge University Press, 2007), 5.
14. See the editors' introduction to *The Plays of David Garrick*, ed. Harry William Perdicord and Fredric Louis Bergmann, 7 vols. (Carbondale: Southern Illinois University Press, 1980–1982), 5:xix–xxii.
15. Arthur Murphy, *The Life of David Garrick, Esq.*, 2 vols. (London: J. Wright, 1801), 2:197. Such sentiments are confirmed in Garrick's correspondence from the 1740s; see David Garrick, *Letters*, ed. David M. Little and George M. Kahrl, 3 vols. (Cambridge, Mass.: Harvard University Press, 1963), particularly Garrick's letters to Francis Hayman and to Somerset Draper, post October 10, 1745 (1:52–57).
16. Thomas Davies, *Memoirs of the Life of David Garrick, Esq.*, 3rd ed., 2 vols. (London, 1781), 1:50–51. For other discussions of this episode, see Jean Benedetti, *David Garrick and the Birth of Modern Theatre* (London: Methuen, 2001), 62–63, and Peter Thomson, "Celebrity and Rivalry: David [Garrick] and Goliath [Quin]," in *Theatre and Celebrity in Britain, 1660–2000*, ed. Mary Luckhurst and Jane Moody (New York: Palgrave, 2005), 127–147.
17. Murphy, *The Life of David Garrick, Esq.*, 1:116.
18. Davies, *Memoirs of the Life of David Garrick, Esq.*, 1:104–105.
19. Richard Cumberland, *Memoirs of Richard Cumberland, Written by Himself* (London, 1806), 35–36.
20. Gentleman, *The Dramatic Censor*, 1:274.
21. Cumberland, *Memoirs of Richard Cumberland*, 35.
22. For the history of the Wilkite furor here and throughout this chapter, I rely on George Rudé, *Wilkes and Liberty: A Social Study of 1763 to 1774* (Oxford: Clarendon Press, 1962); John Brewer, *Party Ideology and Popular Politics at the Accession of George III* (Cambridge: Cambridge University Press, 1976); Linda Colley, *Britons: Forging the Nation, 1707–1837* (New Haven, Conn.: Yale University Press, 1992); Kathleen Wilson, *The Sense of the People: Politics, Culture, and Imperialism in England, 1715–1785* (Cambridge: Cambridge University Press, 1995), 206–236; Peter D. G. Thomas, *John Wilkes: A Friend to Liberty* (New York: Oxford University Press, 1996); Adam Rounce, "'Stuarts without End': Wilkes, Churchill, and Anti-Scottishness," *Eighteenth-Century Life* 29 (2005): 20–43; and John Sainsbury, *John Wilkes: The Lives of a Libertine* (Aldershot, U.K.: Ashgate, 2006).
23. See Colley, *Britons*, 196–207; Brewer, *Party Ideology*, 112–136, and Peter D. G. Thomas, *George III: King and Politicians, 1760–1770* (Manchester: Manchester University Press, 2002).
24. Brewer, *Party Ideology*, 117. For the politics of Bute's personal life and his work with the pro-ministry press, see Brewer, *Party Ideology*, 219–239; John Brewer, "The Misfortunes of Lord Bute," *The Historical Journal* 16 (1973): 3–43; Robert Rea, *The English Press in Politics, 1760–1774* (Lincoln: University of Nebraska Press, 1963), 13–41; and Rounce, "'Stuarts without End.'"

25. Philip Francis, *A Letter from the Cocoa Tree to the Country Gentlemen* (London, 1762), 13; Tobias Smollett, *The Briton*, in *The Works of Tobias Smollett: Poems, Plays, and The Briton*, ed. Byron Gassman (Athens: University of Georgia Press, 1993), 275.
26. *An Address to the Cocoa Tree from a Whig* (London, 1762), 6.
27. See K. Wilson, *The Sense of the People*, 212–228. Accounts since Lewis Namier's *The Structure of Politics at the Accession of George III*, 2nd ed. (New York: St. Martin's Press, 1957), have challenged earlier assumptions of George III's absolutist aspirations; see Thomas, *George III*, 1–23. However, these polemical accusations were extensive; along with K. Wilson, see Brewer, *Party Ideology*, 39–54, and Rudé, *Wilkes and Liberty*, 186–187. The sexual politics of the Wilkite controversy are explored further in Marilyn Morris, *Sex, Money, and Personal Character in Eighteenth-Century British Politics* (New Haven, Conn.: Yale University Press, 2014), and Declan Kavanagh, *Effeminate Years: Literature, Politics, and Aesthetics in Mid-Eighteenth-Century Britain* (Lewisburg, Pa.: Bucknell University Press, 2017).
28. *The North Briton* no. 33, January 15, 1763, in John Wilkes, *The North Briton, from No. I to No. XLVI inclusive: With several useful and explanatory notes, not printed in any former edition* (London, 1763), 219.
29. In a speech Wilkes made outside Westminster after his release from Tower, he declared that "universal liberty" is "not the cause of Peers and Gentlemen only, but of all the middling and inferior class of people, which stand most in need of protection." See "An Account of the proceedings in relation to John Wilkes, Esq; member of Parliament for Aylesbury, as author of the North Briton No. XLV," in *The Annual Register; or, A View of the History, Politicks, and Literature, for the Year 1763* (London, 1764), 139.
30. John Wilkes, *The Correspondence of the Late John Wilkes, with his Friends, Printed from the Original Manuscripts, in which are introduced Memoirs of His Life*, ed. John Almon, 5 vols. (London, 1805), 1:124, 128–129.
31. Wilkes, *The Correspondence of the Late John Wilkes*, 3:110, 113–114.
32. Wilkes, *The Correspondence of the Late John Wilkes*, 3:120.
33. See Rebecca Schneider, *Performing Remains: Art and War in Times of Theatrical Reenactment* (New York: Routledge, 2011), 68.
34. Quoted in Rudé, *Wilkes and Liberty*, 25.
35. See for instance, John Almon, *A Letter to J. Kidgell, containing a full answer to his Narrative*, 3rd ed. (London, 1763), 18, and Charles Churchill, "The Duellist," in *The Poetical Works of Charles Churchill*, 265.
36. For a comprehensive study of Wilkes's libertinism, see Sainsbury, *John Wilkes*.
37. Morris, *Sex, Money, and Personal Character*, 61–62.
38. On Enlightenment sexuality, see Roy Porter, "Mixed Feelings: The Enlightenment and Sexuality in Eighteenth-Century Britain," in *Sexuality in Eighteenth-Century Britain*, ed. Paul-Gabriel Boucé (Manchester: Manchester University Press, 1982), 1–27. On the politics of sexuality and masculinity in Wilkes's case specifically, see K. Wilson, *The Sense of the People*, 218–221; Kavanagh, *Effeminate Years*, 37–98; and John Sainsbury, "Wilkes and Libertinism," *Studies in Eighteenth-Century Culture* 26 (1998): 151–174.
39. Richard Grenville, Earl of Temple, *The Grenville Papers: Being the Correspondence of Richard Grenville Earl of Temple, K.G., and the Right Hon. George Grenville, their Friends and Contemporaries*, ed. William James Smith, 4 vols. (New York: AMS Press, 1970), 1:489.
40. See Ovid, *Metamorphoses*, trans. David Raeburn (New York: Penguin, 2004), 53. As Temple is counseling Wilkes to give up satirical wit in favor of persuasive argument here, however, he is likely thinking of Francis Bacon's similar use of Ovid's quote in his essay "Of Discourse"; see Francis Bacon, *The Essayes or Counsels, Civill and Morall*, ed. Michael Kiernan (Oxford: Oxford University Press, 2000), 104. The translation is Kiernan's. For

Lothario's powers of persuasion, see Nicholas Rowe, *The Fair Penitent*, ed. Malcolm Goldstein (Lincoln: University of Nebraska Press, 1969), 12.

41. Horace Walpole, *Memoirs of the Reign of King George III*, ed. Derek Jarrett, 4 vols. (New Haven, Conn.: Yale University Press, 2000), 1:117.
42. *Wilkes's Jest Book; or, The Merry Patriot* (London, 1769), title page.
43. *The Patriot's Jubilee* (London, 1770), title page.
44. Churchill, *The Poetical Works of Charles Churchill*, 218; *The North Briton* no. 42, March 19, 1763, in Wilkes, *The North Briton*, 279, 286. Bute's defense of economizing measures and attacks on it were widespread; see *The North Briton* nos. 42 and 43; and Kavanagh, *Effeminate Years*, 83–93.
45. Wilkes, *The North Briton*, 285; Wilkes, *The Correspondence of the Late John Wilkes*, 3:93.
46. My argument here intersects with that of Kavanagh, who similarly reads the oppositionist discourse about excise as linked to unproductiveness (*Effeminate Years*, 86–87). Whereas he reads "monster" as "sodomite," however, I contend that Wilkes and his contemporaries would have also been familiar with its traditional context in Restoration drama as referring to a "cuckold."
47. Walpole writes, "The public indignation went so far, that *The Beggar's Opera* being performed at Covent Garden theatre soon after this event, the whole audience, when Macheath says, '*That Jemmy Twitcher should peach me, I own surprises me*' burst out into an applause of application; and the nickname of *Jemmy Twitcher* stuck by the Earl [Sandwich] so as almost to occasion the disuse of his title" (*Memoirs of the Reign of King George III*, 1:207).
48. John Gay, *The Beggar's Opera*, ed. Bryan Loughrey and T. O. Treadwell (New York: Penguin, 1986), 69.
49. Lawrence Stone, *The Family, Sex and Marriage in England, 1500–1800* (New York: Harper and Row, 1977), 258.
50. Gay, *The Beggar's Opera*, 74–75, 49.
51. See John Sainsbury, "John Wilkes, Debt, and Patriotism," *Journal of British Studies* 34 (1995): 165–195.
52. *A New Form of Prayer, and Thanksgiving for the Happy Deliverance of John Wilkes* (London, 1768), 6.
53. *The North Briton* no. 45, April 23, 1763.
54. *The North Briton* no. 45, April 23, 1763.
55. This is perhaps evoked most familiarly in William Hogarth's ironic 1763 engraving of Wilkes wearing the cap of liberty, "symbol," as Shearer West argues, "of the sovereignty of the King"; see "Wilkes's Squint: Synecdochic Physiognomy and Political Identity in Eighteenth-Century Print Culture," *Eighteenth-Century Studies* 33 (1999): 65–84.
56. William Blackstone, in his commentaries of the 1760s, defines prerogative thus: "that special pre-eminence, which the king hath, over and above all other persons, and out of the ordinary course of common law, in right of his regal dignity. . . . It can only be applied to those rights and capacities which the king enjoys alone, in contradistinction to others, and not to those which he enjoys in common with any of his subjects"; Blackstone, *The Oxford Edition of Blackstone: Commentaries on the Laws of England*, book 1: *Of the Rights of Persons*, ed. David Lemmings (Oxford: Oxford University Press, 2016), 155.
57. John Dryden, *The Works of John Dryden*, vol. 3: *Poems, 1685–1692*, ed. Earl Miner and Vinton Dearing (Berkeley: University of California Press, 1969), 101.
58. For histories of Wilkite crowds and criticism of them, see Rudé, *Wilkes and Liberty*; Brewer, *Party Ideology*; and K. Wilson, *The Sense of the People*; and Kavanagh, *Effeminate Years*, 69–98.

59. *An Epistle from Col. John Lilburn, In the Shades, to John Wilkes* (London, 1765), 10; *Another Letter to Mr. Almon, in Matter of Libel* (London, 1770), 143.
60. Brewer, *Party Ideology*, 190.
61. *A Narrative of the Proceedings against John Wilkes, Esq.* (London, 1768), 29.
62. See Walpole, *Memoirs of the Reign of King George III*, 3:207; and the brief biography of Dalrymple in Joanna Major and Sarah Murden, *An Infamous Mistress: The Life, Loves and Family of the Celebrated Grace Dalrymple Elliott* (Barnsley, U.K.: Pen and Sword Books, 2016), 16–17.
63. Hugh Dalrymple, *Rodondo; or, The State Jugglers, Canto III* (London, 1770), 14. Further citations refer to this edition and appear parenthetically in the text.
64. John Vanbrugh, *The Provoked Wife*, in *John Vanbrugh: Four Comedies*, ed. Michael Cordner (New York: Penguin, 1989), 218. Further citations refer to this edition and appear parenthetically in the text. Curt Zimansky describes *The Provoked Wife* as "the most consistently popular Restoration play on the eighteenth-century stage" and notes that it was also considered one of the most immoral. Its performance history includes interpolations of moral sentiments and revisions, including Vanbrugh's own in 1706; see Zimansky, introduction to *The Provoked Wife*, ed. Curt Zimansky (Lincoln: University of Nebraska Press, 1969), xiii, xx, xxi–xxii. See also Antony Coleman, "Sir John Brute on the Eighteenth-Century Stage," *Restoration and Eighteenth-Century Theatre Research* 8 (1969): 41–46.
65. See Erin Mackie, *Rakes, Highwaymen, and Pirates: The Making of the Modern Gentleman in the Eighteenth Century* (Baltimore, Md.: Johns Hopkins University Press, 2009). For an earlier Restoration libertine tavern scene, see act 3 of George Etherege's *She Would If She Could* (1668).
66. John Locke, *A Letter Concerning Toleration*, ed. James H. Tully (Indianapolis, Ind.: Hackett, 1983), 51. Ironically for Lord Rake's gang, Locke counted atheists among those whose creeds were not to be tolerated by civil magistrates.
67. Brean Hammond, introduction to *John Vanbrugh: The Relapse and Other Plays*, ed. Brean Hammond (Oxford: Oxford University Press, 2004), xvii; Michael Cordner, "Playwright versus Priest: Profanity and the Wit of Restoration Comedy," in *The Cambridge Companion to English Restoration Theatre*, ed. Deborah Payne Fisk (Cambridge: Cambridge University Press, 2000), 217.
68. See Sainsbury, "John Wilkes, Debt, and Patriotism," 168–173.
69. Wilkes spent his exile in France, and his libertinism was tied to Francophilia; see Sainsbury, "John Wilkes, Debt, and Patriotism," 171.
70. See Jane Garrett, *The Triumphs of Providence: The Assassination Plot, 1696* (Cambridge: Cambridge University Press, 1980), 41, 121–134.
71. Zimansky notes Thomas Otway's Sir Davy Dunce (*The Soldiers' Fortune*) and George Etherege's Sir Oliver Cockwood (*She Would If She Could*) as prevalent types for Brute (introduction to *The Provoked Wife*, xv–xvi).
72. Works of broad importance on these topics in relation to the *London Journal* include Patricia Meyer Spacks, *Imagining a Self: Autobiography and Novel in Eighteenth-Century England* (Cambridge, Mass.: Harvard University Press, 1976), 227–263; Donald Kay, "Boswell in the Green Room: Dramatic Method in the *London Journal*," *Philological Quarterly* 57 (1978): 195–212; Felicity Nussbaum, *The Autobiographical Subject: Gender and Ideology in Eighteenth-Century England* (Baltimore, Md.: Johns Hopkins University Press, 1989), 103–126; the essays in *James Boswell: Psychological Interpretations*, ed. Donald Newman (New York: St. Martin's Press, 1995); David Weed, "Sexual Positions: Men of Pleasure, Economy, and Dignity in Boswell's *London Journal*," *Eighteenth-Century Studies* 31 (1998): 215–234; Philip Carter, "James Boswell's Manliness," in *English*

Masculinities, 1660–1800, ed. Tim Hitchcock and Michele Cohen (New York: Longman, 1999), 111–130; and Erik Bond, *Reading London: Urban Speculation and Imaginative Government in Eighteenth-Century Literature* (Columbus: Ohio State University Press, 2007), 138–182.

73. James Boswell, *Boswell's London Journal 1762–1763, together with Journal of My Jaunt, Harvest 1762*, ed. Frederick Pottle (London: Heinemann, 1951), 81.
74. Mackie, *Rakes, Highwaymen, and Pirates*, 84.
75. James Boswell, *London Journal, 1762–1763*, ed. Gordon Turnbull (New York: Penguin, 2010), 182. Further citations refer to this edition and appear parenthetically in the text.
76. See Weed, "Sexual Positions."
77. James Boswell, "Sketch of the Early Life of James Boswell, written by Himself for Jean Jacques Rousseau, 5 December 1764," in Frederick Pottle, *James Boswell: The Earlier Years, 1740–1769* (New York: McGraw-Hill, 1966), 2, 4. Originally written in French, the translation here is Pottle's.
78. Gordon Turnbull, introduction to Boswell, *London Journal, 1762–1763*, xxiv. On this aspect of his relation with his father, see also Turnbull, "Boswell and Sympathy: The Trial and Execution of John Reid," in *New Light on Boswell*, ed. Greg Clingham (Cambridge: Cambridge University Press, 1991), 104–115.
79. See Anna Bryson, *From Courtesy to Civility: Changing Codes of Conduct in Early Modern England* (Oxford: Oxford University Press, 1998), 243–275; and James G. Turner, *Libertines and Radicals in Early Modern London: Sexuality, Politics and Literary Culture, 1630–1685* (Cambridge: Cambridge University Press, 2002), 197–251.
80. Boswell in fact disliked tavern riots; see his entry for May 18, 1763 (*London Journal, 1762–1763*, 224).
81. James Boswell, *The General Correspondence of James Boswell, 1757–1763*, ed. David Hankins and James J. Caudle (New Haven, Conn.: Yale University Press, 2006), 237.
82. On the nexus of wit, sexual potency, and sovereignty, see Richard Braverman, *Plots and Counterplots: Sexual Politics and the Body Politic in English Literature, 1660–1730* (Cambridge: Cambridge University Press, 1993), 221–224.
83. See Bryson, *From Courtesy to Civility*, 261–271; and Carter, "James Boswell's Manliness."
84. Philip Dormer Stanhope, Lord Chesterfield, letters to his son Philip, March 27, 1747, and November 8, 1750, in *Lord Chesterfield's Letters*, ed. David Roberts (Oxford: Oxford University Press, 1998), 49, 214–215. The young Boswell was fascinated with "men of pleasure," male role models attached to fashionable urban culture such as the Edinburgh actor West Digges and his early patron Lord Eglinton (see Boswell, *London Journal, 1762–1763*, 13, 23). In contrast, Boswell typically reserves words like "rake" or "libertine" for moments of remorse for or resolutions against unrestrained, often lower-class sexual adventuring or disorderly behavior which he reads as damaging to the genteel and self-controlled character of the *retenu* (see Boswell, *London Journal, 1762–1763*, 69, 188).
85. Chesterfield, letter to his son Philip, March 27, 1747, in *Chesterfield's Letters*, 50.
86. Boswell, *Boswell's London Journal . . . with Journal of My Jaunt*, 62.
87. For a divergent reading of Boswell's "cavalier masculinity," which relies on the gender politics of 1740s critiques of Jacobitism rather than the cultural memory of the Restoration court, see Weed, "Sexual Positions."
88. Boswell's friend Erskine once described him as "a Tory with Whig Principles"; see James Boswell, *Boswell in Extremes, 1776–1778*, ed. Charles McC. Weis and Frederick Pottle (New York: McGraw-Hill, 1970), 252.
89. See Jürgen Habermas, *The Structural Transformation of the Public Sphere: An Inquiry into a Category of Bourgeois Society*, trans. Thomas Burger with the assistance of Frederick Lawrence (Cambridge, Mass.: MIT Press, 1989), 5–14.

90. Frank Brady, *Boswell's Political Career* (New Haven, Conn.: Yale University Press, 1965), 18.
91. See Pottle, *James Boswell*, 108–109.
92. See Mackie's reading of Rochester's "A Ramble in St. James's Park," in *Rakes, Highwaymen, and Pirates*, 49–51.
93. Ironically, this realization confirms what Louisa herself repeatedly tells Boswell about sexual passion; see Boswell, *London Journal, 1762–1763*, 53, 93.
94. Weed suggests that Boswell's "cavalier masculinity" is ultimately replaced by self-controlled masculine role models such as William Temple and Samuel Johnson ("Sexual Positions," 220).
95. See Mackie, *Rakes, Highwaymen, and Pirates*, 94–96.

NOTES TO CHAPTER 4

1. Charles Lamb, "On the Artificial Comedy of the Last Century," in *The Works of Charles and Mary Lamb*, ed. E. V. Lucas, 7 vols. (New York: AMS Press, 1968), 2:141.
2. William Hazlitt, *The Complete Works of William Hazlitt*, ed. P. P. Howe, 21 vols. (New York: AMS Press, 1967), 6:68, 71.
3. Jane Moody, *Illegitimate Theatre in London, 1770–1840* (Cambridge: Cambridge University Press, 2000), 207. See also Jeffrey Cox and Michael Gamer, "'Torn from Its Genus': Hannah Cowley on Comedy, Laughter, and Morality," in *Emancipation, Liberation and Freedom: Romantic Drama and Theatre in Britain, 1760–1830*, ed. Gioia Angeletti (Parma, Italy: Monte Università Parma, 2010), 87–116. For analysis of the changing class/social makeup of audiences and their repertory desires, see Michael Booth, *Prefaces to English Nineteenth-Century Theatre* (Manchester: Manchester University Press, 1980), and Frederick Burwick, *Romantic Drama: Acting and Reacting* (Cambridge: Cambridge University Press, 2009).
4. Allardyce Nicoll, *A History of Early Nineteenth Century Drama, 1800–1850* (Cambridge: Cambridge University Press, 1930), 16, 185.
5. On historical reenactments and trends in scenic realism on the Romantic stage, see Burwick, *Romantic Drama*, 7; Jonathan Lamb, "Historical Reenactment, Extremity, and Passion," *The Eighteenth Century: Theory and Interpretation* 49 (2008): 239–250; and Iain McCalman and Paul A. Pickering, eds., *Historical Reenactment: From Realism to the Affective Turn* (New York: Palgrave, 2010). On the apolitical nature of these comedic Restoration reenactments, see Dorothea Flothow, "Merrying the Monarch: Charles II in Historical Comedies (1800 to the Present)," in *History and Humour: British and American Perspectives*, ed. Barbara Korte and Doris Lechner (Bielefeld, Germany: Transcript, 2013), 87–110. Simon Shepherd and Peter Womack contest this depoliticized reading very briefly in their discussion of Jerrold and Walker's *Nell Gwynne* plays in *English Drama: A Cultural History* (Oxford: Blackwell, 1996), 182–187. On the displacement of political radicalism and the rise of diversionary popular culture after the Regency, see Iain McCalman, *Radical Underworld: Prophets, Revolutionaries and Pornographers in London, 1795–1840* (Cambridge: Cambridge University Press, 1988), and John Marriott's introduction to *Unknown London: Early Modernist Visions of the Metropolis, 1815–45*, ed. John Marriott, vol. 1 (London: Pickering and Chatto, 2000), xxx, xl.
6. C. Lamb, "Artificial Comedy," 2:143.
7. Flothow, "Merrying the Monarch," 91–92.
8. Rebecca Schneider, *Performing Remains: Art and War in Times of Theatrical Reenactment* (New York: Routledge, 2011), 174.

9. Bernard Shaw, preface to *In Good King Charles's Golden Days*, in *Last Plays* (New York: Penguin, 1974), 9; Diana Taylor, *The Archive and the Repertoire: Performing Cultural Memory in the Americas* (Durham, N.C.: Duke University Press, 2003), 13.
10. Taylor, *The Archive and the Repertoire*, 28.
11. Mary Shelley, *Frankenstein*, ed. J. Paul Hunter (New York: Norton, 1996), 110.
12. See, for example, Joseph Nicholes, "Revolutions Compared: The English Civil War as Political Touchstone in Romantic Literature," in *Revolution and English Romanticism: Politics and Rhetoric*, ed. Keith Hanley and Raman Selden (New York: St. Martin's Press, 1990), 261–276, and Timothy Lang, *Victorians and the Stuart Heritage: Interpretations of a Discordant Past* (Cambridge: Cambridge University Press, 1995).
13. See Joseph Nicholes, "Politics by Indirection: Charles Lamb's Seventeenth-Century Renegade, John Woodvil," *The Wordsworth Circle* 19 (1988): 49–55. Gillian Russell notes how much politically subversive drama at the time used tactics of displacement; see *The Theatres of War: Performance, Politics, and Society, 1793–1815* (New York: Oxford University Press, 1995), 53.
14. Edmund Burke, *Reflections on the Revolution in France*, ed. Conor Cruise O'Brien (New York: Penguin, 2004), 248.
15. See Marvin Carlson, *The Haunted Stage: The Theatre as Memory Machine* (Ann Arbor: University of Michigan Press, 2001).
16. Hazlitt, *Complete Works*, 11:64.
17. Hazlitt, "What Is the People?" (1818), in *Complete Works*, 7:260.
18. Hazlitt, "On the Regal Character" (1818), in *Complete Works*, 7:286–287.
19. See Eric J. Evans, *Britain before the Reform Act: Politics and Society, 1815–1832* (New York: Longman, 1989), 1–38; Linda Colley, *Britons: Forging the Nation, 1707–1837* (New Haven, Conn.: Yale University Press, 1992), 334–350; and Michael J. Turner, *British Politics in an Age of Reform* (New York: Manchester University Press, 1999), 106–152.
20. Samuel Taylor Coleridge, *Biographia Literaria*, in *The Collected Works of Samuel Taylor Coleridge*, ed. James Engell and W. Jackson Bate, vol. 7, part 2 (Princeton, N.J.: Princeton University Press, 1983), 221. For readings of Coleridge's views on drama and radicalism, see Jeffrey Cox, "Romantic Drama and the French Revolution," in Hanley and Selden, *Revolution and English Romanticism*, 250–251, and Moody, *Illegitimate Theatre*, 57–62.
21. See Jeffrey Cox's introduction in *Seven Gothic Dramas, 1789–1825*, ed. Jeffrey Cox (Athens: Ohio University Press, 1992), 27.
22. Coleridge, *Biographia Literaria*, 221.
23. See Watson Nicholson, *The Struggle for a Free Stage in London* (New York: Houghton and Mifflin, 1906); E. B. Watson, *Sheridan to Robertson: A Study of the Nineteenth-Century London Stage* (Cambridge, Mass.: Harvard University Press, 1926); Dewey Ganzel, "Patent Wrongs and Patent Theatres: Drama and the Law in the Early Nineteenth Century," *PMLA* 76 (1961): 384–396; Marc Baer, *Theatre and Disorder in Late Georgian London* (Oxford: Oxford University Press, 1992); Moody, *Illegitimate Theatre*; Jane Moody, "'Fine Word, Legitimate!': Toward a Theatrical History of Romanticism," *Texas Studies in Language and Literature* 38 (1996): 223–244; Julia Swindells, *Glorious Causes: The Grand Theatre of Political Change, 1789–1833* (Oxford: Oxford University Press, 2001); and Jacky Bratton, *New Readings in Theatre History* (Cambridge: Cambridge University Press, 2003), 67–91.
24. Moody, *Illegitimate Theatre*, 74.
25. See Moody, "'Fine Word,'" 232–233; Bratton, *New Readings*, 67–91; and David Worrall, *The Politics of Romantic Theatricality, 1787–1832: The Road to the Stage* (New York: Palgrave, 2007).

26. Ganzel, "Patent Wrongs," 388. See also Moody, *Illegitimate Theatre*, 10–47; and Swindells, *Glorious Causes*, 13.
27. *Hansard's Parliamentary Debates*, 3rd series, vol. 13 (London: T. C. Hansard, 1833), 240.
28. For more on the meetings and the Select Committee, see Ganzel, "Patent Wrongs"; Bratton, *New Readings*, 67–91; and Swindells, *Glorious Causes*, 1–17, 176–187.
29. *The Morning Chronicle*, January 4, 1832.
30. *The Morning Chronicle*, January 4, 1832.
31. On the patent theaters' precarious finances, see Moody, *Illegitimate Theatre*, 62–78.
32. *The Morning Chronicle*, January 4, 1832.
33. *The Morning Chronicle*, March 23, 1832.
34. See Hazlitt, *Lectures on the English Comic Writers*, in *Complete Works*, 6:69, and Walter Scott, *An Essay on the Drama*, in *The Miscellaneous Works of Sir Walter Scott*, vol. 6 (Edinburgh, 1861), 217–395.
35. *The Morning Chronicle*, March 23, 1832.
36. *The Morning Chronicle*, March 23, 1832.
37. Melinda Zook, "The Restoration Remembered: The First Whigs and the Making of Their History," *Seventeenth Century* 17 (2002): 215.
38. See Bratton, *New Readings*, 3–16, 67–91.
39. *The Morning Chronicle*, June 1, 1832; Wetherall's comment is in response to Bulwer's May 31, 1832, speech.
40. Douglas Jerrold, *The Bride of Ludgate* (London, 1831), 6. Further citations refer to this edition and appear parenthetically in the text.
41. *The Examiner*, December 18, 1831; *The Athenaeum*, December 10, 1831. For similar comments, see also *The Morning Post*, December 9, 1831.
42. *The Tatler*, December 9, 1831.
43. James Robinson Planché, *The Recollections and Reflections of J. R. Planché*, 2 vols. (London, 1872), 1:237; Planché, *The Court Beauties: A Dramatic Sketch in One Act* (London, 1835), 3. Further citations refer to this edition and appear parenthetically in the text. Accurate historical scenic realism was a goal for many playwrights who flaunted documentary sources as grounds for their representations; see Planché, *Court Beauties*, 3, and William Thomas Moncrieff, *The "Tobit's Dog!"* (London, 1838), iii–iv.
44. Lamb, "Artificial Comedy," 2:142.
45. See Flothow, "Merrying the Monarch."
46. Taylor, *The Archive and the Repertoire*, 13.
47. On these politics of Reform broadly, see John Cannon, *Parliamentary Reform, 1640–1832* (Cambridge: Cambridge University Press, 1973), 242–263; Colley, *Britons*, 334–350; Eric J. Evans, *The Great Reform Act of 1832* (New York: Routledge, 1994); M. Turner, *British Politics*; Arthur Burns and Joanna Innes, introduction to *Rethinking the Age of Reform: Britain, 1780–1850*, ed. Arthur Burns and Joanna Innes (Cambridge: Cambridge University Press, 2003), 1–70; and Swindells, *Glorious Causes*, 1–17.
48. See Giorgio Agamben, *Homo Sacer: Sovereign Power and Bare Life*, trans. Daniel Heller-Roazen (Stanford, Calif.: Stanford University Press, 1998), and Judith Butler, *Precarious Life: The Powers of Mourning and Violence* (London: Verso, 2004), 50–100.
49. *The Examiner*, December 18, 1831.
50. *The Morning Post*, December 9, 1831; *The Tatler*, December 9, 1831.
51. Henry Robert Addison, *The King's Word* (London, 1835), 9. Further citations refer to this edition and appear parenthetically in the text.
52. See Swindells, *Glorious Causes*, 27–35. For the radicalism of Jerrold's prose and social melodrama, see Richard Kelly, *Douglas Jerrold* (New York: Twayne, 1972), and Michael Slater, *Douglas Jerrold: 1803–1857* (London: Duckworth, 2002).

53. Colley, *Britons*, 345–346.
54. John Howard Payne, *Charles the Second; or, The Merry Monarch* (London, 1824), 14, 27. Further citations refer to this edition and appear parenthetically in the text. On nautical drama and its imagining of sailors, see Russell, *Theatres of War*, 7–10, 97–99.
55. Colley, *Britons*, 342.
56. For Jerrold, see Slater, *Douglas Jerrold*, 81–82. For Planché, see his *Recollections*, and John Russell Stephens, *The Profession of the Playwright: British Theatre, 1800–1900* (Cambridge: Cambridge University Press, 1992). For Addison, see John Russell Stephens, "Henry Robert Addison," in *The Oxford Dictionary of National Biography* (Oxford: Oxford University Press, 2004). For Payne, see Gabriel Harrison, *John Howard Payne: Dramatist, Poet, Actor, Author of Home, Sweet Home: His Life and Writings* (New York: B. Blom, 1969), and Grace Overmyer, *America's First Hamlet* (Westport, Conn.: Greenwood Press, 1975).
57. For this reformist discourse, see Ganzel, "Patent Wrongs"; Baer, *Theatre and Disorder*; Moody, *Illegitimate Theatre*, 48–78; Bratton, *New Readings*, 67–91; and Katherine Newey, "Reform on the London Stage," in Burns and Innes, *Rethinking the Age of Reform*, 238–253.
58. Philo-Dramaticus, "A Letter to Charles Kemble Esq., and R. W. Elliston Esq.," *Blackwood's Edinburgh Magazine*, vol. 17 (London, 1825), 727.
59. See *The Modern Stage: A Letter to the Hon. George Lamb, M.P. on the Decay and Degradation of English Dramatic Literature* (London, 1819).
60. Douglas Jerrold, *Nell Gwynne; or, The Prologue* (London, 1833), iii. Further citations refer to the edition and appear parenthetically in the text. See also Kelly, *Douglas Jerrold*, 35.
61. On the co-opting of the language of illegitimacy by radical reform, see Moody, *Illegitimate Theatre*, 62–78.
62. For a similar reading of *Nell Gwynne* as reformist critique, see Shepherd and Womack, *English Drama*, 185.
63. See Agamben, *Homo Sacer*, 81–86, 136–143.
64. For an example of this argument in relation to *Nell Gwynne*, see Slater, *Douglas Jerrold*, 93.
65. On Reform's relation to revolutionary politics, see Cannon, *Parliamentary Reform*, 242–263; Colley, *Britons*, 334–350; and Burns and Innes, introduction to *Rethinking the Age of Reform*, 15.
66. See Joanna Innes, "'Reform' in English Public Life: The Fortunes of a Word," in Burns and Innes, *Rethinking the Age of Reform*, 93–94.
67. See Slater, *Douglas Jerrold*, 92.
68. See Anthony Hamilton, *The Memoirs of Count Grammont*, ed. Gordon Goodwin, 2 vols. (London: A. H. Bullen, 1903).
69. John Walker, *Nell Gywnne* (London, 1830), 17. The discourse of "levelling" is part of contemporary political satires of Reform; see Joseph Grego, *A History of Parliamentary Elections and Electioneering* (London: Chatto and Windus, 1892), 358–359.
70. See J. Douglas Canfield, *Tricksters and Estates: On the Ideology of Restoration Comedy.* (Lexington: University Press of Kentucky, 1997), and Misty G. Anderson, "Genealogies of Comedy," in *The Oxford Handbook of the Georgian Theatre*, ed. Julia Swindells and David Francis Taylor (Oxford: Oxford University Press, 2014), 347–367.
71. For reform's targeting of the middle classes, see Colley, *Britons*, 334–350, and Evans, *Britain before the Reform Act*, 81–94.
72. See Schneider, *Performing Remains*, 30.
73. Walker, *Nell Gwynne*, 34.

74. On the post-Reform propertied middle-class hegemony in the state and on the stage, see Colley, *Britons*, 334–350; Burns and Innes, introduction to *Rethinking the Age of Reform*, 16, 46; and Bratton, *New Readings*, 69, 88.
75. Taylor, *The Archive and the Repertoire*, 28–29.
76. Elliston was known for his rakish personal life and capitalized on this in the parts he played; see Christopher Murray, *Robert William Elliston, Manager* (London: The Society for Theatre Research, 1975). For Moncrieff's claim, see his preface to *Selections from the Dramatic Works of William T. Moncrieff* (London, 1851), iii.
77. See Murray, *Robert William Elliston, Manager*, 63–65.
78. Saint-Évremond's biography may be found in John Wilmot, Lord Rochester, *The Works of the Right Honourable the Late Earls of Rochester and Roscommon*, 2nd ed. (London, 1707).
79. William Thomas Moncrieff, *Rochester; or, King Charles the Second's Merry Days* (London, 1819), 63. Further citations refer to this edition and appear parenthetically in the text.
80. See Swindells, *Glorious Causes*, 32–35; Worrall, *The Politics of Romantic Theatricality*, 135–165; and Newey, "Reform on the London Stage," 251–253.
81. See E. P. Thompson, *The Making of the English Working Class* (New York: Vintage, 1963), 603–710, and M. Turner, *British Politics*, 106–152.
82. Quoted in Thompson, *The Making of the English Working Class*, 639. Liverpool's ministers were quick to suspect treason everywhere; see Evans, *Britain before the Reform Act*, 18–19, and M. Turner, *British Politics*, 125–126, 133–134.
83. James G. Turner, *Libertines and Radicals in Early Modern London: Sexuality, Politics and Literary Culture, 1630–1685* (Cambridge: Cambridge University Press, 2002), 62.
84. Moncrieff, preface to *Selections from the Dramatic Works*, v–vi.
85. Moncrieff, preface to *Selections from the Dramatic Works*, vii–viii.
86. Moncrieff, preface to *Selections from the Dramatic Works*, viii.
87. See Moncrieff's assertions of his own popularity and notoriety in his interviews in Select Committee on Dramatic Literature, *Report from the Select Committee on Dramatic Literature: with the Minutes of Evidence*, in the Parliamentary Papers, *Reports from Committees, 1831–32*, vol. 6 (London: House of Commons, 1832), 175–180.
88. Worrall, *The Politics of Romantic Theatricality*, 153–154.
89. See Moncrieff's preface to his play *Reform; or, John Bull Triumphant*, in *Richardson's New Minor Drama*, ed. William Thomas Moncrieff (London, 1828–1831), v–vii, and Moncrieff's Select Committee interview: Select Committee on Dramatic Literature, *Report from the Select Committee*, 175–180.
90. *The Morning Chronicle*, February 25, 1832.
91. *The Morning Chronicle*, February 25, 1832.
92. Select Committee on Dramatic Literature, *Report from the Select Committee*, 177.
93. Select Committee on Dramatic Literature, *Report from the Select Committee*, 177.
94. Select Committee on Dramatic Literature, *Report from the Select Committee*, 177.
95. Moncrieff, preface to *Reform*, vi.
96. Moody, *Illegitimate Theatre*, 38. For Elliston's renovations, see *The Morning Post*, November 16, 1818, and Murray, *Robert William Elliston, Manager*, 61–65.
97. *The Morning Post*, November 17, 1818. On the pervasiveness of the patents' turn to illegitimate forms, see Moody, *Illegitimate Theatre*, 48–78.
98. *The Morning Post*, November 17, 1818.
99. George Daniel's preface to *Rochester*, in *Cumberland's Minor Theatre*, ed. George Daniel, 16 vols. (London, 1828), 11:5.
100. Moncrieff, *Selections from the Dramatic Works*, iii–iv. For favorable reviews that assert similar sentiments, see *The Morning Post*, November 17, 1818; *The Examiner*, November 22, 1818; *The Times*, January 18, 1819; and *The Morning Chronicle*, January 9, 1819.

101. Eliza Vestris and James Planché were to accomplish something similar at the Olympic in the 1830s with genteel petite comedies set in the Restoration; see Moody, *Illegitimate Theatre*, 197–207.

NOTES TO CONCLUSION

1. See Jim Davis, "Looking towards 1843 and the End of Monopoly," in *The Oxford Handbook of the Georgian Theatre*, ed. Julia Swindells and David Francis Taylor (Oxford: Oxford University Press, 2014), 156–173.
2. Diana Taylor, *The Archive and the Repertoire: Performing Cultural Memory in the Americas* (Durham, N.C.: Duke University Press, 2003), 143.

BIBLIOGRAPHY

NEWSPAPERS

Applebee's Original Weekly Journal
The Athenaeum
The Craftsman
The Examiner
The Freeholder's Journal
The London Chronicle
The London Journal
Mist's Weekly Journal
The Morning Chronicle
The Morning Post
The North Briton
The St. James's Journal
The Tatler
The Times
Weekly Journal, or the British Gazetteer
The Whitehall Evening Post

PRIMARY SOURCES

An Account of the Societies for the Reformation of Manners. London, 1699.

Addison, Henry Robert. *The King's Word*. London, 1835.

Addison, Joseph, and Richard Steele. *The Spectator*. Edited by Donald F. Bond. 5 vols. Oxford: Clarendon Press, 1965.

An Address to the Cocoa Tree from a Whig. London, 1762.

Almon, John. *A Letter to J. Kidgell, containing a full answer to his Narrative*. 3rd ed. London, 1763.

The Annual Register; or, A View of the History, Politicks, and Literature, for the Year 1763. London, 1764.

Another Letter to Mr. Almon, in Matter of Libel. London, 1770.

Bacon, Francis. *The Essayes or Counsels, Civill and Morall*. Edited by Michael Kiernan. Oxford: Oxford University Press, 2000.

Beckingham, Charles. "A Poem to the Memory of Nicholas Rowe, Esq." In *Musarum Lachrymae; or, Poems to the Memory of Nicholas Rowe, Esq.; By Several Hands*, 13–21. London, 1719.

Behn, Aphra. *The Rover and Other Works*. Edited by Jane Spencer. Oxford: Oxford University Press, 1995.

Blackmore, Richard. *Prince Arthur: An Heroick Poem in Ten Books*. London, 1695.

———. *A Satyr against Wit*. London, 1700.

Blackstone, William. *The Oxford Edition of Blackstone: Commentaries on the Laws of England*. Book 1: *Of the Rights of Persons*. Edited by David Lemmings. Oxford: Oxford University Press, 2016.

Boswell, James. *Boswell in Extremes, 1776–1778*. Edited by Charles McC. Weis and Frederick Pottle. New York: McGraw-Hill, 1970.

———. *Boswell's London Journal 1762–1763, together with Journal of My Jaunt, Harvest 1762*. Edited by Frederick Pottle. London: Heinemann, 1951.

———. *The General Correspondence of James Boswell, 1757–1763*. Edited by David Hankins and James J. Caudle. New Haven, Conn.: Yale University Press, 2006.

———. *London Journal, 1762–1763*. Edited by Gordon Turnbull. New York: Penguin, 2010.

———. "Sketch of the Early Life of James Boswell, written by Himself for Jean Jacques Rousseau, 5 December 1764." In *James Boswell: The Earlier Years, 1740–1769*, 1–6, by Frederick Pottle. New York: McGraw-Hill, 1985.

Boyer, Abel. *Letters of Wit, Politicks and Morality*. London, 1701.

Brown, Tom. *The Works of Mr. Thomas Brown, in Prose and Verse; Serious, Moral, and Comical*. 2 vols. London, 1707.

Burke, Edmund. *Reflections on the Revolution in France*. Edited by Conor Cruise O'Brien. New York: Penguin, 2004.

Butler, Samuel. *Satires and Miscellaneous Poetry and Prose*. Edited by René Lamar. Cambridge: Cambridge University Press, 1928.

Chesterfield, Philip Dormer Stanhope, Lord. *Lord Chesterfield's Letters*. Edited by David Roberts. New York: Oxford University Press, 1992.

Chetwood, William Rufus. *A General History of the Stage*. London, 1749.

Churchill, Charles. *The Poetical Works of Charles Churchill*. Edited by Douglas Grant. Oxford: Clarendon Press, 1956.

Cibber, Colley. *An Apology for the Life of Colley Cibber*. Edited by B.R.S. Fone. New York: Dover, 2000.

Cibber, Theophilus. *The Lives of the Poets of Great Britain and Ireland*. London, 1753.

Coleridge, Samuel Taylor. *The Collected Works of Samuel Taylor Coleridge*. Vol. 7, part 2. Edited by James Engell and W. Jackson Bate. Princeton, N.J.: Princeton University Press, 1983.

Collier, Jeremy. *A Short View of the Immorality and Profaneness of the English Stage*. London, 1698.

Commendatory Verses, on the Author of the Two Arthurs, and the Satyr against Wit. London, 1700.

Cumberland, Richard. *Memoirs of Richard Cumberland, Written by Himself*. London, 1806.

Dalrymple, Hugh. *Rodondo; or, The State Jugglers, Canto III*. London, 1770.

Daniel, George, ed. *Cumberland's Minor Theatre*. 16 vols. London, 1828.

Davies, Thomas. *Memoirs of the Life of David Garrick, Esq.* 3rd ed. 2 vols. London, 1781.

Defoe, Daniel. *The Fears of the Pretender turn'd into the Fears of Debauchery*. London, 1715.

———. *More Reformation. A Satyr upon Himself*. London, 1703.

———. *Reformation of Manners, a Satyr*. London, 1702.

———. *Religious and Didactic Writings of Daniel Defoe*. Vol. 6. Edited by J. A. Downie. London: Pickering and Chatto, 2007.

Dennis, John. *The Critical Works of John Dennis*. Edited by Edward Niles Hooker. 2 vols. Baltimore, Md.: Johns Hopkins University Press, 1943.

Downes, John. *Roscius Anglicanus*. Edited by Judith Milhous and Robert D. Hume. London: Society for Theatre Research, 1987.

Dryden, John. *The Works of John Dryden*. Vol. 3: *Poems, 1685–1692*. Edited by Earl Miner and Vinton Dearing. Berkeley: University of California Press, 1969.

An Epistle from Col. John Lilburn, In the Shades, to John Wilkes. London, 1765.

An Epistle from Matt of the Mint, lately deceased, to Captain Macheath. London, 1729.

An Essay upon the Taste and Writings of the Present Times. London, 1728.

Etherege, George. *The Man of Mode; or, Sir Fopling Flutter*. In *Restoration and Eighteenth-Century Comedy*, 2nd ed., edited by Scott McMillin, 87–167. New York: W. W. Norton, 1997.

Fielding, Henry. *Contributions to The Champion and Related Writings*. Edited by W. B. Coley. Oxford: Oxford University Press, 2003.

———. *Joseph Andrews and Shamela*. Edited by Judith Hawley. New York: Penguin, 1999.

Francis, Philip. *A Letter from the Cocoa Tree to the Country Gentlemen*. London, 1762.

Garrick, David. *Letters*. Edited by David M. Little and George M. Kahrl. 3 vols. Cambridge, Mass.: Harvard University Press, 1963.

———. *The Plays of David Garrick*. Edited by Harry William Perdicord and Fredric Louis Bergmann. 7 vols. Carbondale: Southern Illinois University Press, 1980–1982.

Gay, John. *The Beggar's Opera*. Edited by Bryan Loughrey and T. O. Treadwell. New York: Penguin, 1986.

———. *John Gay: Dramatic Works*. Edited by John Fuller. 2 vols. Oxford: Clarendon Press, 1983.

Genest, John. *Some Account of the English Stage from the Restoration in 1660 to 1830*. 10 vols. Bath, U.K., 1832.

Gentleman, Francis. *The Dramatic Censor; or, Critical Companion*. 2 vols. London, 1770.

Gildon, Charles. *A New Rehearsal; or, Bays the Younger*. London, 1714.

———. *The Patriot; or, The Italian Conspiracy*. London, 1703.

Grego, Joseph. *A History of Parliamentary Elections and Electioneering*. London: Chatto and Windus, 1892.

Grenville, Richard, Earl of Temple. *The Grenville Papers: Being the Correspondence of Richard Grenville Earl of Temple, K.G., and the Right Hon: George Grenville, their Friends and Contemporaries*. Edited by William James Smith. 4 vols. New York: AMS Press, 1970.

Hamilton, Anthony. *The Memoirs of Count Grammont*. Edited by Gordon Goodwin. 2 vols. London: A. H. Bullen, 1903.

Hansard's Parliamentary Debates. 3rd series. Vol. 13. London: T. C. Hansard, 1833.

Hazlitt, William. *The Complete Works of William Hazlitt*. Edited by P. P. Howe. 21 vols. New York: AMS Press, 1967.

Hobbes, Thomas. *Leviathan*. Edited by C. B. Macpherson. New York: Penguin, 1985.

Inchbald, Elizabeth. *Remarks for the British Theatre*. Edited by Cecilia Macheski. Delmar, N.Y.: Scholars' Facsimiles and Reprints, 1990.

Jerrold, Douglas. *The Bride of Ludgate*. London, 1831.

———. *Nell Gwynne; or, The Prologue*. London, 1833.

Johnson, Samuel. *A Dictionary of the English Language*. 2nd ed. 2 vols. London, 1756.

———. *The Lives of the Most Eminent English Poets; with Critical Observations on Their Works*. Edited by Roger Lonsdale. 4 vols. Oxford: Clarendon Press, 2006.

Lamb, Charles. *The Works of Charles and Mary Lamb*. Edited by E. V. Lucas. 7 vols. New York: AMS Press, 1968.

Locke, John. *A Letter Concerning Toleration*. Edited by James H. Tully. Indianapolis, Ind.: Hackett, 1983.

———. *The Second Treatise of Government*. In *Two Treatises of Government*, 265–428, edited by Peter Laslett. Cambridge: Cambridge University Press, 1988.

The London Magazine; or, Gentleman's Monthly Intelligencer. Vol. 40. London, 1771.

Memoirs Concerning the Life and Manners of Captain Mackheath. London, 1728.

Milton, John. *Paradise Lost*. In *Complete Poems and Major Prose*, edited by Merritt Y. Hughes, 207–469. Indianapolis, Ind.: Hackett, 1957.

The Modern Stage: A Letter to the Hon. George Lamb, M.P. on the Decay and Degradation of English Dramatic Literature. London, 1819.

Moncrieff, William Thomas. *Reform; or, John Bull Triumphant*. In *Richardson's New Minor Drama*, edited by William Thomas Moncrieff. London, 1828–1831.

———. *Rochester; or, King Charles the Second's Merry Days*. London, 1819.

———. *Selections from the Dramatic Works of William T. Moncrieff*. London, 1851.

———. *The "Tobit's Dog!"* London, 1838.

Murphy, Arthur. *The Life of David Garrick, Esq.* 2 vols. London: J. Wright, 1801.

A Narrative of the Proceedings against John Wilkes, Esq. London, 1768.

A New Form of Prayer, and Thanksgiving for the Happy Deliverance of John Wilkes. London, 1768.

New Monthly Magazine and Literary Journal. Vol. 20. London, 1827.

Ovid. *Metamorphoses*. Translated by David Raeburn. New York: Penguin, 2004.

The Patriot's Jubilee. London, 1770.

Payne, John Howard. *Charles the Second; or, The Merry Monarch*. London, 1824.
Philo-Dramaticus. "A Letter to Charles Kemble Esq., and R. W. Elliston Esq." In *Blackwood's Edinburgh Magazine*, vol. 17. London, 1825.
Planché, James Robinson. *The Court Beauties: A Dramatic Sketch in One Act*. London, 1835.
———. *The Recollections and Reflections of J. R. Planché*. 2 vols. London, 1872.
Pope, Alexander. *The Correspondence of Alexander Pope*. Edited by George Sherburn. 5 vols. Oxford: Clarendon Press, 1956.
———. *Miscellanies: The last volume*. London, 1727.
———. *The Poems of Alexander Pope*. Edited by John Butt. New Haven, Conn.: Yale University Press, 1963.
A Prologue sent to Mr. Row, to his new play, call'd The Fair Penitent. London, 1706.
Proposals for a National Reformation of Manners. London, 1694.
Richardson, Samuel. *Clarissa; or, The History of a Young Lady*. Edited by Angus Ross. New York: Penguin, 2004.
Ridpath, George. *The Stage Condemn'd*. London, 1698.
Rochester, John Wilmot, Lord. *The Works of John Wilmot, Earl of Rochester*. Edited by Harold Love. Oxford: Oxford University Press, 1999.
———. *The Works of the Right Honourable the Late Earls of Rochester and Roscommon*. 2nd ed. London, 1707.
Rowe, Nicholas. *The Ambitious Step-mother*. London, 1701.
———. *The Fair Penitent*. Edited by Malcolm Goldstein. Lincoln: University of Nebraska Press, 1969.
———. *The Tragedy of Jane Shore*. Edited by Harry William Perdicord. Lincoln: University of Nebraska Press, 1974.
Scott, Walter. *An Essay on the Drama*. In *The Miscellaneous Works of Sir Walter Scott*, vol. 6, 217–395. Edinburgh, 1861.
Select Committee on Dramatic Literature. *Report from the Select Committee on Dramatic Literature: with the Minutes of Evidence*. In the Parliamentary Papers, *Reports from Committees, 1831–32*, vol. 6. London: House of Commons, 1832.
The Senator. London, 1728.
Shadwell, Thomas. *The Libertine*. In *Four Restoration Libertine Plays*, edited by Deborah Payne Fisk, 1–84. Oxford: Oxford University Press, 2005.
Shaftesbury, Anthony Ashley Cooper, 3rd Earl of. *Characteristics of Men, Manners, Opinions, Times*. Edited by Lawrence E. Klein. Cambridge: Cambridge University Press, 1999.
Shaw, Bernard. *In Good King Charles's Golden Days*. In *Last Plays*, 7–74. New York: Penguin, 1974.
Shelley, Mary. *Frankenstein*. Edited by J. Paul Hunter. New York: Norton, 1996.
Sidney, Algernon. *Discourses Concerning Government*. Edited by Thomas G. West. Indianapolis, Ind.: Liberty Fund, 1996.
Smollett, Tobias. *The Works of Tobias Smollett: Poems, Plays, and The Briton*. Edited by Byron Gassman. Athens: University of Georgia Press, 1993.
The State of the Case, between the Lord Chamberlain of his Majesty's Household, and Sir Richard Steele, as Represented by that Knight. Restated in Vindication of King George, and the Most Noble the Duke of Newcastle. London, 1720.
Steele, Richard. *The Christian Hero: An Argument Proving that no Principles but those of Religion are Sufficient to make a Great Man*. In *Tracts and Pamphlets by Richard Steele*, edited by Rae Blanchard, 1–62. New York: Octagon Books, 1967.
———. *The Correspondence of Richard Steele*. Edited by Rae Blanchard. London: Oxford University Press, 1941.

———. *The Guardian*. Edited by John Calhoun Stephens. Lexington: University Press of Kentucky, 1982.

———. *The Plays of Richard Steele*. Edited by Shirley Strum Kenny. Oxford: Clarendon Press, 1971.

———. *The State of the Case between the Lord Chamberlain of His Majesty's Household, and the Governor of the Royal Company of Comedians*. In *Tracts and Pamphlets by Richard Steele*, edited by Rae Blanchard, 591–608. New York: Octagon Books, 1967.

———. *The Tatler*. Edited by Donald F. Bond. 3 vols. Oxford: Clarendon Press, 1987.

Thrale, Hester. Annotations in *The Spectator*. 8 vols. London: Payne, Rivington, et al., 1789. GEN MSS Vol. 527. Beinecke Rare Book and Manuscript Library, Yale University, New Haven, Conn.

Trotter, Catharine. *Love at a Loss; or, Most Votes Carry It*. In *The Broadview Anthology of Restoration and Early Eighteenth-Century Drama*, edited by J. Douglas Canfield and Maja-Lisa von Sneidern, 857–902. Peterborough, Ont.: Broadview Press, 2001.

The Twickenham Hotch-Potch. London, 1728.

Vanbrugh, John. *John Vanbrugh: Four Comedies*. Edited by Michael Cordner. New York: Penguin, 1989.

Victor, Benjamin. *An Epistle to Sir Richard Steele*. London, 1722.

A View of the Town; or, Memoirs of London. London, 1731.

Villiers, George. *Plays, Poems, and Miscellaneous Writings associated with George Villiers, Second Duke of Buckingham*. Edited by Robert D. Hume and Harold Love. 2 vols. Oxford: Oxford University Press, 2007.

Walker, John. *Nell Gywnne*. London, 1830.

Walpole, Horace. *Memoirs of the Reign of King George III*. Edited by Derek Jarrett. 4 vols. New Haven, Conn.: Yale University Press, 2000.

———. *The Works of Horatio Walpole, Earl of Orford*. 5 vols. London, 1798.

Welsted, Leonard. *The Works, in Verse and Prose, of Leonard Welsted*. Edited by John Nichols. London, 1787.

Wilkes, John. *The Correspondence of the Late John Wilkes, with his Friends, Printed from the Original Manuscripts, in which are introduced Memoirs of His Life*. Edited by John Almon. 5 vols. London, 1805.

———. *The North Briton, from No. I to No. XLVI inclusive: With several useful and explanatory notes, not printed in any former edition*. 3 vols. London, 1763.

Wilkes, Thomas. *A General View of the Stage*. London, 1759.

Wilkes's Jest Book; or, The Merry Patriot. London, 1769.

Wycherley, William. *The Country Wife and Other Plays*. Edited by Peter Dixon. Oxford: Oxford University Press, 1996.

SECONDARY SOURCES

Agamben, Giorgio. *Homo Sacer: Sovereign Power and Bare Life*. Translated by Daniel Heller-Roazen. Stanford, Calif.: Stanford University Press, 1998.

Anderson, Benedict. *Imagined Communities: Reflections on the Origins and Spread of Nationalism*. London: Verso, 1983.

Anderson, Misty G. "Genealogies of Comedy." In *The Oxford Handbook of the Georgian Theatre*, edited by Julia Swindells and David Francis Taylor, 347–367. Oxford: Oxford University Press, 2014.

Armens, Sven. *John Gay: Social Critic*. New York: Octagon, 1966.

Ault, Norman. "Pope and Addison." *Review of English Studies* 17 (1941): 428–451.

Avery, Emmett. *Congreve's Plays on the Eighteenth-Century Stage*. New York: Modern Language Association, 1951.

———. "The Reputation of Wycherley's Comedies as Stage Plays in the Eighteenth Century." *Research Studies of the State College of Washington* 12 (1944): 131–154.

Backscheider, Paula R. *Spectacular Politics: Theatrical Power and Mass Culture in Early Modern England*. Baltimore, Md.: Johns Hopkins University Press, 1993.

Baer, Marc. *Theatre and Disorder in Late Georgian London*. Oxford: Oxford University Press, 1992.

Bahlmann, Dudley. *The Moral Revolution of 1688*. New Haven, Conn.: Yale University Press, 1957.

Bailes, Sara Jane. *Performance Theatre and the Poetics of Failure: Forced Entertainment, Goat Island, Elevator Repair Service*. New York: Routledge, 2011.

Benedetti, Jean. *David Garrick and the Birth of Modern Theatre*. London: Methuen, 2001.

Bevis, Richard. *The Laughing Tradition: Stage Comedy in Garrick's Day*. Athens: University of Georgia Press, 1980.

Birdsall, Virginia Ogden. *Wild Civility: The English Comic Spirit on the Restoration Stage*. Bloomington: Indiana University Press, 1970.

Blau, Herbert. *Take Up the Bodies: Theater at the Vanishing Point*. Urbana: University of Illinois Press, 1982.

Bond, Erik. *Reading London: Urban Speculation and Imaginative Government in Eighteenth-Century Literature*. Columbus: Ohio State University Press, 2007.

Booth, Michael. *Prefaces to English Nineteenth-Century Theatre*. Manchester: Manchester University Press, 1980.

Bowers, Terence. "Universalizing Sociability: *The Spectator*, Civic Enfranchisement, and the Rule(s) of the Public Sphere." In *The Spectator: Emerging Discourses*, edited by Donald J. Newman, 150–174. Newark: University of Delaware Press, 2005.

Boyce, Benjamin. *Tom Brown of Facetious Memory: Grub Street in the Age of Dryden*. New York: Johnson Reprint, 1968.

Boym, Svetlana. *The Future of Nostalgia*. New York: Basic Books, 2001.

Boys, Richard C. *Sir Richard Blackmore and the Wits*. Ann Arbor: University of Michigan Press, 1949.

Brady, Frank. *Boswell's Political Career*. New Haven, Conn.: Yale University Press, 1965.

Bratton, Jacky. *New Readings in Theatre History*. Cambridge: Cambridge University Press, 2003.

Braverman, Richard. *Plots and Counterplots: Sexual Politics and the Body Politic in English Literature, 1660–1730*. Cambridge: Cambridge University Press, 1993.

———. "The Rake's Progress Revisited: Politics and Comedy in the Restoration." In *Cultural Readings of Restoration and Eighteenth-Century English Theater*, edited by J. Douglas Canfield and Deborah Payne, 141–168. Athens: University of Georgia Press, 1995.

Brewer, John. "The Misfortunes of Lord Bute." *The Historical Journal* 16 (1973): 3–43.

———. *Party Ideology and Popular Politics at the Accession of George III*. Cambridge: Cambridge University Press, 1976.

Brown, Laura. "The Defenseless Woman and the Development of English Tragedy." *Studies in English Literature* 22 (1982): 429–443.

———. *English Dramatic Form, 1660–1760: An Essay in Generic History*. New Haven, Conn.: Yale University Press, 1981.

Bryson, Anna. *From Courtesy to Civility: Changing Codes of Conduct in Early Modern England*. Oxford: Oxford University Press, 1998.

Bueler, Lois, ed. *Clarissa: The Eighteenth-Century Response, 1747–1804*. 2 vols. New York: AMS Press, 2010.

Burns, Arthur, and Joanna Innes. Introduction to *Rethinking the Age of Reform: Britain, 1780–1850*, edited by Arthur Burns and Joanna Innes, 1–70. Cambridge: Cambridge University Press, 2003.

Burwick, Frederick. *Romantic Drama: Acting and Reacting*. Cambridge: Cambridge University Press, 2009.

Butler, Judith. *Excitable Speech: A Politics of the Performative*. New York: Routledge, 1997.

———. *Gender Trouble: Feminism and the Subversion of Identity*. New York: Routledge, 1990.

———. *Precarious Life: The Powers of Mourning and Violence*. London: Verso, 2004.

Canfield, J. Douglas. "The Critique of Capitalism and the Retreat into Art in Gay's *Beggar's Opera* and Fielding's *Author's Farce*." In *Cutting Edges: Postmodern Critical Essays on Eighteenth-Century Satire*, edited by James E. Gill, 320–334. Knoxville: University of Tennessee Press, 1995.

———. "Nicholas Rowe." In *Restoration and Eighteenth-Century Dramatists*, second series, edited by Paula Backscheider, 262–289. Detroit, Mich.: Gale Research, 1989.

———. *Nicholas Rowe and Christian Tragedy*. Gainesville: University Press of Florida, 1977.

———. "Shifting Tropes of Ideology in English Serious Drama, Late Stuart to Early Georgian." In *Cultural Readings of Restoration and Eighteenth-Century English Theater*, edited by J. Douglas Canfield and Deborah Payne, 195–227. Athens: University of Georgia Press, 1995.

———. *Tricksters and Estates: On the Ideology of Restoration Comedy*. Lexington: University Press of Kentucky, 1997.

Cannan, Paul D. *The Emergence of Dramatic Criticism in England: From Jonson to Pope*. New York: Palgrave, 2006.

Cannon, John. *Parliamentary Reform, 1640–1832*. Cambridge: Cambridge University Press, 1973.

Carlson, Marvin. *The Haunted Stage: The Theatre as Memory Machine*. Ann Arbor: University of Michigan Press, 2001.

Carter, Phillip. "James Boswell's Manliness." In *English Masculinities, 1660–1800*, edited by Tim Hitchcock and Michele Cohen, 111–130. New York: Longman, 1999.

———. *Men and the Emergence of Polite Society, Britain 1660–1800*. New York: Pearson, 2000.

Case, Arthur. "Pope, Addison, and the 'Atticus' Lines." *Modern Philology* 33 (1935): 187–193.

Certeau, Michel de. *The Practice of Everyday Life*. Translated by Steven Rendall. Berkeley: University of California Press, 1984.

Chernaik, Warren. *Sexual Freedom in Restoration Literature*. Cambridge: Cambridge University Press, 1995.

Claydon, Tony. *William III and the Godly Revolution*. Cambridge: Cambridge University Press, 1996.

Coleman, Antony. "Sir John Brute on the Eighteenth-Century Stage." *Restoration and Eighteenth-Century Theatre Research* 8 (1969): 41–46.

Colley, Linda. *Britons: Forging the Nation, 1707–1837*. New Haven, Conn.: Yale University Press, 1992.

Cordner, Michael. "Playwright versus Priest: Profanity and the Wit of Restoration Comedy." In *The Cambridge Companion to English Restoration Theatre*, edited by Deborah Payne Fisk, 209–225. Cambridge: Cambridge University Press, 2000.

Corman, Brian. "Interpreting and Misinterpreting *The Man of Mode*." *Papers on Language and Literature* 13 (1977): 35–53.

———. "Restoration Drama after the Restoration: The Critics, the Repertory and the Canon." In *A Companion to Restoration Drama*, edited by Susan J. Owen, 177–192. Oxford: Blackwell, 2001.

Cowan, Brian. "Mr. Spectator and the Coffeehouse Public Sphere." *Eighteenth-Century Studies* 37 (2004): 345–366.

Cox, Jeffrey. Introduction to *Seven Gothic Dramas, 1789–1825*, edited by Jeffery Cox, 1–77. Athens: Ohio University Press, 1992.

———. "Romantic Drama and the French Revolution." In *Revolution and English Romanticism: Politics and Rhetoric*, edited by Keith Hanley and Raman Selden, 241–260. New York: St. Martin's Press, 1990.

Cox, Jeffrey, and Michael Gamer. "'Torn from Its Genus': Hannah Cowley on Comedy, Laughter, and Morality." In *Emancipation, Liberation and Freedom: Romantic Drama and Theatre in Britain, 1760–1830*, edited by Gioia Angeletti, 87–116. Parma, Italy: Monte Università Parma, 2010.

Davis, Jim. "Looking towards 1843 and the End of Monopoly." In *The Oxford Handbook of the Georgian Theatre*, edited by Julia Swindells and David Francis Taylor, 156–173. Oxford: Oxford University Press, 2014.

DeGabriele, Peter. *Sovereign Power and the Enlightenment: Eighteenth-Century Literature and the Problem of the Political*. Lewisburg, Pa.: Bucknell University Press, 2015.

Denning, Michael. "Beggars and Thieves." *Literature and History* 8 (1982): 41–55.

Diamond, Elin. Introduction to *Performance and Cultural Politics*, edited by Elin Diamond, 1–13. New York: Routledge, 1996.

Dickinson, H. T. *Liberty and Property: Political Ideology in Eighteenth-Century Britain*. New York: Holmes and Meier, 1977.

Dillon, Elizabeth Maddock. *New World Drama: The Performative Commons in the Atlantic World, 1649–1849*. Durham, N.C.: Duke University Press, 2014.

Dobrée, Bonamy. *Restoration Comedy, 1600–1720*. Oxford: Oxford University Press, 1924.

Doody, Margaret Anne. *A Natural Passion: A Study of the Novels of Samuel Richardson*. Oxford: Clarendon Press, 1974.

Downer, Alan. "Nature to Advantage Dressed: Eighteenth-Century Acting." *PMLA* 58 (1943): 1002–1037.

Downie, J. A. "Defoe's *Review*, the Theatre, and Anti-High-Church Propaganda." *Restoration and Eighteenth-Century Theatre Research* 15 (1976): 24–32.

Dugaw, Dianne. *Deep Play: John Gay and the Invention of Modernity*. Newark: University of Delaware Press, 2001.

Empson, William. *Some Versions of Pastoral*. London: Chatto and Windus, 1950.

Evans, Eric J. *Britain before the Reform Act: Politics and Society, 1815–1832*. New York: Longman, 1989.

———. *The Great Reform Act of 1832*. New York: Routledge, 1994.

Fisk, Deborah Payne. Introduction to *Four Restoration Libertine Plays*, edited by Deborah Payne Fisk, xi–xliv. New York: Oxford University Press, 2005.

Flothow, Dorothea. "Merrying the Monarch: Charles II in Historical Comedies (1800 to the Present)." In *History and Humour: British and American Perspectives*, edited by Barbara Korte and Doris Lechner, 87–110. Bielefeld, Germany: Transcript, 2013.

Foucault, Michel. *Power/Knowledge: Selected Interviews and Other Writings, 1972–1977*. Edited by Colin Gordon. New York: Pantheon, 1980.

———. *Security, Territory, Population: Lectures at the Collège de France, 1977–1978*. Edited by Michael Senellart. Translated by Graham Burchell. New York: Picador, 2004.

———. *"Society Must Be Defended": Lectures at the Collège de France, 1975–1976*. Edited by Mauro Bertani and Alessandro Fontana. Translated by David Macey. New York: Picador, 2003.

Freeman, Lisa. *Antitheatricality and the Body Public*. Philadelphia: University of Pennsylvania Press, 2017.

———. *Character's Theater: Genre and Identity on the Eighteenth-Century English Stage*. Philadelphia: University of Pennsylvania Press, 2002.

———. "Jeremy Collier and the Politics of Theatrical Representation." In *Players, Playwrights, Playhouses: Investigating Performance, 1660–1800,* edited by Michael Cordner and Peter Holland, 135–151. New York: Palgrave, 2007.

Fujimura, Thomas H. *The Restoration Comedy of Wit.* Princeton, N.J.: Princeton University Press, 1952.

Gallagher, Catherine. "Embracing the Absolute: The Politics of the Female Subject in Seventeenth-Century England." *Genders* 1 (1988): 24–39.

Ganzel, Dewey. "Patent Wrongs and Patent Theatres: Drama and the Law in the Early Nineteenth Century." *PMLA* 76 (1961): 384–396.

Garrett, Jane. *The Triumphs of Providence: The Assassination Plot, 1696.* Cambridge: Cambridge University Press, 1980.

Gavin, Michael. *The Invention of English Criticism, 1650–1760.* Cambridge: Cambridge University Press, 2015.

Goldgar, Bertrand. *Walpole and the Wits: The Relation of Politics to Literature, 1722–1742.* Lincoln: University of Nebraska Press, 1976.

Gollapudi, Aparna. *Moral Reform in Comedy and Culture, 1696–1747.* Burlington, Vt.: Ashgate, 2011.

Gray, Charles Harold. *Theatrical Criticism in London to 1795.* New York: Columbia University Press, 1931.

Habermas, Jürgen. *The Structural Transformation of the Public Sphere: An Inquiry into a Category of Bourgeois Society.* Translated by Thomas Burger with the assistance of Frederick Lawrence. Cambridge, Mass.: MIT Press, 1989.

Halberstam, Judith. *The Queer Art of Failure.* Durham, N.C.: Duke University Press, 2001.

Hammond, Brean. Introduction to *John Vanbrugh: The Relapse and Other Plays,* edited by Brean Hammond, vii–xxx. Oxford: Oxford University Press, 2004.

———. *Professional Imaginative Writing in England, 1670–1740: "Hackney for Bread."* Oxford: Clarendon Press, 1997.

Hardt, Michael, and Antonio Negri, *Commonwealth.* Cambridge, Mass.: Harvard University Press, 2009.

Harol, Corrinne. "1688: Literature, Politics, and the Long Restoration." *Restoration* 39 (2015): 5–16.

Harris, Jocelyn. "Protean Lovelace." In *Passion and Virtue: Essays on the Novels of Samuel Richardson,* edited by David Blewett, 92–113. Toronto: University of Toronto Press, 2001.

Harris, Susan Cannon. "Outside the Box: The Female Spectator, *The Fair Penitent,* and the Kelly Riots of 1747." *Theatre Journal* 57 (2005): 33–56.

Harris, Tim. *Politics under the Later Stuarts: Party Conflict in a Divided Society, 1660–1715.* New York: Longman, 1993.

———. *Revolution: The Great Crisis of the British Monarchy, 1685–1720.* New York: Penguin, 2006.

———. "'There Is None that Loves Him but Drunk Whores and Whoremongers': Popular Criticism of the Restoration Court." In *Politics, Transgression, and Representation at the Court of Charles II,* edited by Julia Marciari Alexander and Catharine MacLeod, 35–60. New Haven, Conn.: Yale University Press, 2007.

Harrison, Gabriel. *John Howard Payne: Dramatist, Poet, Actor, Author of Home, Sweet Home: His Life and Writings.* New York: B. Blom, 1969.

Harth, Phillip. *Pen for a Party: Dryden's Tory Propaganda in Its Contexts.* Princeton, N.J.: Princeton University Press, 1993.

Harwood, John. *Critics, Values, and Restoration Comedy.* Carbondale: Southern Illinois University Press, 1982.

Highfill, Philip H., Jr., Kalman A. Burnim, and Edward A. Langhans, eds. *A Biographical Dictionary of Actors, Actresses, Musicians, Dancers, Managers, and Other Stage Personnel in London, 1660–1800.* 16 vols. Carbondale: University of Southern Illinois Press, 1973–1993.

Hohendahl, Peter Uwe. *The Institution of Criticism.* Ithaca, N.Y.: Cornell University Press, 1982.

Hoppit, Julian. *A Land of Liberty? England, 1689–1727.* Oxford: Oxford University Press, 2000.

Houston, Alan. *Algernon Sidney and the Republican Heritage in England and America.* Princeton, N.J.: Princeton University Press, 1991.

Hoxby, Blair, and Ann Baynes Coiro, eds. *Milton in the Long Restoration.* Oxford: Oxford University Press, 2016.

Hughes, Derek. *English Drama, 1660–1700.* Oxford: Clarendon Press, 1996.

Hume, Robert D. *The Development of English Drama in the Late Seventeenth Century.* Oxford: Clarendon Press, 1976.

———. *The Rakish Stage: Studies in English Drama, 1660–1800.* Carbondale: Southern Illinois University Press, 1983.

———. "Theatres and Repertory." In *The Cambridge History of British Theatre,* vol. 2, edited by Joseph Donohue, 53–70. Cambridge: Cambridge University Press, 2004.

———. "Theory of Comedy in the Restoration." *Modern Philology* 70 (1973): 302–318.

Hume, Robert D., and Harold Love. "General Introduction." In George Villiers, *Plays, Poems, and Miscellaneous Writings associated with George Villiers, Second Duke of Buckingham,* vol. 1, xlii–xliv. Oxford: Oxford University Press, 2007.

Innes, Joanna. "'Reform' in English Public Life: The Fortunes of a Word." In *Rethinking the Age of Reform: Britain, 1780–1850,* edited by Arthur Burns and Joanna Innes, 71–97. Cambridge: Cambridge University Press, 2003.

Jordan, Robert. "The Extravagant Rake in Restoration Comedy." In *Restoration Literature: Critical Approaches,* edited by Harold Love, 69–90. London: Methuen, 1972.

Kachur, B. A. *Etherege and Wycherley.* New York: Palgrave, 2004.

Kaiser, Thomas. "The Drama of Charles Edward Stuart, Jacobite Propaganda, and French Political Protest, 1745–1750." *Eighteenth-Century Studies* 30 (1997): 365–381.

Kavanagh, Declan. *Effeminate Years: Literature, Politics, and Aesthetics in Mid-Eighteenth-Century Britain.* Lewisburg, Pa.: Bucknell University Press, 2017.

Kay, Carol. *Political Constructions: Defoe, Richardson, and Sterne in Relation to Hobbes, Hume, and Burke.* Ithaca, N.Y.: Cornell University Press, 1988.

Kay, Donald. "Boswell in the Green Room: Dramatic Method in *The London Journal.*" *Philological Quarterly* 57 (1978): 195–212.

Kelly, Richard. *Douglas Jerrold.* New York: Twayne, 1972.

Kenny, Shirley Strum. "Humane Comedy." *Modern Philology* 75 (1977): 29–43.

Kenyon, J. P. *Revolution Principles: The Politics of Party, 1689–1720.* Cambridge: Cambridge University Press, 1977.

Keymer, Tom. *Richardson's "Clarissa" and the Eighteenth-Century Reader.* Cambridge: Cambridge University Press, 1992.

King, Thomas. *The Gendering of Men, 1600–1750.* Vol. 1: *The English Phallus.* Madison: University of Wisconsin Press, 2004.

———. *The Gendering of Men, 1600–1750.* Vol. 2: *Queer Articulations.* Madison: University of Wisconsin Press, 2008.

Kinkead-Weekes, Mark. *Samuel Richardson: Dramatic Novelist.* Ithaca, N.Y.: Cornell University Press, 1973.

Kinservik, Matthew J. *Disciplining Satire: The Censorship of Satiric Comedy on the Eighteenth-Century London Stage.* Lewisburg, Pa.: Bucknell University Press, 2002.

———. "Reconsidering Theatrical Regulation in the Long Eighteenth Century." In *Players, Playwrights, Playhouses: Investigating Performance, 1660–1800*, edited by Michael Cordner and Peter Holland, 152–171. New York: Palgrave, 2007.

Klein, Lawrence. "Liberty, Manners, and Politeness in Early Eighteenth-Century England." *The Historical Journal* 32 (1989): 583–605.

———. "Property and Politeness in the Early Eighteenth-Century Whig Moralists: The Case of *The Spectator*." In *Early Modern Conceptions of Property*, edited by John Brewer and Susan Staves, 221–233. New York: Routledge, 1995.

———. *Shaftesbury and the Culture of Politeness: Moral Discourse and Cultural Politics in Early Eighteenth-Century England*. Cambridge: Cambridge University Press, 1994.

Knight, Charles. *A Political Biography of Richard Steele*. London: Pickering and Chatto, 2009.

Koselleck, Reinhart. *The Practice of Conceptual History: Timing History, Spacing Concepts*. Translated by Todd Samuel Presner. Stanford, Calif.: Stanford University Press, 2002.

Kraft, Elizabeth. *Restoration Stage Comedies and Hollywood Remarriage Films: In Conversation with Stanley Cavell*. New York: Routledge, 2017.

Kramnick, Isaac. *Bolingbroke and His Circle: The Politics of Nostalgia in the Age of Walpole*. Cambridge, Mass.: Harvard University Press, 1968.

Kramnick, Jonathan. *Making the English Canon: Print-Capitalism and the Cultural Past, 1700–1770*. Cambridge: Cambridge University Press, 1998.

Krapp, Robert C. "Class Analysis of a Literary Controversy: Wit and Sense in Seventeenth-Century English Literature." *Science and Society* 10 (1946): 80–92.

Krutch, Joseph Wood. *Comedy and Conscience after the Restoration*. Rev. ed. New York: Columbia University Press, 1949.

Lamb, Jonathan. "Historical Reenactment, Extremity, and Passion." *The Eighteenth Century: Theory and Interpretation* 49 (2008): 239–250.

Lang, Timothy. *Victorians and the Stuart Heritage: Interpretations of a Discordant Past*. Cambridge: Cambridge University Press, 1995.

Lillywhite, Bryant. *London Coffee Houses: A Reference Book of Coffee Houses of the Seventeenth, Eighteenth, and Nineteenth Centuries*. London: G. Allen and Unwin, 1963.

Loar, Christopher. *Political Magic: British Fictions of Savagery and Sovereignty, 1650–1750*. New York: Fordham University Press, 2014.

Loftis, John. *Comedy and Society from Congreve to Fielding*. Stanford, Calif.: Stanford University Press, 1959.

———. *The Politics of Drama in Augustan England*. Oxford: Clarendon Press, 1963.

———. *Steele at Drury Lane*. Berkeley: University of California Press, 1952.

Lynch, James J. *Box, Pit, and Gallery: Stage and Society in Johnson's London*. Berkeley: University of California Press, 1953.

Mackie, Erin. *Market à la Mode: Fashion, Commodity, and Gender in "The Tatler" and "The Spectator."* Baltimore, Md.: Johns Hopkins University Press, 1997.

———. *Rakes, Highwaymen, and Pirates: The Making of the Modern Gentleman in the Eighteenth Century*. Baltimore, Md.: Johns Hopkins University Press, 2009.

Major, Joanna, and Sarah Murden. *An Infamous Mistress: The Life, Loves and Family of the Celebrated Grace Dalrymple Elliott*. Barnsley, U.K.: Pen and Sword Books, 2016.

Markley, Robert. "The Canon and Its Critics." In *The Cambridge Companion to English Restoration Theatre*, edited by Deborah Payne Fisk, 226–242. Cambridge: Cambridge University Press, 2000.

———. *Two-Edg'd Weapons: Style and Ideology in the Comedies of Etherege, Wycherley, and Congreve*. Oxford: Clarendon Press, 1988.

Marriott, John. Introduction to *Unknown London: Early Modernist Visions of the Metropolis, 1815–45*, vol. 1, edited by John Marriott, xv–xlix. London: Pickering and Chatto, 2000.

Marsden, Jean. *Fatal Desire: Women, Sexuality, and the English Stage, 1660–1720.* Ithaca, N.Y.: Cornell University Press, 2006.

McCalman, Iain. *Radical Underworld: Prophets, Revolutionaries and Pornographers in London, 1795–1840.* Cambridge: Cambridge University Press, 1988.

McCalman, Iain, and Paul A. Pickering, eds. *Historical Reenactment: From Realism to the Affective Turn.* New York: Palgrave, 2010.

McGirr, Elaine. *Eighteenth-Century Characters: A Guide to the Literature of the Age.* New York: Palgrave, 2007.

———. *Heroic Mode and Political Crisis, 1660–1745.* Newark: University of Delaware Press, 2009.

———. "Why Lovelace Must Die." *NOVEL: A Forum on Fiction* 37 (2003–2004): 5–23.

McKeon, Michael. *The Secret History of Domesticity: Public, Private, and the Division of Knowledge.* Baltimore, Md.: Johns Hopkins University Press, 2005.

Mijers, Esther, and David Onnekink, eds. *Redefining William III: The Impact of the King-Stadholder in International Context.* Burlington, Vt.: Ashgate, 2007.

Milhous, Judith, and Robert D. Hume, eds. *The London Stage, 1660–1800: A New Version of Part 2, 1700–1729.* http://personal.psu.edu/faculty/h/b//hbl/London%20Stage%202001/.

Moody, Jane. "'Fine Word, Legitimate!': Toward a Theatrical History of Romanticism." *Texas Studies in Language and Literature* 38 (1996): 223–244.

———. *Illegitimate Theatre in London, 1770–1840.* Cambridge: Cambridge University Press, 2000.

Morillo, John. "John Dennis: Enthusiastic Passions, Cultural Memory, and Literary Theory." *Eighteenth-Century Studies* 34 (2000): 21–41.

Morris, Marilyn. *Sex, Money, and Personal Character in Eighteenth-Century British Politics.* New Haven, Conn.: Yale University Press, 2014.

Murray, Christopher. *Robert William Elliston, Manager.* London: Society for Theatre Research, 1975.

Namier, Lewis. *The Structure of Politics at the Accession of George III.* 2nd ed. New York: St. Martin's Press, 1957.

Neill, Michael. "Heroic Heads and Humble Tails: Sex, Politics, and the Restoration Comic Rake." *The Eighteenth Century: Theory and Interpretation* 24 (1983): 115–139.

Newey, Katherine. "Reform on the London Stage." In *Rethinking the Age of Reform: Britain, 1780–1850,* edited by Arthur Burns and Joanna Innes, 238–253. Cambridge: Cambridge University Press, 2003.

Newman, Donald J., ed. *James Boswell: Psychological Interpretations.* New York: St. Martin's Press, 1995.

———, ed. *The Spectator: Emerging Discourses.* Newark: University of Delaware Press, 2005.

Nicholes, Joseph. "Politics by Indirection: Charles Lamb's Seventeenth-Century Renegade, John Woodvil." *The Wordsworth Circle* 19 (1988): 49–55.

———. "Revolutions Compared: The English Civil War as Political Touchstone in Romantic Literature." In *Revolution and English Romanticism: Politics and Rhetoric,* edited by Keith Hanley and Raman Selden, 261–276. New York: St. Martin's Press, 1990.

Nicholson, Watson. *The Struggle for a Free Stage in London.* New York: Houghton and Mifflin, 1906.

Nicoll, Allardyce. *A History of Early Nineteenth Century Drama, 1800–1850.* Cambridge: Cambridge University Press, 1930.

Nokes, David. *John Gay: A Profession of Friendship.* Oxford: Oxford University Press, 1995.

Novak, Maximillian. "Margery Pinchwife's 'London Disease': Restoration Comedy and the Libertine Offensive of the 1670s." *Studies in the Literary Imagination* 10 (1977): 1–23.

Nussbaum, Felicity. *The Autobiographical Subject: Gender and Ideology in Eighteenth-Century England*. Baltimore, Md.: Johns Hopkins University Press, 1989.

———. *Rival Queens: Actresses, Performance, and the Eighteenth-Century British Theater*. Philadelphia: University of Pennsylvania Press, 2010.

Olshen, Barry. "The Original and 'Improved' Comedies of Sir John Vanbrugh: Their Nineteenth-Century London Stage History." *Restoration and Eighteenth-Century Theatre Research* 13 (1974): 27–52.

O'Quinn, Daniel. *Entertaining Crisis in the Atlantic Imperium, 1770–1790*. Baltimore, Md.: Johns Hopkins University Press, 2011.

———. *Staging Governance: Theatrical Imperialism in London, 1770–1800*. Baltimore, Md.: Johns Hopkins University Press, 2005.

Overmyer, Grace. *America's First Hamlet*. Westport, Conn.: Greenwood Press, 1975.

Owen, Susan J. *Restoration Theatre and Crisis*. Oxford: Clarendon Press, 1996.

Pacheco, Anita. "Reading Toryism in Aphra Behn's Cit-Cuckolding Comedies." *Review of English Studies* 55 (2004): 690–708.

Peck, James. "Anne Oldfield's Lady Townly: Consumption, Credit, and the Whig Hegemony of the 1720s." *Theatre Journal* 49 (1997): 397–416.

Phelan, Peggy. *Unmarked: The Politics of Performance*. London: Routledge, 1993.

Pincus, Steve. *1688: The First Modern Revolution*. New Haven, Conn.: Yale University Press, 2009.

Pocock, J.G.A. *Virtue, Commerce, and History: Essays in Political Thought and History, Chiefly in the Eighteenth Century*. Cambridge: Cambridge University Press, 1985.

Porter, Roy. "Mixed Feelings: The Enlightenment and Sexuality in Eighteenth-Century Britain." In *Sexuality in Eighteenth-Century Britain*, edited by Paul-Gabriel Boucé, 1–27. Manchester: Manchester University Press, 1982.

Pottle, Frederick. *James Boswell: The Earlier Years, 1740–1769*. New York: McGraw-Hill, 1966.

Rea, Robert. *The English Press in Politics, 1760–1774*. Lincoln: University of Nebraska Press, 1963.

Ridout, Nicholas. *Stage Fright, Animals, and Other Theatrical Problems*. Cambridge: Cambridge University Press, 2006.

Roach, Joseph. *Cities of the Dead: Circum-Atlantic Performance*. New York: Columbia University Press, 1996.

———. *It*. Ann Arbor: University of Michigan Press, 2007.

———. *The Player's Passion: Studies in the Science of Acting*. Ann Arbor: University of Michigan Press, 1993.

———. "Power's Body: The Inscription of Morality as Style." In *Interpreting the Theatrical Past: Essays in the Historiography of Performance*, edited by Bruce McConachie and Thomas Postlewait, 99–118. Iowa City: University of Iowa Press, 1989.

Robinson, John, and Hunter Robinson. *The Life of Robert Coates*. London, 1891.

Rose, Craig. *England in the 1690s: Revolution, Religion, and War*. Malden, Mass.: Blackwell, 1999.

Rosenthal, Laura. "'All Injury's Forgot': Restoration Sex Comedy and National Amnesia." *Comparative Drama* 42 (2008): 7–28.

Rounce, Adam. "'Stuarts without End': Wilkes, Churchill, and Anti-Scottishness." *Eighteenth-Century Life* 29 (2005): 20–43.

Rudé, George. *Wilkes and Liberty: A Social Study of 1763 to 1774*. Oxford: Clarendon Press, 1962.

Russell, Gillian. *The Theatres of War: Performance, Politics, and Society, 1793–1815*. New York: Oxford University Press, 1995.

Sainsbury, John. *John Wilkes: The Lives of a Libertine*. Aldershot, U.K.: Ashgate, 2006.

———. "John Wilkes, Debt, and Patriotism." *Journal of British Studies* 34 (1995): 165–195.

———. "Wilkes and Libertinism." *Studies in Eighteenth-Century Culture* 26 (1998): 151–174.

Schechner, Richard. *Between Theater and Anthropology*. Philadelphia: University of Pennsylvania Press, 1985.

Schneider, Rebecca. *Performing Remains: Art and War in Times of Historical Reenactment*. New York: Routledge, 2011.

Schultz, William Eben. *Gay's Beggar's Opera: Its Content, History, and Influence*. New York: Russell and Russell, 1967.

Scott, Jonathan. *England's Troubles: Seventeenth-Century English Political Instability in European Context*. Cambridge: Cambridge University Press, 2000.

Shapira, Yael. "Shakespeare, *The Castle of Otranto*, and the Problem of the Corpse on the Eighteenth-Century Stage." *Eighteenth-Century Life* 36 (2012): 1–29.

Shepherd, Simon, and Peter Womack. *English Drama: A Cultural History*. Oxford: Blackwell, 1996.

Slater, Michael. *Douglas Jerrold: 1803–1857*. London: Duckworth, 2002.

Smith, Hannah. *Georgian Monarchy: Politics and Culture, 1714–1760*. Cambridge: Cambridge University Press, 2006.

Sofer, Andrew. *The Stage Life of Props*. Ann Arbor: University of Michigan Press, 2003.

Spacks, Patricia Meyer. *Imagining a Self: Autobiography and the Novel in Eighteenth-Century England*. Cambridge, Mass.: Harvard University Press, 1976.

Spencer, Jane. "*The Rover* and the Eighteenth Century." In *Aphra Behn Studies*, edited by Janet Todd, 84–107. Cambridge: Cambridge University Press, 1996.

Staves, Susan. *Players' Scepters: Fictions of Authority in the Restoration*. Lincoln: University of Nebraska Press, 1979.

Stephens, John Russell. "Henry Robert Addison." In *The Oxford Dictionary of National Biography*. Online ed. Oxford: Oxford University Press, 2004.

———. *The Profession of the Playwright: British Theatre, 1800–1900*. Cambridge: Cambridge University Press, 1992.

Stewart, Susan. *On Longing: Narratives of the Miniature, the Gigantic, the Souvenir, the Collection*. Durham, N.C.: Duke University Press, 1993.

Stocker, Margarita. "Political Allusion in *The Rehearsal*." *Philological Quarterly* 67 (1988): 11–35.

Stone, George Winchester, Jr. "The Making of the Repertory." In *The London Theatre World, 1660–1800*, edited by Robert D. Hume, 181–209. Carbondale: Southern Illinois University Press, 1980.

Stone, Lawrence. *The Family, Sex and Marriage in England, 1500–1800*. New York: Harper and Row, 1977.

Strohmer, Shaun. "'My Eyes Take Pleasure to Behold Thee': Spectatorship and the Mastery of Passion in *The Fair Penitent*." *Restoration and Eighteenth-Century Theatre Research* 14 (1999): 55–65.

Swindells, Julia. *Glorious Causes: The Grand Theatre of Political Change, 1789–1833*. Oxford: Oxford University Press, 2001.

Swindells, Julia, and David Francis Taylor, eds. *The Oxford Handbook of the Georgian Theatre, 1737–1832*. Oxford: Oxford University Press, 2014.

Tasch, Peter. "*The Beggar's Opera* and *The Libertine*." *Notes and Queries* 36 (1989): 52.

Taylor, Diana. *The Archive and the Repertoire: Performing Cultural Memory in the Americas*. Durham, N.C.: Duke University Press, 2003.

Thomas, Peter D. G. *George III: King and Politicians, 1760–1770*. Manchester: Manchester University Press, 2002.

———. *John Wilkes: A Friend to Liberty*. New York: Oxford University Press, 1996.

Thompson, E. P. *The Making of the English Working Class*. New York: Vintage, 1963.

Thomson, Peter. "Acting and Actors from Garrick to Kean." In *The Cambridge Companion to British Theatre, 1730–1830*, edited by Jane Moody and Daniel O'Quinn, 3–20. Cambridge: Cambridge University Press, 2007.

———. "Celebrity and Rivalry: David [Garrick] and Goliath [Quin]." In *Theatre and Celebrity in Britain, 1660–2000*, edited by Mary Luckhurst and Jane Moody, 127–147. New York: Palgrave, 2005.

Traugott, John. "The Rake's Progress from Court to Comedy." *Studies in English Literature* 6 (1966): 381–407.

Tumir, Vaska. "She-Tragedy and Its Men: Conflict and Form in *The Orphan* and *The Fair Penitent*." *Studies in English Literature, 1500–1900* 30 (1990): 411–428.

Turnbull, Gordon. "Boswell and Sympathy: The Trial and Execution of John Reid." In *New Light on Boswell*, edited by Greg Clingham, 104–115. Cambridge: Cambridge University Press, 1991.

———. Introduction to *London Journal, 1762–1763*, by James Boswell, edited by Gordon Turnbull, xv–xlvii. New York: Penguin, 2010.

Turner, James G. *Libertines and Radicals in Early Modern London: Sexuality, Politics and Literary Culture, 1630–1685*. Cambridge: Cambridge University Press, 2002.

———. "Lovelace and the Paradoxes of Libertinism." In *Samuel Richardson: Tercentenary Essays*, edited by Margaret Anne Doody and Peter Sabor, 70–88. Cambridge: Cambridge University Press, 1989.

———. "The Properties of Libertinism." *Eighteenth-Century Life* 9 (1985): 75–87.

Turner, Michael J. *British Politics in an Age of Reform*. New York: Manchester University Press, 1999.

Van Lennep, William, Emmett L. Avery, Arthur H. Scouten, George Winchester Stone Jr., and Charles Beecher Hogan, eds. *The London Stage, 1660–1800: A Calendar of Plays, Entertainments, and Afterpieces*. 5 parts in 11 vols. Carbondale: Southern Illinois University Press, 1960–1968.

Visconsi, Elliott. *Lines of Equity: Literature and the Origins of Law in Later Stuart England*. Ithaca, N.Y.: Cornell University Press, 2008.

Wanko, Cheryl. *Roles of Authority: Thespian Biography and Celebrity in Eighteenth-Century Britain*. Lubbock: Texas Tech University Press, 2003.

Watson, E. B. *Sheridan to Robertson: A Study of the Nineteenth-Century London Stage*. Cambridge, Mass.: Harvard University Press, 1926.

Weber, Harold. *The Restoration Rake-Hero: Transformations in Sexual Understanding in Seventeenth-Century England*. Madison: University of Wisconsin Press, 1986.

Webster, Jeremy. *Performing Libertinism in Charles II's Court: Politics, Drama, Sexuality*. New York: Palgrave, 2005.

Weed, David. "Sexual Positions: Men of Pleasure, Economy, and Dignity in Boswell's *London Journal*." *Eighteenth-Century Studies* 31 (1997): 215–231.

Weil, Rachel. *Political Passions: Gender, the Family, and Political Argument in England, 1680–1714*. Manchester: Manchester University Press, 1999.

West, Shearer. "Wilkes's Squint: Synecdochic Physiognomy and Political Identity in Eighteenth-Century Print Culture." *Eighteenth-Century Studies* 33 (1999): 65–84.

Williams, Abigail. *Poetry and the Creation of a Whig Literary Culture, 1681–1714*. Oxford: Oxford University Press, 2005.

Williams, Raymond. *Marxism and Literature*. Oxford: Oxford University Press, 1977.

Wilson, Brett. "Bevil's Eyes; or, How Crying at *The Conscious Lovers* Could Save Britain." *Eighteenth-Century Studies* 45 (2012): 497–518.

———. *A Race of Female Patriots: Women and Public Spirit on the British Stage, 1688–1745*. Lewisburg, Pa.: Bucknell University Press, 2012.

Wilson, Kathleen. "Rowe's *Fair Penitent* as Global History: Or, a Diversionary Voyage to New South Wales." *Eighteenth-Century Studies* 41 (2008): 231–251.

———. *The Sense of the People: Politics, Culture, and Imperialism in England, 1715–1785*. Cambridge: Cambridge University Press, 1995.

Wilson, Michael. "Garrick, Iconic Acting, and the Ideologies of Theatrical Portraiture." *Word and Image* 6 (1990): 368–394.

Winton, Calhoun. *John Gay and the London Theatre*. Lexington: University Press of Kentucky, 1993.

Worrall, David. *The Politics of Romantic Theatricality, 1787–1832: The Road to the Stage*. New York: Palgrave, 2007.

Wyman, Lindley. "The Tradition of Formal Meditation in Rowe's *The Fair Penitent*." *Philological Quarterly* 42 (1963): 412–416.

Zimansky, Curt. Introduction to *The Provoked Wife*, edited by Curt Zimansky, xiii–xxii. Lincoln: University Press of Nebraska, 1969.

Zomchick, John. "Force, Contract, and Power in *The Woman-Captain*." *Restoration* 20 (1996): 175–188.

Zook, Melinda. "The Restoration Remembered: The First Whigs and the Making of Their History." *Seventeenth Century* 17 (2002): 213–234.

INDEX

ABOUT THE AUTHOR

DANIEL GUSTAFSON is an assistant professor of English at The City College of New York.